Renaissance and Seventeenth-Century Studies

Renaissance and Seventeenth-Century Studies

by

JOSEPH ANTHONY MAZZEO

NEW YORK: Columbia University Press
LONDON: Routledge & Kegan Paul
1964

First published 1964
by Columbia University Press
Columbia University, New York
and Routledge & Kegan Paul Ltd
68–74 Carter Lane, London, E.C.4
Made and printed in Great Britain
by William Clowes and Sons, Limited
London and Beccles

Library of Congress
Catalog Card Number: 64–13195

Contents

vii

Preface

THE essays in this volume fall into two groups. The first
four turn on problems of metaphor and style, and treat of two
eras in which these problems underwent critical reformulation
and re-examination. St. Augustine marks the classical attempt
to take account of what might be called 'biblical poetics' while
the two essays on the theory of 'metaphysical' poetry treat of
the attempt of seventeenth-century critics to comprehend, at the
level of theory, the expansion of metaphorical and analogical
possibilities that marked the so-called 'metaphysical' movement
as, indeed, it also characterized the growth of the cultural
influence of the Bible. Some of the intellectual presuppositions
of the later movement will be seen to have been implicit in the
thought of St. Augustine, although much had to happen before
they became actual. The essay on Donne's alchemical imagery
is an example of the way a 'metaphysical' poet used fresh
metaphorical material and of how the richly analogical structure
of Renaissance proto-science facilitated such a use.

The second group of essays are, in general, about Machiavelli and Machiavellism and about Andrew Marvell. However,
I have again been essentially concerned with the way in which
crucial metaphors and idea-images serve as principles for
organizing experience both in Machiavelli's own writings and
in that work of Marvell which reflects his influence. Each group
begins with a retrospective glance at a medieval analogue or
forerunner, St. Augustine in one case and Dante in the other.
The final essay, 'Cromwell as Davidic King,' weaves together
the Machiavellian and Augustinian strands as they are manifested
in the work of a poet of wit, the 'various light' of whose mind
responded harmoniously to the different currents of thought and
taste that I have examined in these essays.

The two groups of essays are unified by their common concern with the relations between thought and literary structure, of the way in which ideas generate new metaphorical, stylistic, and structural possibilities in literary works of art, or the way in which functional imagery gives a literary dimension to works of thought.

In revising, sometimes markedly, what has been published before in journals, and in writing what here appears for the first time, I have been assisted by the generous criticisms of many colleagues at Columbia University and elsewhere. They stand absolved from my errors and obscurities but I hope that there is much in this book that they will wish to acknowledge.

J. A. M.

Columbia University
New York City

Acknowledgements

THOSE chapters or portions of chapters first published elsewhere and covered by previous copyrights are here reprinted with some changes, by permission of the original publishers.

'St. Augustine's Rhetoric of Silence' first appeared in *Journal of the History of Ideas*, XXIII (1962), 175–96; 'A Seventeenth-Century Theory of Metaphysical Poetry,' in *Romanic Review*, XLII (1951), 245–55; 'Metaphysical Poetry and the Poetic of Correspondence,' in *Journal of the History of Ideas*, XIV (1953), 221–34; 'Notes on John Donne's Alchemical Imagery,' in *Isis*, XLVIII (1957), 103–23; 'Hell vs. Hell: From Dante to Machiavelli,' in *Symposium*, XVII (1963), 245–267; 'Machiavelli: The Artist as Statesman,' in *University of Toronto Quarterly*, XXXI (1962), 265–82; 'Cromwell as Machiavellian Prince in Marvell's "An Horatian Ode",' in *Journal of the History of Ideas*, XXI (1960), 1–17; 'Cromwell as Davidic King,' in *Reason and the Imagination*, ed. J. A. Mazzeo (New York, Columbia University Press, and London, Routledge and Kegan Paul, 1962), 29–56.

I would also like to thank Sheed and Ward for permission to quote from F. J. Sheed's translation of St. Augustine's *Confessions* (1943), the Oxford University Press and Bodley Head Ltd. for permission to quote from J. D. Sinclair's translation of the *Divine Comedy* (1948), Holt, Rinehart and Winston Inc. for permission to quote from Morris R. Cohen's *A Preface to Logic* (1944) and the University of California Press for permission to quote from Ernst Kantorowicz' *Laudes regiae* (1946).

CHAPTER I

St. Augustine's Rhetoric of Silence
Truth vs. Eloquence and Things vs. Signs

B UT sight shall displace faith; and hope shall be swallowed up in that perfect bliss to which we shall come: love on the other hand shall wax greater when these others fail.[1]

Medieval rhetorical principles developed within three different traditions. First of all there was the strictly literary tradition of the Roman rhetoric of Cicero and Quintilian. The second was based on a fusion of Aristotle's logic (on terms and propositions) and Cicero (on definitions and principles). The third and, until the late Middle Ages, the most important from the theological and philosophical point of view was the Augustinian tradition, a blend of Platonism with Cicero.[2]

We are concerned here with St. Augustine's attempt to assimilate classical rhetoric to Christian needs and with the profound transformations he made in the doctrine he received. From one point of view he brought rhetoric back to where Plato had left it in the *Phaedrus*, where eloquence and rhetoric are based on truth in contrast to mere show. St. Augustine's analysis of rhetoric reveals an authentic platonism which he re-created out of the contemporary materials furnished by

---

[1] Sed fidei succedit species, quam videbimus; et spei succedit beatitudo ipsa, ad quam perventuri sumus: charitas autem etiam istis decedentibus augebitur potius (*De doctrina Christiana*, I, 38, 42; *PL*, XXIV, col. 35).

[2] Richard McKeon, 'Rhetoric in the Middle Ages,' in *Critics and Criticism*, ed. R. S. Crane (Chicago, 1952), pp. 260–96, 263.

neoplatonists and Academics. On the other hand, he established or cast into authoritative form, often verbalistic conceptions of allegory, typology, symbolism, and metaphor which, as Beryl Smalley said referring to *De doctrina Christiana*, 'made Scripture into a divine encyclopedia written in cipher.'[1]

While the historian of thought will always find St. Augustine's greatness in his concern for a rhetoric based on truth, the historian of culture and taste is compelled to reflect on the enormous influence exerted on medieval literature and art by the analogical modes of thought and interpretation he did so much to disseminate as well as by the manner in which he reflected and created a new influential sensibility.

Every student of the *Confessions* recalls how St. Augustine was originally convinced of the incompatibility of Christianity and philosophy because of the extreme difference in the styles of the Bible and Cicero (III, 3, 5–5, 9; *PL*, XXXII, cols. 685–86), and how he took his first step towards a resolution of this conflict under the influence of St. Ambrose's teachings on the allegorical and symbolic modes of interpreting Scripture (V, 13, 23, and VI, 4, 5–6; *PL*, XXXII, cols 717 and 721–22).[2] Yet in some ways the conflict was never fully resolved. St. Augustine's exegetical and hermeneutic practices led him into some extraordinarily elaborate symbolic and 'rhetorical' interpretations which he would never have tolerated in his philosophy or sermons where he disparaged spending too much time on rhetorical problems in the pursuit of truth.[3]

In any case St. Augustine always remained under the influence of Cicero and treated all of the basic problems of rhetoric in Ciceronian terms, although he freely adapted his source to platonic and Christian contexts. His basic questions of inquiry are those of Cicero (*an sit*, *quid sit*, *quale sit*), and again following Cicero the subject of inquiry is either concerned with realities or signs (*res et signa*). However, he reduced Cicero's five parts of rhetoric to the two concerning discovery and state-

---

[1] Smalley, *The Study of the Bible in the Middle Ages* (2nd ed; Oxford, 1952), p. 294.

[2] Cf. the change in Victorinus' rhetoric effected by his conversion in *Conf.*, VIII, 2, 5; *PL*, XXXII, col. 751.

[3] Cf. *Epist.* CXVIII *ad Dioscurum*, I, 2 and V, 34; *PL*, XXXIII, cols. 432–33.

ment, and it is in this change and its consequences that we see St. Augustine's originality and the great importance for the future of his *De doctrina Christiana*.[1]

That work, especially the fourth book, not only brought rhetoric back to its ancient concern for truth by re-creating a platonic view of rhetoric in the midst of fourth-century sophistic, but it also became the final statement of St. Augustine's view of the relations of rhetoric to Christianity by expressing a profound adaptation of the language of rhetoric to his metaphysics and theology. The nature and uses of signs became strictly related to the realities to be sought (discovery) and to their formulation (statement), so that the use of the arts of language is utterly dependent on the structure of reality, a relationship with which no classical rhetorician other than Plato had been concerned.[2]

Thus the theme that underlies the whole of Book IV is that of the eloquence of words (*verba*) versus the immeasurably greater eloquence of realities (*res*), of truth. Nevertheless, since the eloquence of words may be used for both good and evil, St. Augustine allows Christians to learn to be eloquent.[3] Skill in speaking, or eloquence, is something best learned when we are young. However, when we are older, we can still learn;

---

[1] Cf. McKeon, *op. cit.*, pp. 264–65. The Ciceronian divisions of rhetoric (*inventio, dispositio, elocutio, memoria* and *actio*) became two, the *modus inveniendi* treated in the first three books of *De doctrina* and roughly equivalent to classical *inventio*, and the *modus proferendi* mostly concerned with *elocutio* but also touching on *memoria* and *actio* treated in the fourth book. St. Augustine omits *dispositio* altogether, perhaps feeling that the arrangement of religious discourse was given in the texts of Scripture expounded and did not require the technique necessary in the organization of evidence and argument for forensic speeches. See Sister M. T. Sullivan, *S. Aurelii Hipponiensis episcopi de doctrina christiana liber quartus*, a commentary, with a revised text, introduction, and translation, *Catholic University of America Patristic Studies*, vol. XXIII (Washington, D.C., 1930), pp. 8–13, 44.

[2] McKeon, *op. cit.*, pp. 265–66. We must recall that book four of *De doctrina* was completed in A.D. 426, many years after the composition of the first three books in 397. It is therefore the fruit of a lifetime of thought. On the significance of the work see C. S. Baldwin, *Medieval Rhetoric and Poetic* (New York, 1928), p. 51; Sullivan, *op. cit.*, pp. 41–42, and McKeon, *op. cit.*, pp. 264–65.

[3] *De doctrina Christiana*, IV, 2, 3; *PL*, XXXIV, col. 89. In the many future references to this work I shall omit '*PL*, 34' for the sake of brevity.

and the best method is to read and listen to eloquent speakers rather than to learn a lot of rules. Indeed, skill in speaking or eloquence (*facundia vel eloquentia*) precedes the rules, and eloquent men embody only those rules which are merely generalizations based on their practice. One cannot use rules to become eloquent and, if you do speak well, it is not by thinking of the rules as you speak, for this is patently impossible.[1]

It is not only true that eloquence cannot be taught by manuals but, St. Augustine insists, to emphasize eloquence is to stress what is of lesser importance. Wisdom is more important by far than eloquence and wisdom comes from a true, thorough understanding of Scripture.[2]

Nevertheless, with the proper provisos rhetoric is useful to the Christian preacher. Indeed, we can even find examples of rhetorical figures in St. Paul, Amos, and Christian writers.[3]

We find in all this an exact distinction between the truth of a proposition and the skill with which it is expressed, between practising the arts of rhetoric and dialectic with skill and coming to a knowledge of the truth. A man can walk quite well, St. Augustine had said at the writing of Book II of *De doctrina*, without making a minute analysis of the act of walking, and a man who cannot walk will derive no benefit from making such an analysis. Similarly an intelligent man can see quite well that an inference is unsound even if he cannot analyse his act and formulate rules of inference.[4]

In the last analysis, we can say that St. Augustine teaches that eloquence is useful but not indispensable to preachers. A preacher can find what models he needs in Scripture and in Christian authors and he can ignore the technical treatises on

---

[1] *De doctrina Christiana*, 3, 4; cols. 90–91. Note that by the time of the Empire *eloquentia* meant literary expression in general. See the remarks of H.-I. Marrou, *St. Augustin et la fin de la culture antique*, 2 vols. (Paris, 1949), pp. 498 ff. All citations from this work are from volume I.

[2] *Ibid.*, 5, 7–8; cols. 91–92.

[3] *Ibid.*, 7, 11–21; cols. 93–98. Cf. *De doctrina Christiana*, III, 29, 40; col. 80, where St. Augustine tells us that Scripture has an abundance of tropes and even the names of some of them such as *allegoria, aenigma* and *parabola*. Marrou warns that we are not to conclude from such statements that St. Augustine advocated a formal rhetorical analysis of Scripture (*op. cit.*, pp. 476 n. 1 and 519–20 n. 1).

[4] *Ibid.*, II, 34, 52 to II, 37, 55; cols. 59–61.

rhetorical theory and learn, so to speak, by immersion in the text. In the process of learning the truth and realities (*res*) of Scripture, he will inevitably learn to master the *verba*. The distinction in St. Augustine's rhetorical theory is thus carried over into pedagogical practice. This was a revolutionary doctrine for its time, a time in which rhetoric was virtually an end in itself, in which the teaching of rhetoric was extremely formalistic, and we can recognize in it the modern sentiment about the teaching of the arts of language.[1]

Words vs. Things in Allegorical Exegesis

The first and most important thing to say about St. Augustine's conception of allegory and his techniques of biblical exegesis is that he considered them, in the last analysis, relatively unimportant. All of the teaching on faith and morals necessary to salvation is quite plain in Scripture. Such teachings are the essence of revelation and, along with the operation of the law of love in the interpreter, the key to correct exegesis. The plain and unequivocal texts, applied in the spirit of love, are to be used to explain the obscure ones.[2] Having established this principle, St. Augustine goes on to make many subtle distinctions. Let us return to the distinction between things and signs and see how it is applied to the interpretation of Scripture.

All teaching is either about things or about signs, but knowledge of things is gained by means of signs. In the strict sense, a thing (*res*) is never employed as a sign of any other such as wood, stone, cattle, etc. However, in the case of Scripture this does not apply. The wood which Moses cast into the bitter waters to make them sweet, the stone which Jacob used as a pillow, the ram which Abraham offered up instead of his son are all, to be sure, things. But they are also signs of other things. Now words are also realities; otherwise they would not exist at all, but they are never employed except as signs of something else. Hence while every sign is also a thing, not every thing is also a sign.[3]

---

[1] Marrou, *op. cit.*, pp. 515–18; *De doctrina Christiana*, IV, 1, 2 to IV, 3, 5; cols. 89–91: IV, 5, 8; col. 98 and IV, 21, 50; col. 114.

[2] *De doctrina Christiana*, II, 9, 14 to II, 15, 22; col. 42–46. Cf. *ibid.*, I, 32 to 35; col. 32 and I, 35, 39 to I, 40, 44; cols. 34–36.

[3] *Ibid.*, I, 2, 2; col. 19–20.

Some signs are natural and others conventional (*data*). Natural signs are those which lead to knowledge of something else, like all signs, but which were not intended to do so as, for example, smoke when it indicates fire. This use of natural signs is a result of our association of the two through experience.[1] Conventional signs, on the other hand, are those which living beings exchange with one another for communicating thoughts and feelings with each other as best as they can. There is no other use for signs but communication. Even the signs which God has given us and which are contained in Scripture were communicated through men—the men who wrote the Scriptures.[2]

It is clear that St. Augustine here refers to God's unique power to confer on realities their significance as signs. A stone is a sign only if Jacob sleeps on it in the particular circumstances in which God made him sleep on it in order to make the event a sign. A careful reading of St. Augustine would clear up some of the confusion in modern literary studies of medieval allegory which fail to distinguish between man's allusions and references to the divine allegory of realities as signs, and man's power to *create* such signs. The latter, in strict theology, is impossible. They can only be discovered, in Scripture or in life, and they can be used, but they cannot be invented.

Most of the signs by which men communicate to one another are related to the sense of hearing, some relate to sight, and a very few to the other senses. Thus gestures, actions, and military standards may be called visible words (*verba visibilia*). There are also some musical signs such as military bugle-calls, but they are very few in number. St. Augustine's examples for the use of signs relating to the sense of smell and taste are both, significantly enough, drawn from the life of Christ. Thus he employed odour as a sign when ointment was poured on his feet and employed taste as a sign through the eating of the bread and drinking of the wine in the sacrament of the Eucharist. He even employed touch as a sign during the miracles of healing.[3]

What is striking in these examples from the life of Christ is

[1] *De doctrina Christiana*, II, 1, 2; col. 36.
[2] *Ibid.*, II, 2, 3; col. 37.
[3] *Ibid.*, II, 3, 4; col. 37.

that they should be drawn from Scripture for precisely those senses which it is most difficult to conceive as possessing value as signs in ordinary human life. Is it the case that the only certain use of such *sensibilia* as signs can be found in the life of Christ whose every gesture, according to St. Augustine, had some bearing on his mission of revelation? One is inclined to suspect that this may be so, and it would be in harmony with St. Augustine's conviction that only the Divinity can use things as signs in an intrinsic and natural, and not conventional meaning. I suppose some conventional signs adapted to the senses of smell, touch, and taste might have been found if St. Augustine had been willing to imagine a situation which would provide the metacommunicative context for a gesture, an odour or touch acquiring value as a sign. Such a context is of course immediately given in the doctrine of the Incarnation, for no divine act whatever could be meaningless.

St. Augustine's Theory of the Sacraments as Signs

St. Augustine applies his distinctions between signs and things and between divine and human signs to a theory of the sacraments in a most interesting way. He begins by pointing out that any man is in bondage to a sign (*sub signo enim servit*) who uses or pays homage to any significant object (*aliquam rem significantem*) without knowing what it signifies. The free and spiritual man honours signs because of what they refer to, and this was true even of the patriarchs and prophets who did not know the final clear set of signs but who referred what signs they had to the right transcendental reality in the right way. The Christian dispensation clarifies all of the older divine signs and frees us from the burden of attending to the older signs whose meaning has now become clear. Instead we have a few simple signs, established by Christ himself, easy to perform, most august to the intellect (*intellectu Augustissima*) and most sacred. Such are the sacraments of baptism and of the Eucharist. We revere these signs in spiritual freedom because we know that to which they refer. To take such signs for the things they signify is to be in bondage and weakness; to misinterpret them is to be misled by error. Even the man who does not understand them but nevertheless knows they are signs is better off in that he is not in bondage. It is better to be in bondage to

7

misunderstood but useful signs than to interpret them wrongly so that you escape from the yoke of bondage to the object but fall into the coils of error.[1]

St. Augustine here makes the term sacrament synonymous with divine (and, of course, efficacious) sign. This broad use of 'sacrament' which flows from his rhetorical theories is one of the three categories into which we can classify the contents of Scripture. There are things to be known and believed, that is to say, dogma; things to be observed and done or things prohibited lest they be done; and finally, things veiled in the mysteries of sacraments (*sacramentorum velata mysteriis*), the last disclosed in the spiritual and transcendental reference of divinely ordained signs. In this sense the term extends beyond the traditional sacraments of Church tradition to include the transcendental meaning of the events and realities of Scripture, all of which, like the sacraments, are to be understood as pointing beyond themselves.[2]

Such signs are not conventional with a meaning extrinsically conferred by men—and extrinsic meaning is the only kind of meaning men can confer—but they are, as it were, the language of God who creates the reality and its intrinsic meaning simultaneously. While men are free to understand and refer to such signs, they are not able to make them. If men pronounce them they do so entirely under divine inspiration. Only the eternal meanings, the true realities of all divine signs, are really important. While knowledge of temporal things and of the various branches of knowledge is useful in scriptural exegesis, we must not forget that the Sacraments are signs only in so far as they are an adaptation to human sensibility of eternal truths. They are otherwise immutable in their significance of the immutable things of God.[3]

It is clear that St. Augustine thereby creates a further distinction within the distinction of words and things. There are things or realities which are temporal and others which are changeless. Similarly there are signs which are temporal and signs which are changeless. The latter are divinely instituted just as the changeless realities are themselves the divine, or

---

[1] *De doctrina Christiana*, III, 9, 13; cols. 70–71.
[2] *De scriptura sacra speculum*, praef. *PL*, XXXIV, cols. 887–89.
[3] *Epist.* CXXXVIII *ad Marcellinum*, I, 7; *PL*, XXXIII, col. 527.

aspects of it. Words, temporal signs, are in some respects less useful to designate other signs than to express truths and persuade minds. Therefore, the real utility of knowledge of things lies in the clarification of signs rather than *vice versa*.[1] We must thus pass, as it were, from the voices of men to the silent voice of God's creation.

This movement from words to silence, from signs to realities, is the fundamental presupposition of Augustinian allegorical exegesis. It is of course true, that one of the impulses behind St. Augustine's allegorism, as in that of Origen, is to save the morality of certain portions of the Bible repugnant to a later moral consciousness. Nevertheless, his allegorism has a firmly worked out philosophical basis and it became so important an instrument of exegesis in his eyes that he demanded the allegorizing of everything in Scripture which did not specifically refer to faith or morals.[2]

While modern theologians are not so extreme, they still distinguish between the literal and spiritual sense of Scripture and very much in Augustinian terms.[3] They also make further distinctions between the literal sense proper, that is the immediate sense of the words, and the figurative literal sense which is the meaning of a metaphorical expression or a figure of speech. Thus an expression like 'the hand of God was upon him' is an instance of an expression whose literal sense is simply what it says and whose figurative literal sense could be rendered as 'he was divinely inspired.' Note that this is not, in modern exegesis, a spiritual sense. To find that we have to have an event or reality which in turn will be a sign. As an example let us take the phrase 'Israel went out of Egypt.' In addition to a literal sense referring to an historical event this would have one or more spiritual senses such as the passage of the soul from vice to virtue or, in death, from earth to heaven. Such spiritual senses were not presumed to be arbitrary and were certainly not man-made. There is a sense in which it would have been true to say that God made Israel pass out of

[1] Cf. the remarks of Etienne Gilson, *Introduction à l'étude de St. Augustin*, 2nd ed. (Paris, 1943), 151–53.

[2] *De doctrina Christiana*, III, 10, 14; col. 71.

[3] S. M. Zarb, O.P., 'Unité ou multiplicité des sens litteraux de la Bible ?' *Revue Thomiste* (1932), 251–300, esp. 251–52.

Egypt in order to signify to later generations what they discovered in that event.

While St. Augustine recognizes these distinctions he is not very precise in formulating them. His usual classification for exegesis is between *signa propria* and *signa translata*. The former are the object of a more or less philological study of the text while the latter include everything else, the figurative literal sense and the higher spiritual senses or allegorical senses.[1]

From another point of view the division between *signa propria* and *signa translata* corresponds generally to two kinds of information needed in the interpretation of Scripture. The first category requires *linguarum notitia*, the philological equipment needed to examine what we would call the literal sense proper and also to answer such problems as the meaning of names (sacred onomastics), and the etymology of words, often far-fetched and edifying. The second category usually requires *rerum notitia*, the information furnished by the other sciences which deal with the nature of things. These other sciences furnish information as to the symbolic value, moral or dogmatic, of the things signified by the words of Scripture so as to double the meaning of a text by adding the meaning of things to the meaning of words.[2] Thus, it is from physical science that we

---

[1] Cf. E. Moirat, *Notion augustinienne de l'herméneutique* (Clermont-Ferrand, 1906). Cf. *De doctrina Christiana*, II, 9, 14 to II, 15, 22; cols. 65–68. St. Augustine makes some further distinctions such as *signa ignota* which are unknown words whether in Latin or other languages, *signa obscura* which are difficult words but which will yield a satisfactory meaning. *Signa ambigua*, fully discussed in book III of *De doctrina*, are those words which have a plurality of meanings and which either in the original or in translation lead to a diversity of interpretations of certain passages of Scripture. They are in turn divided in *signa ambigua propria* and *signa ambigua translata*. St. Augustine allows that diversity of interpretation is correct within the limits of parallel or complementary meanings even if the author's intention was to give the text only one meaning. This sort of ambiguity is to be sharply distinguished from an incorrect or mistranslated text. Philological study, grammar, helps to clarify ambiguous literal expression while rhetoric helps us to recognize and interpret figurative ambiguous expressions. The ultimate rule is, as always, the guide of faith and morals and the law of love. Cf. *De doctrina Christiana*, II, 10, 15 to II, 21; cols. 42–45 and III, 1, 1 to III, 15, 23; cols. 65–74. On literal and figurative senses see III, 5, 9 to III, 24, 34; cols. 74–78.

[2] *De doctrina Christiana*, II, 16, 23 to II, 16–26; cols. 47–48.

learn that the phases of the moon are an allegory of the human soul or of the Church, both of which variously reflect the light of God, the Sun of Justice.[1]

Linguistic knowledge would help the interpreter to find out the actual meaning of Hebrew names and places and help him discover the secret meaning hidden in those names. Natural history would help us understand what Scripture means when it tells us to be as wise as serpents when we learn that the serpent will sacrifice its body to protect its head. The head is obviously Christ and we should be glad to sacrifice the body for the head. Mathematics, i.e. of a neopythagorean sort, will help us explain why Moses, Elijah, and Jesus all fasted for forty days and of the meaning of the number ten in reference to the Psaltery with ten strings.[2]

While such techniques of interpretation could be applied to fables as well as to facts, to events as well as to things, they were essentially adapted to the revelation of the higher spiritual senses of the things and events of Scripture, of the meaning of the silent words of God. Not only was Scripture itself an endless allegory but the world that Scripture described was itself a further silent, wordless allegory of the eternal. The whole created world is a set of symbols of the divine, a sublime poem whose words are things, whose silent voice is the voice of its creator.[3]

The most philosophical form of such a conception is to be found in the Trinitarian exemplarism of St. Augustine's *De Trinitate* where the traces of the Trinity in creation are arranged as triads such as unity, goodness, truth or mode, measure, form. But along with this very abstract exemplarism we find, as we have seen, the kind of allegorizing of things which is so much a part of medieval natural history with its bestiaries and lapidaries. By the time of Rabanus Maurus (*c.* 800) the fusion of allegorism and exemplarism was complete, and this way of looking at the world as well as Scripture became the most dominant one in medieval culture.

[1] *Enarratio in Psalm.* X; *PL*, XXXVI, cols. 131–33 and *Epist.* LX, 5, 8; *PL*, XXXIII, col. 208.

[2] *De doctrina Christiana*, II, 16, 23 to II, 16, 25; cols. 47–48. Cf. II, 29, 45; cols. 56–57.

[3] Cf. *Epist.* LV, 7, 13; *PL*, XXXIII, col. 210, and *De civ. Dei*, XI, 18; *PL*, XLI, col. 332.

The Theory of Styles

Let us now turn to an examination of St. Augustine's reinterpretation of the traditional Ciceronian conception of the aims of the orator, the *officia oratoris*, and see how this rigorous devotion to truth and its quest affected the classical theory of decorum in style.

To teach, delight, and persuade (*docere, delectare, flectere*) are the three aims of the orator, and these St. Augustine adopts unchanged from Cicero.[1] Corresponding to the three *officia* are three styles which respectively accomplish the three aims: the *submissum* which serves *ad docendum*, the *temperatum, ad delectandum* and the *grande*, also called the *sublime, ad flectendum*.[2] Like the ideal pagan orator the Christian orator must meet moral requirements, although they are the superior requirements of Christian morality.[3] However, it is not only in the more stringent morality he requires that St. Augustine modifies Cicero, but he changes his thought on the question of style itself. Thus he says that the truth needs no adornment to give pleasure but gives pleasure because it is the truth.[4] Where Cicero taught that each style was particularly adapted to a special subject-matter, little things in a subdued style in order to teach, moderate things in a temperate style in order to please, and great arguments in a majestic style in order to sway the mind or persuade, St. Augustine maintained that this cannot apply to ecclesiastical orators. Their subject-matter is always of great moment and the Ciceronian analysis is suitable only for forensic matters.[5] At this point St. Augustine makes a revolutionary change in the theory of styles with consequences which the student of later literature cannot underestimate. For if the subject-matter is always great in the discourse of ecclesiastical orators, then the three styles appear as simple technical devices regarding the treatments of a uniformly great subject-matter and not as modes appropriate to different categories of subject.

Thus the subdued style is good for teaching great things, the

---

[1] *De doctrina Christiana*, IV, 12–14, 27–31; cols. 101–03, and cf. Sullivan, *op.cit.*, pp. 6–7.

[2] *Ibid.*, IV, 17, 34; cols. 104–05.

[3] *Ibid.*, IV, 27–30, 59–63; cols. 118–20.

[4] *Ibid.*, IV, 12, 28; col. 101.

[5] *Ibid.*, IV, 17–18, 34–37; cols. 104–06.

moderate style for praise and blame in regard to great things, and the grand style for persuading the reluctant in regard to great things.[1] The way is opened to the notion of a variety of styles or a mixture of styles in the treating of a uniform subject-matter, and St. Augustine even takes the step of saying that, although a speech or piece of writing may appropriately have a prevailing style, the mixture of styles is good for the sake of variety itself.[2] We have thus passed, in principle, from the poetic practice of Virgil to that of Dante. The break-up of classical genre theory was, as the brilliant studies of Erich Auerbach have shown, implicit in Christianity itself so that it is somewhat surprising to find that St. Augustine's practice is at considerable variance with his new theories.[3] If the style of the preacher is to be in some sense a biblical style, for this is what St. Augustine's reinterpretation of classical style theory meant, then St. Augustine shows little evidence of taking the Bible as his primary literary inspiration. While the presence of parallelisms and antitheses in his style and in that of other Christian authors would indicate some biblical influence, we are much more aware of the carefully wrought classical periods inspired by the old pagan authors.

H.-I. Marrou has very ably discussed the conflict between St. Augustine's theory of a new rhetoric and his life-long practice of the old, and decided that there is not as much contradiction as might appear if we examine the writings of his contemporaries. St. Augustine certainly allowed incorrect Latin if it were necessary to reach the unlearned and if it already existed in the Latin version of Scripture. Indeed, though the Old Latin versions, hallowed by liturgical use, were full of barbarisms, St. Augustine thought it was correct to use them, for one did not need to be elegant and eloquent in order to be wise.[4]

Certainly, there was no reason for St. Augustine to write bad Latin simply in order to do so, and he seems to have felt no need to disguise his superior culture. His violent criticism of

[1] *De doctrina Christiana*, IV, 19, 38; cols. 106–07.

[2] *Ibid.*, IV, 22, 51; cols. 114–15.

[3] For Auerbach's thesis see his *Mimesis*, trans. W. R. Trask (Princeton, 1953), and his references to some of his earlier studies.

[4] *De doctrina Christiana*, IV, 28, 6; col. 119: Sed qui utrumque non potest, dicat sapienter quod non dicit eloquenter, potius quam dicat eloquenter, quod dicit insipienter. Cf. Marrou, *op. cit.*, pp. 533 ff.

literary culture, in spite of the fact that it included Homer and Virgil, is in large part an attack on synthetic and artificial literature. St. Augustine felt finally no very severe conflict over the competing Christian and pagan cultures. He felt free to take and adapt whatever elements of pagan culture would be useful and to discard the rest, unlike St. Jerome who was tormented by guilt over his Ciceronianisms.[1]

Whatever the case may be, St. Augustine certainly came to grips with the great problem in converting intellectuals, namely, their repugnance towards the strange and rustic character of Scripture. He recommends that those who have been trained in the schools to judge literature by the norms of classicism should be taught to listen to divine Scriptures so that they will not denigrate solid diction simply because it does not possess the rhetorical showiness they expect. By listening, without reading, they will discover that although Scripture may seem plain and humble, exactly because of its absence of windiness, it is truly elevated by the solidity of its content.[2]

When the learned have problems in the interpretation of Scripture, use is to be made of allegorical interpretation, a device of course already quite familiar to them in their reading of the classics, and they are to be taught that the meaning of Scripture is superior to the letter as the spirit is to the body. They ought to prefer to listen to true rather than eloquent discourses, just as they ought to choose their friends for their wisdom rather than their good looks.[3]

---

[1] Marrou, op. cit., pp. 352–56. Marrou has a strong tendency to undervalue the religious motives in St. Augustine's attack on poetry. In this connection we might remind ourselves that St. Augustine's most famous and extensive attacks on literature would seem to be in the Confessions.

[2] De catechizandis rudibus, 9, 13; PL, XL, col. 320; Maxime autem isti docendi sunt Scripturas audire divinas, ne sordeat eis solidum eloquium, quia non est inflatum. Cf. De doctrina Christiana, IV, 6, 9; col. 92, Marrou, op. cit., pp. 473 and Pierre Labriolle, Histoire de la littérature latine chrétienne, 3rd ed., 2 vols. (Paris, 1947), vol. I, pp. 22, 31–32.

[3] Ibid., 9, 13, PL, XL, col. 320: cum aliquid eis quod in promtu positum non ita movebat, enodatione allegoriae alicujus eruitur. His enim maxime utile est nosse, ita esse praeponendas verbis sententias, ut praeponitur animus corpori. Exquo fit, ut ita malle debeant veriores quam disertiores audire sermones, sicut malle debent prudentiores quam formosiores habere amicos.

The learned, too, must understand that no voice reaches God save that of the heart (*animi affectum*), so that they should not condemn preachers if they hear them make grammatical errors or do not understand the words that they are pronouncing. While such faults should be corrected they should also be accepted in a spirit of tolerance. If in the law courts eloquence is manifested through the spoken voice, in church it is manifested through prayer (*ut sono in foro, sic voto in ecclesia bene dici*).[1]

That this attitude represents St. Augustine's resolution of his own experience with Scripture is, of course, certain. We have only to recall his own difficulty in reconciling Christ and Cicero (*Confessions*, III, 5, 9) and compare it with his final views on the question. Nevertheless, in spite of his rejection of the canons of literary judgment of the classical rhetoricians, he never quite gave up the attempt to justify the greatness of the Bible in terms of the concepts of classical genre and style theory. Thus in *De doctrina Christiana* he insists on the actual rhetorical beauty of Scripture—in addition, as we have seen, to finding rhetorical figures in it—but has to agree that its eloquence is of its own peculiar kind (*alteram quamdam eloquentiam suam*).[2]

What is abundantly clear is that St. Augustine attempted, and with a good deal of success, to work out a theory of literary beauty which would penetrate below the level of sound, and of style in the 'external' sense, to the level of truth, that is, to the fidelity of the author's language in capturing and interpreting reality. St. Augustine would have said that the greatest writers survive translation, not without loss to be sure, but with their greatness essentially intact. Because of this point of view he does not hesitate to point out that solecisms and barbarisms are necessary to translate Scripture since both single words and idioms would be impossible to translate into the Latin of the classical authors.[3]

Such a viewpoint reveals more than anything else how bold

---

[1] *De catechizandis rudibus*, 9, 13; *PL*, XL, col. 320.

[2] IV, 6, 9 to IV, 7, 21; cols. 92–98. Cf. Marrou, *op. cit.*, pp. 476.

[3] Cf. *De doctrina Christiana* II, 13, 19 and II, 15, 22; col. 46, where St. Augustine prizes the *Vetus Latina* Bible above the Septuagint and the latter above the original Hebrew because of the story of the miraculous agreement of all its translators each translating independently.

an apology *De doctrina Christiana* is to the classically trained intellectual for the apparently pedestrian and crude literary quality of Scripture, just as the *Confessions* are an equally bold apology for the fact that Christianity did not present itself as a formal philosophic system.[1]

The Rhetoric of Silence and the Pleasures of Obscurity

We have seen that St. Augustine sharply distinguished between eloquence and truth, words and realities, and that he based all of his thinking concerning rhetoric on this distinction. But there are some further distinctions to be made. Given the fact that eloquence is useful, there are two kinds of possible eloquence which correspond to two kinds of wisdom. While the classical rhetorical tradition at its best tried to join wisdom and eloquence on the grounds that only the combination of the two would be safe and efficacious, St. Augustine introduced a distinction between eternal and temporal wisdom which would correspond to a knowledge of eternal and temporal realities (*res*). Analogously, there are two kinds of *verba*, those which are man-made and conventional, what we customarily call language in the broadest sense of the term, and which contrast with the second category of internal, silent words by which the inner teacher, Christ, teaches us the truth.[2]

Like *De magistro*, *De doctrina Christiana* culminates in a laudation of the eloquence of things. The analysis of the *modus inveniendi* in the first three books begins with a division of things or realities into those which can be final goals and may be enjoyed (*frui*) and those which are simply means to be used (*uti*). Only God is the final end; the lesser realities and words themselves are merely means to that end. Hence, after a theological section, *De doctrina* proceeds in Book II to an analysis of the nature of words in both sacred and secular writing, and in Book III to exegetical techniques of clarification which take account of both verbal difficulties and difficulties of

---

[1] Cf. Glanville Downey, 'Education in the Christian Roman Empire: Christian Education under Constantine and His Successors,' *Speculum* XXXII (1957), 48–61, esp. 55, and the classic study of A. D. Nock, *Conversion: The Old and New in Religion, from Alexander the Great to Augustine of Hippo* (Oxford, 1933), esp. pp. 164 ff.

[2] *De magistro*, III, 5–6 and XI, 36 to XII, 46; *PL*, XXXII, cols. 1197–98 and 1215–20. Cf. McKeon, *op. cit.*, pp. 266.

fact and circumstance. Book IV, on the *modus proferendi*, has little to say of technique but stresses 'an eloquence in which words are supplied by things and by wisdom itself and the speaker is unlearnedly wise.[1]

Thus true rhetoric culminates in silence, in which the mind is in immediate contact with reality. We shall return to the question of silence later on after we consider some of the paradoxical consequences of things or realities as words, whereby the rhetoric of silence simultaneously encouraged greater clarity on the one hand and long flights of symbolic interpretation of the things mentioned in Scripture on the other, flights which obscured any immediacy of perception. The latter consequence was reinforced by the presence of many obscure and obviously symbolic passages of Scripture itself. It is this very phenomenon which impelled St. Augustine to create new categories for the evaluation of obscurity not quite consistent with the fundamental movement of the rhetoric of silence toward maximal immediacy and clarity.

As always, St. Augustine adapts himself freely to the demands of Scripture for new categories of literary value. Whence, he asks, the obscurity of Scripture? God made it obscure because he wished to polish and exercise the pious intellect. The obscurities of Scripture are, in fact, stylistic virtues which have the function of exciting our desire to know more and to prevent the boredom we might otherwise feel in studying Scripture.[2] In this statement we have the germ of a new sensibility based on the positive evaluation of obscurity, or at least of what later developed into a new sensibility. Dante's admiration of the *trobar clus* of Arnaut Daniel is only one illustration of an attitude which runs right through the medieval sensibility, together, of course, with other more luminous ideals of expression and thought which we also find, as we have seen, in St. Augustine himself. We are not unfamiliar with a modern revival (based on quite different cultural presuppositions) of such a positive valuation of obscurity, as any reader of *Finnegans Wake* or of Empson's *Seven Types of Ambiguity* can testify. In Joyce's book

[1] McKeon, *op. cit.*, pp. 266 and *De doctrina Christiana*, III, 48 and III, 12, 18; cols. 68 and 72–73, and IV, 1, 1 to IV, 7, 11; cols. 89–94.

[2] *De doctrina Christiana*, IV, 8, 22; col. 98 and II, 6, 7; col. 38. Cf. Marrou, *op. cit.*, pp. 486–88.

we have a work written to be read with exegetical methods which would not have seemed unfamiliar to St. Augustine.[1]

In an interesting example of the pleasure of figurative and obscure expression, St. Augustine comments on the following verse from *Canticles* (IV, 2) 'Thy teeth are like a flock of sheep that are shorn, which come up from the washing, thereof everyone bears twins, and none is barren among them.' He asks why he should feel so much pleasure in viewing the holy man of the Church under the figure of teeth which tear sinners away from error, and under the figure of sheep that have been shorn, laying down the burden of the world like fleeces and arising from the washing of baptism bearing the twin commandments of love. Literally expressed, the truth he finds in the verse would be just as true, and he finds it difficult to answer just why he should feel such pleasure. Nevertheless, no one doubts that it is, at least in some cases, more pleasant to have knowledge communicated through figures and that there is greater satisfaction in overcoming the difficulty of such passages. The Holy Spirit has so written Scripture as to satisfy our hunger with the plainer passages and stimulate our appetite by the more difficult ones, but the truths contained in all the hard passages are elsewhere simply expressed, so that all of the saving truths of Scripture are presumably available in clear form.[2]

We can see from this passage the way in which the rhetoric of silence, which should have culminated—and frequently did—in clarity and immediacy, which should transcend words and arrive at things, could sometimes lead to verbal ingenuities and apparently arbitrary elaborations of relatively plain texts. We can also see that this took place when the things signified by the words, such as teeth and sheep, were in such contexts so bluntly simple that they could not easily bear the weight of meaning which every word of Scripture was presumed to possess.

[1] St. Augustine calls our attention to the peculiar pleasure to be found in unravelling obscurity, a pleasure he can't explain (*De doctrina Christiana*, II, 6, 7–8; cols. 38–39). Unlike St. Thomas who much later felt himself compelled to defend St. Augustine's views of obscurity, St. Augustine seems to have felt no need to take an apologetic stand on the question. As Marrou points out this reflects something of the intellectual temper of his times, pagan as well as Christian (*op. cit.*, p. 489 f).

[2] *De doctrina Christiana*, II, 6, 7; cols. 38–39.

We might point out here that such allegorical readings, even though they served to make much of Scripture intelligible to gentiles, were by no means unfamiliar to St. Augustine's contemporaries, pagan or Christian. The war between biblical and classical poetics concerned the surface of the text, so to speak, and not the possibility of allegorical exegesis.[1] Whether or not the text was obscure or clear, the movement of thought was through the words to the realities themselves, from the temporal realities to the eternal realities, from talk to silence, and from discourse to vision. Let us now consider briefly some other aspects of St. Augustine's revaluation of silence.

One of the most striking passages of the *Confessions* (VI, 3, 3; *PL*, XXXII, cols. 720–72), describes St. Augustine's bewilderment when he comes upon St. Ambrose reading in silence. Yet his reaction, which at first may bewilder us, would have been typical of that of most men of his time. From the very beginning, Greek and Latin literature was not only read aloud, as is well known, but the reader thought of it as something spoken.[2]

This tendency was reinforced by the age one lived in and Hellenistic culture was clearly a rhetorical one. Its characteristic literary pursuit was the public lecture and the cultivation of the spoken word long after it had ceased to have any political efficacy. Not only did the ancient orators from Isocrates to the end of antiquity carefully prepare their speeches as literary works, but the ideals and categories of rhetorical eloquence affected all the forms of literary activity including philosophy.[3]

It was only in the late Empire that silent reading began to

---

[1] The history of the conflict between biblical and classical poetics has yet to be written. For a study of a much later version of the conflict see M. H. Abrams, *The Mirror and the Lamp* (New York, 1953), esp. pp. 76 ff. and 147 ff. on Keble and the transfer of theological ideas to the uses of criticism.

[2] In his *Retractationes* (I, 6; *PL*, XXXII, col. 591) St. Augustine tells us that the first five books of his *De Musica* must be read aloud in order to understand his analysis of metre, for the reader must listen to the silences between the syllables. It is interesting that he did not feel it necessary to recommend this practice earlier at the time of writing *De Musica*.

[3] H. L. Marrou, *History of Education in Antiquity*, trans. by George Lamb (New York, 1956), esp. pp. 81 ff. and 195 ff.

come into existence, and it seems to have remained an exceptional practice throughout the Middle Ages. There is abundant evidence that medieval *scriptoria* were noisy places filled with the sounds of the copyists reciting their texts. In addition, the character of medieval orthography clearly shows that the scribe's memory was auditory rather than visual. Richard of Schöntal vividly describes his troubles in learning to read silently as follows: 'Oftentimes when I am reading straight from the book and in thought only . . . they [devils] make me read aloud word by word, that they may deprive me so much the more of the inward understanding thereof, and that I may the less penetrate into the interior force of the reading, the more I pour myself out in exterior speech.'[1]

Here we find a positive compulsion in trying to read silently which is quite the reverse of St. Augustine's bewilderment at St. Ambrose's practice. I think, however, that we can detect a similar although less violent reversal of values in St. Augustine himself if we compare his reaction to St. Ambrose with the famous account of his conversion in the *Confessions*. First let us look at his account of St. Ambrose's silent reading.

I could not ask of him [Ambrose] what I wished as I wished, for I was kept from any face to face conversation with him by the throng of men with their own troubles, whose infirmities he served. The very little time he was not with these he was refreshing either his body with necessary food or his mind with reading. When he read, his eyes travelled across the page and his heart sought into the sense, but voice and tongue were silent. No one was forbidden to approach him nor was it his custom to require that visitors should be announced: but when we came into him we often saw him reading and always to himself; and after we had sat long in silence, unwilling to interrupt a work on which he was so intent, we would depart again. We guessed that in the small time he could find for the refreshment of his mind, he would wish to be free from the distraction of other men's affairs, and not called away from what he was doing. Perhaps he was on his guard (if he read aloud) that someone listening should be troubled and want an explanation if the

---

[1] Bernhard Pez, *Theasurus anec. nov.*, 1721 vol. I, pt. 2, pp. 376 ff. cited in H. J. Chaytor, *From Script to Print* (Cambridge, 1945), 14–15. See also 7–15 for reading practices in the Middle Ages.

author he was reading expressed some idea over obscurely, and it might be necessary to expound or discuss some of the more difficult questions. And if he had to spend time on this, he would get through less reading than he wished. Or it may be that his real reason for reading to himself was to preserve his voice, which did in fact readily grow tired. But whatever reason for doing it, that man certainly had a good reason.[1]

Let us now turn to St. Augustine's account of his conversion:

And suddenly I heard a voice from some nearby house, a boy's voice or a girl's voice, I do not know: but it was a sort of singsong, repeated again and again, 'Take and read, take and read.' I ceased weeping and immediately began to search my mind most carefully as to whether children were accustomed to chant these words in any kind of game, and I could not remember that I had ever heard any such thing. Damming back my flood of tears I arose, interpreting the incident as quite certainly a divine command to open my book of Scripture and read the passage at which I should open. For it was part of what I had been told about Anthony, that from the Gospel which he happened to be reading he had felt he was being admonished as though what he read was spoken directly to himself: *Go, sell what thou hast and give to the poor and thou shalt have treasure in heaven; and come follow Me.* (Matt. 19.21) By this experience he had been in that instant converted to You. So I was moved to return to the place where Alypius was sitting, for I had put down the Apostle's book there when I arose. I snatched it up, opened it and in silence read the passage upon which my eyes first fell: *Not in rioting and drunkenness, not in chambering and impurities, not in contention and envy, but put ye on the Lord Jesus Christ and make not provision for the flesh in its concupiscences* (Rom. 13.13). I had no wish to read further, and no need. For in that instant, with the very ending of the sentence, it was as though a light of utter confidence shone in all my heart, and all the darkness of uncertainty vanished away.[2]

We notice that at this crucial juncture of his life, at the very moment that St. Augustine is waiting for the voice of the silent

---

[1] *Confessions*, VI, 33; *PL*, XXXII, cols. 720–21. I cite the translation of F. J. Sheed (New York, 1943).

[2] *Ibid.*, VIII, 12, 29; *PL*, XXXII, col. 762.

inner teacher, he reads in silence. It is hard not to seem to make too much of this detail, yet we must recall that the account of St. Augustine's conversion in his *Confessions* is not the only one, and that it is a highly self-conscious and literary account in which every detail is intended to carry weight and to assimilate his own experience to archetypal models in the tradition of conversion. The famous episode, in part, is an artfully constructed symbolic event which subsumes the actual raw autobiographical details into an artistic and theological unity, into a literary form which is partly 'fictional.' The voice in the garden, the conversion by reading a book, these and other details would seem to be in part sacred fictions somewhat removed from the unquestionable real basis which inspired them.[1]

I think, therefore, that it is safe to say that we are to understand that St. Augustine had finally learned the meaning of silence and that St. Ambrose's 'good reason' for silence was nothing else than listening to the instruction of the inner teacher. A philosophical theology of silence was present in both Platonism and Christianity, and the latter began to develop it quite early. Its roots can be found in Pauline texts such as Romans 6.25–26 'the revelation of the mystery which was kept secret since the world began' and Hebrews 3.11–18 and 4.1–11 where St. Paul describes the inability of the Israelites to rest in Canaan and the superior rest available to the believer, of which God's rest after the creation is a type.[2]

Such conceptions were developed by Ignatius Martyr to include the notion that revelation continued in silence and that the Incarnation was a descent from silence into 'speech' or *logos*.

It is better to be silent and be real, than to talk and to be unreal. Teaching is good, if the teacher does what he says. There is then one teacher who 'spoke and it came to pass,' and what he has done even in silence is worthy of the Father. He who has heard the word of Jesus for a true possession can also hear his silence, that he may be perfect that he may act through his

[1] Pierre Courcelle, *Recherches sur les Confessions de St. Augustin* (Paris, 1950), 'Le "tolle, lege"; fiction littéraire et réalité,' pp. 188–202.

[2] On the theology of silence see the indications of C. Pera, ed. *S. Thomae Aquinatis in librum beati Dionysii de divinis nominibus expositio* (Turin–Rome, 1950), p. 338.

speech, and be understood through his silence. Nothing is hid from the Lord, but even our secret things are near him. Let us therefore do all things as though he were dwelling in us, that we may be his temples, and that he may be our God in us.[1]

For St. Augustine all dialectic, true rhetoric, and thought itself were but attempts to reascend to that silence from which the world fell into the perpetual clamour of life as fallen men know it. There is, however, no gnosticism or pelagianism in St. Augustine. All of the rules of exegesis are subordinated to the one great rule, the law of love in the heart of the interpreter, and all the truths needed for salvation were perfectly clear in Scripture, for they too were subsumed into the law of love which is the teaching of all the prophets and saints.[2]

The Mimetic Dialectic and the Ladder of Arts

We shall now consider St. Augustine's rhetoric of silence in its more dialectical form and some of the implications of this scheme of interpreting experience for his classification of the arts.

It is important for us at this point to clarify the sense in which St. Augustine uses the mimetic dialectic. It is, exactly as in Plato, the making of images of an eternal and intelligible reality. The images are more or less accurate, closer or farther from the realities they imitate, but they are always merely images of an absolute reality made up of pure forms. This is to be carefully distinguished from the Aristotelian concept of *mimesis*. Such imitation is always of a particular thing, of a substance in the primary sense, and it is the essence of all

---

[1] Ignatius Martyr, *Epist. ad Ephesios*, 15, 1–3 with text and translation of Kirsopp Lake in *The Apostolic Fathers* (London, 1912), 2 vols. in the Loeb Classical Library, vol. 1. Cf. the same epistle, 19, 1: 'And the virginity of Mary, and her giving birth were hidden from the Prince of this world, as was also the death of the Lord. Three mysteries of a cry which were wrought in the stillness of God. Also cf. Ignatius' *Epist. ad Magnesios*, 8, 2: 'For the divine prophets lived according to Jesus Christ. Therefore they were also persecuted, being inspired by his grace, to convince the disobedient that there is one God, who manifested himself through Jesus Christ his son, who is his Word proceeding from silence, who in all respects was pleasing to him that sent him.'

[2] Cf. *De doctrina Christiana*, II, 9, 14 to II, 15, 22; cols. 42–46: II, 27, 38; col. 80.

artistic activity, of all making. The subject of such imitation in poetry is actions in men.[1]

The platonic concept of *mimesis* culminates in a mystical theology in which ultimate reality is beyond rational comprehension and in which all things and all linguistic potentialities are simply symbols of a reality which transcends them but to which they serve to elevate the soul. Everything thus is a metaphor for the unseen and the incomprehensible, whether a word or a thing, an intelligible or sensible reality, a 'literal' or a metaphorical statement.[2]

From another point of view St. Augustine is employing the structural principle of the philosophical gradation of forms, a hierarchical structure which combines differences of degree as well as of kind. Thus the moral virtues are not merely different in kind but also in degree so that they can be arranged on an ascending scale of values. The variable in such a scale is the same as the generic essence so that the lower forms are simply imperfect specifications of the generic essence which is more and more perfectly realized as we move to the top of the scale.[3]

A major point of division on this scale for St. Augustine, as for Plato, is between the sensible and the intelligible which corresponds to the distinction in rhetoric between things and signs, 'silence' and speech, realities and words. In St. Augustine's treatment of sensation we discover the same pattern of ascent to the intelligible, the silent, that we have found in his rhetoric.

We need sensation in order to know corporeal things, and there is no need to deny that there is action on the body from without and that the body suffers this action.[4] The soul, however, does not suffer change, but simply acts in the body. It is observant of the changes induced in the body from external objects of sensation and changes itself in correspondence with

[1] R. McKeon, 'Literary Criticism and the Concept of Imitation in Antiquity,' in *Critics and Criticism*, ed. R. S. Crane (Chicago, 1952), pp. 147–75, esp. pp. 152, 161, 170.

[2] Cf. R. McKeon, 'Poetry and Philosophy in the Twelfth Century,' in Crane, *op. cit.*, pp. 297–318, 317.

[3] R. G. Collingwood, *An Essay on Philosophical Method* (Oxford, 1933), 54 ff.

[4] *Epist*. XIII, 4; *PL*, XXXIII, col. 178 and *De Trinitate*, XI, 5, 9; *PL*, XLII, col. 42: XI, 8, 14; col. 970.

the changes in the body.[1] Although we need sensation to know corporeal things—God teaches us intelligible things—there is an innate element in sensitive cognition itself. Indeed, the analysis of sensation leads to soul and pure thought, that of pure thought to God.[2]

Thus no one can teach us an idea without making us discover it, nor a thing without making us see it. Whether of an object of sense or thought, Augustine affirms that apprehension is from within. Apprehension may need external signs but only that it may turn within in its spontaneity to find the substance of what it seems to receive.

Beauty, too, is both sensible and intelligible, although it is of course primarily intelligible. It exists when both the unity and order of a thing, its ontological truth and goodness, are manifested. It is the delightful illumination of goodness and truth which simultaneously enlightens and gladdens the perceiver.[3] The world is God's poem (*Civ. Dei*, XI, ch. 18; *PL*, XLI, col. 332) and the beauty of creation derives from the unity and arrangement of parts as does the beauty of a poem (*De musica*, VI, 17, 56, *PL*, 32, col. 1191). The artist contains the image of God in a special way because he continues God's work (*Conf.*, VII, 7, 11; *PL*, XXXII, col. 740) and all beautiful objects, natural or artificial, are but means of ascent to self-subsistent beauty (*De vera religione*, XXIV, 45; *PL*, XXXIV, col. 141 and *De ordine*, II, 14, 39; *PL*, XXXII, col. 1013).

The arts, through which men make beautiful objects serving like all beautiful things to mediate between the many and the one, derive from a rational activity and not from a simply imitative one. Indeed, aesthetic pleasure is filled with the intelligible and with the rational.[4]

---

[1] *De quantitate animae*, I, 32, 71; *PL*, XXXII, col. 1074.

[2] *De magistro* XII, 40; *PL*, XXXII, col. 1217. Cf. Etienne Gilson, *Introduction a l'étude de St. Augustin*, 2nd ed. (Paris, 1943), pp. 88, 102.

[3] *De immortalitate animae*, XII, 19; *PL*, XXXII, col. 1031. Cf. *Epist. classis*, I, 3, 4; *PL*, XXXIII, col. 65, where corporeal beauty is defined as a proportion of parts together with a certain agreeableness (*suavitas*) of colour. This Ciceronian definition is repeated in *Civ. Dei*, XXII, 19, 2; *PL*, 41, col. 781.

[4] *De musica*, I, 4, 5; *PL*, XXXII, cols. 1085–86: *De ordine* II, 34; *PL*, XXXII, cols. 1010–11. Cf. Emmanuel Chapman, *Saint Augustine's Philosophy of Beauty* (New York, 1939), pp. 69, 7. St. Augustine's

The various arts contain or embody different grades of rationality and are also imitative in different degrees. Their relative position on the scale of forms depends precisely on the grade of rationality they contain, so that painting and sculpture rank well below music or literature, and these last two are truly superior only in their transcendental forms as the silence of both truth and that unheard cosmic music of which heard music is only a pale reflection. It was this unheard music which David truly loved.[1] The art of music is thus really timeless and only its phenomenal manifestation is in time. Music itself, like rhetoric, must tend toward silence, from the sensible to the intelligible. So too with the beauties of the world of which the beauties of a painting are a mere copy. The beauty of the world like all beauty must assist us to rise to God.

It would be a mistake to see in this a kind of puritanical didacticism. On the scale of forms all grades of reality imitate each other with higher and higher degrees of intelligibility and being. Man's duty and privilege is to rise to the absolute reality. St. Augustine's judgment is always relative to the position, implied or expressed, of the activity under consideration on a scale of forms. Thus, all 'poetical' works in the sense

---

[1] *De civitate Dei*, XVII, 14; *PL*, XLI, col. 547.

conception of degrees of rationality in sensation is, of course, closely related to his conception of the imagination. Unlike his predecessors he insists on the difference between the simple sensory image (*visio*) and the reproductive imagination with its freedom to make its own synthesis of sense. He also distinguished between sense, phantasy proper (pictorial representations, myths) and phantasy in the service of reason (figures of geometricians, etc.). Three kinds of vision are analogous to this triad: corporeal, spiritual, and intellectual. Corporeal vision corresponds to the first two categories of sense and phantasy, spiritual vision to the third, and intellectual vision transcends the imagination altogether. This last is the only one which is not deceptive. The experience of Sinai (Exod. 19.18) is an example of corporeal vision, while the Apocalypse of John and the experience recorded in Isaiah 6.1 are examples of spiritual vision. In Numbers 12.8 there is an example of vision of the highest sort, in which God is above all imagination (*De Gen. ad litt.*, 12, 27; *PL*, XXXIV, col. 477). There is an analogous classification of kinds of prophetic vision, the most intellectual being the highest. (*De Gen. ad litt.* 12, 9–11; *PL*, XXXIV, cols. 461 ff.). Cf. M. W. Bundy, *The Theory of Imagination in Classical and Medieval Thought* in *University of Illinois Studies in Language and Literature*, XII (1927), nos. 2–3, pp. 1–289, 158–71.

of works of art are works of the imagination to the extent that they have their origin in the life of the senses, although they are elaborated and truly exist in the mind.. Some such works are formed directly from sensation, others from suppositions, and still others from reflection. The mind of the painter obviously remained at the first level while the poet and musician ascended to the more reflective and hence more rational level.[1]

St. Augustine clearly favoured the 'time' arts, literature and music, for they not only allow for more 'rationality' but because of the special position time has in the philosophy of St. Augustine. Time is more of an image of eternity than space. Further, it is a kind of distension of the soul, its very dimension of life. It is significant in this regard that St. Augustine employed literature and 'music,' that is, poetic metrics in the broadest sense, in his analysis of time and memory, for memory is not of the past but is synonymous with the divine, present within, the inner teacher.[2]

St. Augustine's sometimes contradictory evaluation of the arts, and his generally consistent preference for the arts of time over those of space, are consequences of his adoption of the 'mimetic dialectic' proceeding from the sensible exterior to the intelligible interior and finally to God. The progress is from sense to thought, from a lower 'imitation' to a more real archetype which may in turn be 'mimetic' relative to something still higher. All thought moves 'from the exterior to the interior, from the lower to the higher.'[3]

Thus the problem as to whether St. Augustine turned away from sensible beauty in the course of his life to find justification only for intelligible beauty is in some respects a pseudo-problem.[4] In any philosophical scale of forms, classes overlap and a

---

[1] Cf. *Epist. Classis*, I, 8; *PL*, XXXII, cols. 68–71.

[2] *Conf.*, XI, 26, 33; *PL*, XXXII, col. 822, and *De musica*, VI, 8, 21, *PL*, XXXII, col. 1174. Cf. Gilson, *op. cit.*, pp. 138, 249, 253–54.

[3] *Enarr. in Ps.*, 14, 5; *PL*, XXXVII, col. 1887: ab exterioribus ad interiora, ab inferioribus ad suprema.

[4] For this problem and references to the literature on the question see Chapman, *op. cit.*, nn. 1–3, pp. 102–03. St. Augustine is careful to point out in *De ordine* that the term 'beautiful' is used for an object agreeable to sight while the term 'harmonious' is used for an object agreeable to hearing. However, reason is not present in such a single sight or sound, but only when proportion and harmony are present, that is to say in an

concept—truth, beauty, being—admits of degrees and runs through the whole scale. Terms like 'imitation' then are dialectical instruments and their meaning depends on what degree of the scale the thinker is using for his angle of vision, whether he is looking up to the next higher rung or down on the one below. There is no question that, for St. Augustine, the thinker is always impelled up, and that the nature of St. Augustine's thought led him to look more and more to the intelligible, the eternal, and the 'silent.'

---

arrangement of sights or sounds (II, 32; *PL*, XXXII, col. 1010). It is interesting to note that, although St. Augustine, following Aristotle and Plato, gave a kind of primacy to the sense of sight as the most rational of the senses, he still had little regard for the arts of this sense, since his criterion of value was rationality. During the Renaissance, Leonardo and others used the same doctrine of the primacy of sight to justify another and diametrically opposed evaluation of painting.

CHAPTER II

A Seventeenth-century Theory
of Metaphysical Poetry

In treating the problem of the nature of poetry, the vast majority of the critics of the High Renaissance made a long, painful and sometimes useless attempt to interpret the *Poetics* of Aristotle for guidance on this subject. Compared to the attention the *Poetics* received, the *Phaedrus* and *Ion* of Plato were virtually neglected. The notion of divine madness, 'enthusiasm,' or *'furor poeticus'* can be found in many critical works of the Renaissance, but the great effort of criticism was directed toward an interpretation of the concept of 'imitation.' Plato was more often consulted as the authority on all questions concerning the idea of beauty.

The result of this extensive elaboration of the doctrine of 'mimesis' was that most critics of the *cinquecento* maintained the conception of poetry as the imitation of a 'reality' defined as the essential characteristics of human nature and human events. However, this same 'reality' was also the concern of the historian who treated it in a less 'poetic' way than did the poet. According to this analysis only one task really remained to the poet: the provision of *eloquentia* for the *doctrina* supplied by the historian. Thus Renaissance criticism did not go much further than previous criticism in giving poetry any kind of independence among the creations of the human spirit, and still sought for the 'poetic' in the notion of an intrinsically poetic subject-matter.

The development of *seicento* criticism in Italy and Spain was conditioned by the need for a fresh theory of poetry after the exhaustion of the concept of imitation, a need analogous to that felt by creative writers during an epoch of imitation of classics. Among the few kinds of poetry free from the weight of tradition during the Renaissance were the romantic Christian epic and the vernacular epic, both modern creations for which no classical precedents existed. Practically everything else was subject to the authority of the ancients. Both writers and critics began to demand something new and their needs were reflected in the shift in taste which marks the opening decades of the seventeenth century.

The critics still relied heavily on Aristotle but they placed their emphasis on the *Rhetoric* instead of the *Poetics*, and in particular on the theory of metaphor advanced in the third book. The new movement, sparked like the old one by Aristotle but with emphasis on other aspects of his work, ultimately produced a body of critical tracts in which some of the new literary tendencies of the age achieved theoretical formulation.

The major writers on the theory of the conceit, or metaphor (the terms are synonymous), were Baltasar Gracián in Spain and Emmanuele Tesauro, Cardinal Sforza-Pallavicino, Pierfrancesco Minozzi and Matteo Pellegrini in Italy. Their collective efforts helped effect the liberation of poetry from a narrow conception of subject-matter and of rules, placing more emphasis on those aspects of poetic creation included in the concept of *manike*. [1]

This new movement reinterpreted the previous critical vocabulary. The poetic faculty was identified with *ingegno* or 'wit,' the human faculty which creates metaphors and discovers similitudes and identities. [2] *Gusto* or 'good taste' was that aspect of *ingegno* which made judgments and determined the worth of

---

[1] Two of these authors, Gracián and Sforza-Pallavicino, are better known in other capacities than as literary critics. Gracián achieved his European reputation as a moralist while Sforza-Pallavicino became famous as the papal historian of the Council of Trent.

[2] *Ingegno* in poetry and *ingenium* in logic were intimately connected, for in both cases the thing aimed at is a 'novelty.' *Ingenium* in logic is always defined as *inventio novi*.

a metaphor and therefore of a poem, since the theorists conceived of the poem as simply a group of metaphorical statements. The interest in metaphor was not only the dominant theme of the theorists of the conceit but was one of the major interests of the humanists as well. Renaissance theory of metaphor always emphasized the pedagogic aspects of Aristotle's pronouncements on the subject, sometimes to the point of pedantry. Both Castiglione and Erasmus, for example, especially praised the power of metaphor to please while teaching. It was the best means of impressing the reader with an important subject-matter, *doctrina*, by means of *eloquentia*, and thereby facilitated the retention of knowledge.

The writers of tractates on the conceit also began, like their predecessors of the *cinquecento*, by dividing the 'form' of a literary creation from its content. They stated the problem in the same way and agreed that the content was either moral or immoral and consisted of things, actions or thoughts. The 'form,' however, was for our theorists the true key to the work of art. It was imparted by the activity of *ingegno* or 'wit,' and created that element of the work of literary art which is esthetically pleasing. This conception reversed the emphasis of the *cinquecento* critics. It was as a reaction to their predecessors that the *concettisti* turned most of their attention to the study and analysis of the 'form.'

It was this same emphasis on 'form' that led Cardinal Sforza-Pallavicino to observe that the originality of an author is always to be determined by the 'form,' since the content *qua* content is never original.[1]

Pierfrancesco Minozzi, another important critic, says of the 'form':

La forma è più bella della materia; e perciò si devono più apprezzare gl'ingegnosi i quali sono i fabri dei componimenti, che gli eruditi; poichè questi dan la materia, se pur la danno, da comporre e quelli danno la forma di ben comporre.[2]

[1] Cardinal Sforza-Pallavicino, *Trattato del dialogo e dello stile* (Modena, 1819), p. 83. The first edition of this work is dated 1646 and was published in Rome. A third edition was issued in 1662.

[2] Pierfrancesco Minozzi, *Gli sfogamenti dell'ingegno* (Venezia, 1641), pp. 254–55.

Thus the learned man provided the material for the poet, whereas the 'witty' man, the man gifted with *ingegno*, was the man who could actually write well or 'compose' (the Italian word is usually *favellare*). While art for *cinquecento* criticism consisted in a representation of nature which would possess 'verisimilitude' or capture the idea or essence of the subject, for the *seicento* the essence of poetry lay in a formal relationship of words and statements to one another. In poetry, words or representations were not placed in their everyday relationship to one another and the concept of 'wit' or *ingegno* was evolved to explain a particular 'poetic' choice and arrangement of the linguistic elements of a poem.[1] By the side of this formal conception the critics occasionally introduced the notion of a 'witty' subject-matter. However, this seems accidental, for all of the critics of the conceit agreed in denying the existence of a poetic subject-matter.

Baltasar Gracián, much read and studied in seventeenth-century Italy, provides us with another keynote of the new poetic. The different representations joined in metaphor were, for the universally acknowledged father of the new movement, two 'knowable extremes,' while the faculty capable of binding them was *ingegno* or 'wit.' In binding extremes, the *ingegno* produced a metaphor or conceit. Gracián defined the conceit:

es un acto del entendimiento que esprime la correspondencia que se halla entre los objectos.[2]

The conceit is thus the harmonic correlation between two or three knowable extremes, the act whereby the understanding discerns the correspondences between things. Gracián developed this notion in the following analogy:

. . . lo que es para los ojos la hermosura y para los oídos la consonancia, eso es para el entendimiento el concepto.[3]

[1] Giulio Marzot, *L'Ingegno e il genio nel seicento* (Firenze, 1944), ch. II, *passim*.

[2] Baltasar Gracián, *Arte de ingenio* (Madrid, 1944), p. 47. First edition, Madrid, 1642.

[3] *Ibid.*, p. 42. The definition of the conceit as the expression of the correspondences to be found between objects (and it must be remembered that the conceit is the essence of poetry for these theorists) reveals the point of contact of this critical movement with certain aspects of the scientific and philosophical methodology of the Renaissance. The theory of

This analogy indicates that Gracián believed the poetic faculty was rooted in the understanding, although the critics of the conceit attempted to dissociate the understanding conceived as *ingegno* from the understanding conceived as the faculty seeking logical truth. The correspondences which the artist both discovered and created are not the products of discursive reason but of the creative insight of *ingegno*. Pallavicino said that the main function of the conceit is to show how things which appear unconnected are really similar and to arouse thereby a certain sensation of wonder.[1] For Tesauro the purpose of the conceit was to make occult couplings by discovering wondrous similitudes and he describes similitude as the mother of wit and of metaphor.[2]

It is clear then that for the theorists there was a nondiscursive form of the understanding called 'wit' or *ingegno* which is the artistic faculty par excellence. The *ingegno* joined the representations of all things and even when it joined them by antithesis, the antithesis always resolved itself into an 'artful' (*artificioso*) revelation of the correspondences between objects.

With minor modifications, this doctrine was central to all tractates on the conceit. However, the theorists agreed that the *ingegno*, although intimately connected with the understanding, did not aspire to simple, logical truth but rather to a beauty or *acutezza* (wit) which it found in the *relationship* between the same knowable extremes that it discovered. Having found a marvellous and unforeseen relationship, the *ingegno* then developed it in all its concordances and gave it eloquent expression. The conceit, then, also meant the *elaboration* of 'witty' (*ingegnoso*) correspondences.

[1] Sforza-Pallavicino, *Trattato*, p. 16.
[2] Tesauro, *Il cannochiale aristotelico*, 2nd ed. (Venezia, 1663), pp. 245–58; 1st ed. (1654).

the conceit seems to be, in part, the application of the principle of universal analogy and correspondences to the problems of literary criticism and poetics. The notion of cosmic affinities has, of course, a long history but I think it is safe to say that it dominated the intellectual life of the Renaissance more than that of any other period. This parallelism was by no means consciously articulated, but it none the less existed and is itself analogous to the remarkable parallel Ernst Cassirer has demonstrated between Renaissance mathematico-physical theory and theory of art.

Matteo Pellegrini in *I fonti dell'ingegno* emphasized the non-discursive and formal nature of the conceit.

L'acutezza non consiste in un ragionimento, ma in un detto, il quale, può, sì aver molte parti, ma con tutto ciò, almeno virtualmente, sarà sempre una . . .[1]

Thus he sharply distinguished the conceit from discursive statement and defined it in terms of the manner in which its various parts are joined together to create a unity. The artistic merit of a conceit has nothing to do with the quality of the various parts taken by themselves but is a function of the 'form' (*artificio e forma del favellare*). The primacy of form over content is a guiding principle for the critics of the conceit, and they not only apply this notion to the evaluation of a poem as a whole but to each individual metaphor as well.

One of the further requirements of the conceit was that it be 'marvellous' (*mirabile*) or extraordinary. As we have seen, the conceit was expected to furnish some remarkable new similitude or insight and arouse wonder. Some scholars have interpreted this as a desire on the part of the theorists to justify a rather perverse desire for the shocking, the recondite and the extravagant. This is in part true and verifiable in poetic practice. However, in terms of the theory of the *ingegno* and of the conceit, this desire for the *mirabile* is no more than the desire for those very qualities of insight and 'vision' which every good metaphor must possess. Tesauro distinguished very carefully between the sensation of wonder and marvel derived from the perception of the development of correspondences and the surprise derived from some kind of unusual reflection.[2] The true metaphor was brief, intense and established a remarkable identity. For Pallavicino, it had to be 'una osservazione mirabile raccolta in un detto breve.'[3] Pellegrini, suggesting Horace, said that the conceit should 'lightly wound the intellect of the hearer' (*dolcemente ferir l'intelletto di chi ode*) and 'esser raro, e cioè sfuggire il comune.' Tesauro also agreed that it had to be brief to prick the intellect of the hearer and please by its revelation of correspondences.

---

[1] Cited in Croce, *Problemi di estetica*, 4th ed. (Bari, 1949), pp. 329–30.
[2] Tesauro, *op. cit.*, p. 455.
[3] Pallavicino, *Trattato*, p. 79 and p. 103.

However, the theorists warn against making the conceit too obscure. In condemning excessive obscurity, Tesauro said that the terse and 'dark' style of a Tacitus or a Sallust could be excessive, but elsewhere added that their writings also demonstrate how two obscure sayings joined together can become luminous.[1]

The concepts I have discussed are common to all the theorists and among the Italian theorists the terminology is quite uniform. Gracián the Spaniard used some slightly different terms but his ideas are the same as those of Tesauro. The latter's *significazione ingegnosa* is the same as the 'knowable extremes' of Gracián. The notion that the conceit may also harmoniously unfold or develop a set of correspondences was well developed in the work of Gracián and we find a similar notion in Tesauro's concept of the *sillogismo urbanamente fallace*, called *fallace* to distinguish it from the logical syllogism whose purpose is to investigate the truth and not to create beauty. The enthymeme of traditional rhetoric was thus adopted by Tesauro to express the conception of what we today would call the 'logically expanded metaphor.' Poetry belonged to the art of rhetoric and it is not surprising to find rhetorical terms adapted to the use of literary criticism. Rhetoric in turn was connected to logic as the science of 'decurtated syllogisms.'

Among the theorists of the conceit there were also those who were quite critical of exaggerated conceits and all of them recognized some criterion of decorum by which to judge a display of *ingegno*. The most acute critics of excesses were Matteo Pellegrini and Cardinal Sforza-Pallavicino, but we must remember that their adverse criticism was directed only against excesses; they agree on all fundamentals with the more ardent exponents of *concettismo* such as Gracián and Tesauro. It is interesting to observe, however, that Tesauro was the only theorist who offered to explain why excesses take place. The explanation is to be found in the nature of the *ingegno* itself which once set in motion is difficult to control and inevitably tends to excess if not disciplined.[2]

The work of Sforza-Pallavicino provided a curious kind of exception to the general unanimity of opinion among our

[1] Tesauro, *op. cit.*, p. 276 and p. 60; p. 252 and p. 60.
[2] Tesauro, *op. cit.*, p. 232.

theorists. In his *Trattato del dialogo e dello stile*, a book primarily on style, he expounded all of the orthodox ideas about poetry and literary creation that we find in the general theory of *concettismo*. But in his *Del bene*, a book primarily concerned with morality but with brief sections containing scattered comments and observations on literature, he formulated a poetic which Croce considers an anticipation of the aesthetic theories of modern idealism. This strange deviation from the norm must be examined in the light of Pallavicino's rejection of this theory for conventional *concettismo* in the final form of the *Trattato* published after *Del bene*.

In the latter work he began by making the traditional tri-partite division of the human spirit as to its modes of knowing. They are the following:

1. First apprehension: knowledge of the object before any judgment is made as to its truth or falsity, 'senza peró autenticarlo per vero né riprovarlo per falso.'

2. Judgment (giudicio): the faculty which 'proferisce sentenza intorno alla verità o falsità dell'oggetto . . . contien solo quei giudicii . . . che alla sola apparenza dell'obietto sorgono in noi.'

3. Discourse: the faculty by means of which the intellect, 'per mezzo di quelle proposizioni immediate e postagli quasi a canto della natura, discorre di mano in mano a altre verità più remote.'[1]

First apprehension is the moment of art. The nature of art is therefore to represent the object with such vivacity and vigour that memories and impressions are evoked and concentrated together making our emotions more vivid and more intense. Art does not seek after the 'good' or the 'true' but holds up for contemplation the spectacle of beauty. Since first apprehension is prior to judgment, it is capable of neither truth nor error:

. . . nulla rileva al vagheggiatore del bello per verificar le sue cognizioni, che l'oggetto da lui appreso sia o non sia difatto qual ei nell'animo se'l figura.

[1] Pallavicino, *Del bene* (Milano, 1831), Book III, Part 2, chs. 49, 50. 1st ed. (Roma, 1644). Prof. P. O. Kristeller has observed that the notion of 'first apprehension' strongly suggests an adaptation of the stoic epistemology to the use of poetic theory.

Pallavicino reaffirmed the non-utilitarian nature of poetry by repeating that its only purpose is the adornment of the intellect with images of great beauty and splendour.

. . . l'unico scopo delle poetiche favole sì è l'adornare l'intelletto d'immagini o vogliam dire d'appresioni sontuose, nuove, mirabili, splendide. E ciò è gradito per sì gran bene al genere umano, ch'egli ha voluto rimunerare i poeti con gloria superiore a tutte l'altre professioni.

Finally, Pallavicino rejected that version of the theory of verisimilitude which tended to identify poetry with history. He says that even that which is logically false acquires poetic verisimilitude if it partakes of the unity of artistic representation. Since art as first apprehension is prior to any logical judgment, Pallavicino with great consistency rejected the identification of poetry with morality, history, theology, and all the things with which much of previous criticism had tended to identify it. He returned to the orthodox didactic theory of the conceit in the final edition of the *Trattato* and I suspect that the good cardinal did so because his piety would not permit him to accept a clear dissociation of art from morality.[1]

But even in the midst of expounding his non-cognitive view of poetry, he gives warm praise to the virtues of the conceit; and not without the loss of some consistency, for he defines the conceit as an intellectual creation that can give cognition as well as aesthetic pleasure. The inconsistencies between Pallavicino as orthodox and unorthodox *concettista* can be somewhat mitigated if we take the idea of 'first apprehension' as a development of the notion of the *mirabile* instead of as exclusively foreshadowing the idea of an autonomous aesthetic activity. In *Del bene*, the same work in which he explains his theory of first apprehension, Pallavicino says of the conceit:

. . . poichè quel dono di natura, che si chiama ingegno, consiste appunto in congiungere, per mezzo di scaltre apprensioni, oggetti che pareano sconessi, rintracciando in essi gli occulti vestigi d'amicizia fra la stessa contrarietà, la non avvertita unità di special simiglianza nella somma dissimilitudine,

[1] *Ibid.*, chs. 53, 49, 51; cf. *Trattato*, p. 216.

qualche vincolo, qualche parentela, qualche confederazione, dove altri non l'avrebbe mai sospettato.[1]

The term apprehension is here used to describe the *ingegno* in its usual function of discerning correspondences. Many of what Pallavicino described as the qualities of 'first apprehension' are precisely those qualities which the good conceit or metaphor was said to give and which the theorists usually described as the *mirabile*.

Pallavicino represents the only case of theoretical duality among the theorists of the conceit as well as the only one of our critics to display any considerable philosophical originality. They generally spoke as one man and, having touched upon his heterodoxy, we can again consider them as a group.

As the theorists made more and more rules and classifications, they became aware of the danger of falling into an excessively rationalistic approach to literature, and, with considerable literary acumen, they cautioned the reader against thinking that one can be a poet by following precepts. Pallavicino warned against this error in both the *Del bene* and in the *Trattato*:

. . . Che giovano i precetti dell'arte dove manca l'abilità dell'ingegno? Perciò la più vera topica e più sagace è la perspicacia che ne dà la natura . . .
Che siccome ad un braccio debole niun arte di schermire basta per maneggiar la spada, così ad un intelletto debole niun arte di comporre basta per maneggiar bene la penna.[2]

Pellegrini denied that the poet must share the critics' conception of the rules in order to write poetry and write it well. Tesauro agreed with this, affirming that formal study is not enough and that the gift of nature is higher than any rules.

---

[1] Pallavicino, *Del bene*, Book III, Part 2, ch. 55. Note the omission of emphasis on the pedagogic properties of the conceit so apparent in the *Trattato*, and instead the heavy emphasis on those qualities I have described as 'vision' and 'wonder' (Pallavicino, *Trattato*, p. 216). When, as in the *Trattato*, he praises Dante and says that he is read with special interest by *ingegnosi*, he is perhaps only directing our attention to those qualities of poetry which he subsumed under the concept of 'first apprehension,' qualities of intensity, clarity and vividness which characterize Dante's metaphors. *Ibid.*, p. 109.
[2] Pallavicino, *Del bene*, Book III, Part 2, ch. 55; *Trattato*, p. 248.

However, even *ingegno* and formal study together were not enough, for *furore* or poetic madness was also required. Tesauro, wishing to escape from the threat of a purely intellectualistic and cognitive view of poetry, introduced the *furor poeticus* alongside the concept of *ingegno* thereby supporting the view that poetry is the result of a special state of the human spirit. The following passage from Tesauro brings this aspect of his theory into evidence:

Le passioni dell'animo arruotono l'acume dell'ingegno umano . . . Et la ragione è che l'affetto accende gli spiriti, i quali son le facelle dell'intelletto; e la immagine, affetta a quel solo obbietto, in quell'uno minutamente osserva tutte le circostanze, benchè lontane. Et come alterato, stranamente alterandole, accrescendole e accopiandole, ne fabrica iperbolici e capricciosi figurati concetti.[1]

In order to seize the hidden relationships between things and thereby make a conceit, the poet had first to have his *ingegno* sharpened by the 'passions of the soul.' Tesauro took Plato at his word and maintained that the insane are especially gifted at making metaphors and being *ingegnosi*, defining insanity itself as a kind of metaphor where the insane person is continually taking one thing for another.

I matti, meglio che i sani (chi lo crederebbe?) sono condizionati a fabricar nella loro fantasia metafore facete e simboli arguti; anzi la pazzia altro non è che la metafora la quale prende una cosa per altra. Quindi ordinariamente succede che i matti son di bellissimo ingegno, e gl'ingegni più sottili come poeti e matematici, son proclivi ad ammatire. Perocchè quanto la fantasia è più gagliarda, tanto è veramente più disposta ad imprimirsi li fantasmi delle scienze.[2]

[1] Tesauro, *op. cit.*, p. 83.

[2] *Ibid.*, p. 86. Among examples of men of *bellissimo ingegno* Tesauro placed the poets alongside the mathematicians. In this context *ingegno* seems to be identified with a more extensive notion of the process of creative thought and the basic similarity of all creative thought is at least momentarily perceived. Dimly perceived is perhaps a better description of this insight, for this is his only explicit reference of this kind.

He said elsewhere that even the inspirations and visions of the prophets—like those of madmen—were divine *acutezze*.

Although these notions may seem like a fully developed doctrine of poetic inspiration similar to the doctrine Plato advanced in the *Phaedrus*, the *furore* only served to put the faculty of *ingegno* into operation and was not itself a kind of preternatural visitation or illumination. Ignoring the logic of their position, most theorists strongly desired to join this new poetic to the most notable names of Western culture, and indeed they could do this to a certain extent. The poets of the *dolce stil nuovo*, Petrarch and, in classical times, Martial, all could afford a kind of precedent for the desire for 'wit' which had then achieved its greatest effect in literary production and criticism. Tesauro, however, hailed Aristotle as his intellectual father and the man from whom he learned all that it was important to know about poetry. Pallavicino also looked to Aristotle as the source of his theories and complained in his *Trattato* that the criticism of his own time was not philosophical enough. Pellegrini, the theorist most critical of *concettismo*, although in essence a defender of the movement, reviewed the literary theories of antiquity and what they had to say on the subject of 'wit'; he praised the ancients for not having spent too much time on the subject, concluding that antiquity offered no real precedent for poets like Marino.[1]

Pellegrini alone acknowledged this truth. The other theorists reveal a conflict between theory and taste. Tesauro even admired Cicero's prose for its 'wit' (*sic*). However, he also praised it for its smoothness and rotundity, temporarily forgetting the implications of his poetic and betraying the humanist. He usually showed more consistency and preferred the more eccentric Latin authors in his effort to find a noble pedigree for *concettismo*. The theorists really admired authors like Tacitus, Persius, Sallust, Seneca, and Martial.[2]

This desire for classical ancestry was also coupled to a doctrine of sobriety in poetry in the more 'Apollonian' moments of our theorists. Pallavicino warned against excesses of style, addressing his warning especially to philosophers. He repeated this

---

[1] Tesauro, *op. cit.*, p. 17; Pellegrini, *Delle acutezze* (Genoa e Bologna, 1639), p. 156.

[2] Tesauro, *op. cit.*, pp. 216–39. Pallavicino, *Trattato*, p. 103.

warning in *Del bene* saying further that the duty of the writer
is the clear expression of all that can be expressed.[1] Pellegrini
added his voice to the general appeal for sobriety and attempted
to find a criterion for excess in the verdict of popular judgment.[2]

The theory of the conceit also entered into that widespread
phenomenon of seventeenth-century European culture called the
'Battle of the Books.' Our theorists took a curious pride in
concettismo for they felt it was the only way in which the
'moderns' might be able to excel the 'ancients.' It is obvious
that the theorists were not very strongly pro-modern, at least
in theory if not in taste. Their position is really a conservative
one and *concettismo* is for them what the romantic Christian
epic was for the *cinquecento*, a literary genre which the 'moderns'
could point to when they wanted to salvage their pride. They
were still, in some essentials, humanists, although they often
admired even the most extravagant creations of Marino and
Góngora.

In his discussion of the ancestry of wit, Tesauro as humanist
had to agree that as the Latin style became more 'witty' with
the advent of authors like Tacitus, it became less 'Latin.'
However, he suppressed the humanist long enough to acknowledge that the Latin language, like all languages, is beautifully
written when it is written by a person who knows how to write
well regardless of the age or place in which it is written. He
also admitted that terms like 'barbarism' and 'decadent' are
more indicative of personal taste than of any absolute judgment
concerning the worth of the creation to which they are applied.[3]

Pallavicino noted that his contemporaries were able to sur-
pass the ancients in the use of the conceit, thereby making
concettismo the only literary theory enabling the contemporary
writer to write elegantly, especially if he writes in Latin.

E questo modo di parlar metaforico o figurato oggi per avventura è l'unico che a noi rimanga per ornar le Scritture latine
con qualche eleganza non ricopiata servilmente dagli Autori
che vissero in vita di quella lingua.[4]

---

[1] Pallavicino, *Trattato*, p. 14, p. 23, and p. 107; *Del bene*, Book III,
Part 1, ch. 4.

[2] Pellegrini, *Delle acutezze*, p. 250.

[3] Tesauro, *op. cit.*, pp. 218–28.

[4] Pallavicino, *Trattato*, p. 77.

Like Pallavicino, Tesauro carefully conceded the greatest achievements to the ancients. The creations of Virgil, Horace, Cicero, Livy, and the other classical authors are so fine that 'indarno fatica ogni mortal penna di potervi poggiare.' He admired the contemporary Latin literature of the Jesuits, but warned that whoever wished to write vigorous Latin could do so 'potendo superar la vivacità de' concetti, che pareggiar la purità dello stile dell'Aureo Secolo.' However, even though the humanist in Tesauro was ultimately unsuppressible, his sensibility was more than a shade 'modern,' a fact supported by his strong defence of the Italian tongue as a vehicle for literary expression.[1]

It is clear that the tractates do not represent a 'Copernican revolution' in poetic theory or criticism and the conscious attitudes of the theorists certainly do not indicate such a tendency. The tractates agreed with tradition in many essentials and were intended as guidebooks for poets, but were to be used as such with the largest liberty. From a different point of view, the tractates do seem to be rough drafts of a later poetic to the extent that they foreshadow some of the conceptions of eighteenth-century idealistic aesthetics. However, our theorists were not primarily interested in abandoning the problems of *cinquecento* criticism, the problems of fable and history, poetry and morality, imagination and reason, and especially the problem of structure and form. They rather sought to put the question of metaphor and expression at the forefront of criticism, make it the subject of their inquiry, and to increase thereby the possibilities of metaphorical expression.

This emphasis implied a different response to experience in the general sensibility of the time. The direct reaction of an Ariosto to his experience was no longer satisfying and there was little comprehension or sympathy for his art in the *seicento*. There was a demand for a more analytical, self-conscious, exploratory poetry; a conviction that new sentiments and new situations had to be expressed. Shifts in taste are shifts in ways of feeling, and these tractates are records of a new sentiment in literature and life. Dissatisfied with a conception of art as imitation of nature, the *seicento* pictured the artist as the man who must modify nature before it becomes art. While the man

[1] Tesauro, *op. cit.*, pp. 219-20, p. 225, pp. 244-45.

who reproduces nature perfectly is learned, the man of *ingegno*, who modifies it with his wit, is the artist.[1]

By emphasizing the individuality of the 'form' and its exclusive power to confer aesthetic merit on a work, the critics permitted the personality of the artist to play a greater rôle in the theory of literary creation. The relation between the object and its representation was relatively clear in the criticism of the *cinquecento*. For our theorists the relationship was more complex. By finding the correspondences which exist between objects, by his power, to 'join,' the poet created both the object and its representation. The true, in the meaning of the word in which history attempts to treat the true, was no longer an important element in poetry. The poet, in a sense, corrected the defects of nature, a nature which had to be explored and whose objects had to be 'joined' to be given conceptual as well as poetic reality. Art was thus the elaboration of experience and not its mere representation. The more passive rôle assigned to the poet by much of the criticism of the Renaissance and which had theoretically made his personality disappear in the work, was overthrown and the poet emerged in a more active and creative rôle. The *ingegno*, by means of the conceit, conferred 'form' and was the instrument for the creative and poetic exploration of reality.

[1] Tesauro, *op. cit.*, p. 48.

CHAPTER III

Metaphysical Poetry and the Poetic of Correspondence

THE inquiry into the nature of metaphor remains a vital intellectual problem in our time, and the development of science and philosophy since the time of Kant has tended to make ever more evident the important rôle which metaphors and analogies play in the sciences as well as in the arts. Morris Cohen in his *Preface to Logic* says:

. . . metaphors are not merely artificial devices for making discourse vivid and poetical, but are also necessary for the apprehension and communication of new ideas. This is confirmed by the history of language and of early poetry as well as by the general results of modern psychology.

The prevailing view since Aristotle's *Rhetoric* regards metaphor as an analogy from which the words of comparison, *like* or *as*, etc. are omitted. This presupposes that the recognition of the literal truth precedes the metaphor, which is always a conscious transference of the properties of one thing to another. But history shows that metaphors are generally older than expressed analogies. If intelligence grows from the vague and confused to the more definite by a process of discrimination, we may well expect that the mere motion common to animate and inanimate beings should impress us even before we have made a clear distinction between these two kinds of being . . . metaphors may thus be viewed as expressing the vague and confused but primal perception of identity which subsequent processes of discrimination transform into a clear assertion of an identity or a common element (or relation) which the two different things possess. This helps us to explain the proper function of metaphors in science as well as in religion and art, and cautions us against fallacious arguments for or against views expressed in metaphorical language.[1]

Cohen goes on to say that metaphor may be, and often is, the way in which any creative mind perceives new relationships, and that the awareness of dealing with an analogy rather than with an identity comes later, if at all.[2] We must bear in mind, however, that Cohen is primarily interested in the function of analogical thinking in philosophical and scientific investigation. His analysis does not apply with equal validity to the function of metaphor in poetry, where metaphor exists as a final kind of statement and not as statement in need of further intellectual clarification or organization. However, he does establish the cardinal point about metaphorical statement and its relationship to literal and mathematical statement with considerable clarity, demonstrating the present-day reversal of the prevailing view of metaphor. In any case, his kind of approach is essential for a thorough understanding of past investigations of the nature of metaphor.

The seventeenth century witnessed a revival of interest in metaphor among literary critics and rhetoricians similar in intensity to that of our own time. The major seventeenth-century theorists of metaphor or conceit were all continental Europeans: Baltasar Gracián in Spain and Emmanuele Tesauro, Cardinal Sforza-Pallavicino, Pierfrancesco Minozzi, and Matteo Pellegrini in Italy. These critics faced a problem that some seventeenth-century English critics might have faced, but never so far as I can find, did face: what was the theoretical basis of the 'metaphysical' style so widespread in the poetry of the seventeenth century?

If, in the seventeenth century, literature in Italy and elsewhere in Europe rebelled against the old forms and struck out along new paths, the criticism, in spite of its opposition to the Aristotle of the *Cinquecento*, remained in some essentials the

---

[1] Morris R. Cohen, *A Preface to Logic* (New York, 1944), p. 83.
[2] *Ibid.*, p. 85.

same as that of the preceding century. This would seem to be true in investigations concerning metaphor, for our theorists generally *defined* it as a modification of literal statement or its ornamentation.[1] This conception of metaphor was not their only one, but it is the one most easily discerned and the only conception of metaphor which would emerge from a superficial reading of their works. Whenever they define, they take their cue from Aristotle and describe metaphor as the pleasant ornamentation of a literal statement of fact. This adornment helps us to learn the 'plain' truth easily and pleasantly.[2] Metaphor was such a great good that the theorists felt that the accumulation of conceits in abundance was also a great good. Other elements in written expression which were theoretically found to be good, elements such as rhythm, 'invention' and stylistic traits, were duly praised and their development in abundance was encouraged.[3] The foregoing characterization is fairly typical of the evaluation of the tractates given by Borinski, Croce, and Menéndez y Pelayo. [4]

Although it is true that there was often discussion of metaphor in terms of ornament in the tractates on the conceit, Gracián and his Italian followers as well made the attempt to separate the poetic faculty of *ingegno* from any subservience to rhetorical notions of ornamentation. Gracián in particular often explicitly

[1] B. Croce, *Problemi di estetica*, 4th ed. (Bari, 1949), p. 313.

[2] E. Tesauro, *Il cannochiale aristotelico*, 2nd ed. (Venezia, 1663), p. 112.

[3] Croce, *Problemi*, pp. 313–14.

[4] Marcellino Menéndez y Pelayo, *Historia de las ideas esteticas en España*, 9 vols. (Madrid, 1928–1933), vol. II, part II, p. 536. Karl Borinski, *Baltasar Gracián und die Hoffliteratur in Deutschland* (Halle, 1894), 39. Croce, *Problemi*, p. 315. Menéndez y Pelayo calls the work of Gracián a more or less unsuccessful attempt to substitute an 'ideological' rhetoric for the purely formal, ornamental conception of rhetoric which dominated literary theory in Gracián's time. Karl Borinski saw in Gracián's conception of *gusto* a special faculty of aesthetic judgment distinct from logical judgment; he calls it the major single contribution to aesthetics in modern times. Benedetto Croce, though he is in partial agreement with Borinski, regards the work of Gracián and of most of his Italian followers as specimens of seventeenth-century preciosity rather than critical works concerned with poetic theory. This general estimate of the theorists seems to be that, although they foreshadowed certain aesthetic and philosophical theories, they really never transcended the traditional ideas of their own time.

affirmed that *ingegno* does not serve to ornament thought but to create beauty (beauty in the sense that 'wit' is poetic beauty for out theorists).[1] However, in developing this conception Gracián ended with an analogy between 'wit' and architecture in which the solidity of a structure was compared to literal statement while 'wit' furnished the ornamentation. If this analogy from architecture is compared to the analogy from harmony quoted below, it will be noticed that the two analogies are quite different in meaning.

lo que es para los ojos la hermosura y para los oídos la consonancia, eso es para el entendimiento el concepto [i.e. la correspondencia que se halla entre los objetos].

In the one case we have wit defined as the ornamentation of plain and literal statements, in the other case, the analogy from harmony, we have wit as the faculty which seeks out and realizes the hidden resemblances between things.[2]

This antithesis is to be found in one way or another in all the theorists and is based on the inability to transcend the distinction between plain and metaphorical speech. The idea that 'plain' expression is studied by the science of grammar while rhetoric rules the domain of all ornate or non-literal expression was still dominant. The hegemony of this idea in all thinking about literary criticism made it inevitable that, when discussing all 'ornate' expression including poetry, the theorists should fall back on the abstract schemes and definitions of traditional rhetoric.

Tesauro as well as Gracián fell into this same kind of difficulty. For him the essence of wit resided in the 'figure,' or in all that raised expression above the level of plain discourse.[3] The same raising of expression also constituted the distinction between prose and poetry.[4] Tesauro further divided the notion of 'figure' into three separate classifications: those that delight the ear by mellifluous periods, those that delight the affections by the vivacity of the images they present, and those that delight

---

[1] Croce, *Problemi*, pp. 315–16.

[2] Cf. Tesauro, *op. cit.*, p. 248; Baltasar Gracián, *Arte de ingenio* (Madrid, 1944), pp. 40 and 46.

[3] Tesauro, *op. cit.*, p. 112.

[4] G. Cesareo, *Storia delle teorie estetiche in Italia* (Bologna, 1924), p. 37.

the intellect by their wit. The essence of 'witty' figures was metaphor, and Tesauro distinguished eight species in the course of his analysis of 'witty' expression.[1] It is obvious that Tesauro's elaboration of the kinds of figures did not transcend the antithesis between 'plain' and 'ornate' speech.

A similar antithesis is revealed by the difficulty our critics had in formulating a criterion for determining what constitutes excess in the use of the conceit, a difficulty especially present to those critics like Matteo Pellegrini who had a more temperate view of *Concettismo* than his colleagues. They failed to solve this problem because the determination of excess in the use of the conceit demanded other critical principles than the ones with which they were working. On the one hand, as we have seen, it was necessary to transcend the distinction between plain and metaphorical speech, and on the other, to acquire a functional conception of metaphor. These changes would have established poetry as a unique form of statement irreducible to any prose paraphrase. The criterion of excess would then have become a function of whether all the statements in a poem succeed together in giving a 'coherent and powerful structure of attitudes.'[2] But the theorists accepted the conventional distinction between plain and metaphorical speech and were therefore committed, at least in theory, to a conception of poetry as the accumulation of ornamental metaphor; and the more metaphor one could accumulate the better the poem.

It was these theoretical difficulties that led to the covert introduction of other aesthetic faculties by the side of *ingegno*, faculties which were to judge deficiencies and excesses in poetry. There was an appeal to *furore*, poetic genius, and *gusto*, all concepts which served to deny the omnipotence of the rules in the production of a work of art. When Pellegrini ultimately renounced the attempt to formulate rules for the production of good *concetti* he could only come up with the statement that

[1] Tesauro, *op. cit.*, pp. 113 *et seq*. See also pp. 278–79 for the subdivision of the class of 'witty' figures into the following eight: Hiperbole, Hipotiposi, Metafora di Somiglianza, Equivoco, Opposito, Decettione, Metafora di Attributione, Laconismo. Tesauro devotes a chapter to each of these subdivisions.

[2] I have borrowed the phrase 'a coherent and powerful structure of attitudes' from Mr. Cleanth Brooks' *The Well Wrought Urn* (New York, 1947), p. 225.

they must be *leggieri* or graceful, and regretted not being able to say how remote the analogies of a conceit can be before they become excessive.[1] The very fact that he posed the question in this manner is further evidence of the inadequacy of the critical criteria with which he was working.

Minozzi, a minor theorist of the conceit, who staunchly defended *concettismo* against the mild criticism of Pellegrini, was compelled to admit that the extravagant conceits Pellegrini condemned were after all best used in treating the lives of the saints, because unlike profane subjects, religious subjects cannot be praised to excess. He says:

... essi Santi sono meritevole d'ogni qualunque artifizioso ingrandimento, e di loro sempre favellasi daddovero, ed eglino stessi per tanto sono superiori ad ogni umana adulazione. Onde nelle vite de'santi eziando gli scherzi hanno forza di persuadere e di commuovere, essendo presi per serietà non per ischerzi. Ed alle volte è più atto a commuovere uno scherzo perchè dilette che una semplice purità perchè non ha del lusinghiero.[2]

It is clear, then, that this theory of poetry tended, as the theorists themselves realized, to fall on the one hand into a purely legalistic conception of poetry, and on the other into an exclusively intellectualistic account of the process of literary creation. They attempted to avoid the first pitfall by the formulation of concepts like *furore*, and to avoid the second by attempting to distinguish between logical and aesthetic judgments, *ingegno* and intellect.

Although the theorists tried to distinguish *ingegno* from intellect, they always finished up by finding a kind of intellectual truth in the conceit. This was a logical conclusion drawn from their purely intellectualistic definition of the conceit itself.[3] As long as the product of the *ingegno* was defined in exclusively intellectualistic terms, there was scant hope of considering the *ingegno* a faculty sharply divorced from the intellect and its operations. The inability to distinguish between the function of metaphor in poetry and the function of metaphor in philosophy

---

[1] Cf. Croce, *Problemi*, p. 332.
[2] Pierfrancesco Minozzi, *Gli sfogamenti dell'ingegno* (Venezia, 1641), cited in Croce, *Problemi*, 334.
[3] Croce, *Estetica*, Bari, 1945, 8th ed., p. 216.

and science is at the root of this particular dilemma. The attempted solution of this problem introduced a modified notion of the *ingegno* as a kind of creative or super-intellect distinct from ratiocinative intellect. But a final solution of the problem awaited the realization of the way in which all metaphors are alike as well as the way in which they differ in function when metaphorical thought occurs in poetry, science, and religion.[1]

The thought of our theorists on the distinctions between logical and aesthetic judgments deserves some scrutiny. Pallavicino, Tesauro, and Minozzi all warn that there is a difference between the syllogism as it functions in logic and the rhetorical syllogism. Tesauro adapted the enthymeme to describe the notion of the expanded conceit.[2] He then discussed the difference in purpose that distinguished these two kinds of syllogism, a distinction which, for Croce, foreshadowed the later distinction between logic and aesthetics, the one ratiocinative and the other expressive. Thus the enthymeme, equivalent for Tesauro to the expanded conceit in some contexts, aimed at producing aesthetic pleasure, while the logical syllogism arrived at the truth through dialectic. The *enthymema urbanum* had the function of delighting; also called *cavillazione retorica*, it proceeded by leaps and bounds which delighted the reader whereas *cavillazione dialettica* proceeded by regular intervals.[3]

In Tesauro's view, it was not proper to consider a literary statement as a logical affirmation. It is possible to say that poems are ugly or beautiful, but not that they are false or sophistic. The nature of *cavillazione retorica* tells us that one does not inquire into truth with literary statement, but simply states that which is to be enjoyed.[4] One should combat false philosophers, but leave orators alone to adopt splendid and eloquent forms.[5] The positive aspect of this analysis of Tesauro lies in the attempt to distinguish between aesthetic and logical judgments. On the other hand, the distinction between plain and

---

[1] Cf. Wilbur Marshall Urban, *Language and Reality* (New York, 1939), for a general discussion of the philosophy of language and the rôle of metaphor in the various branches of creation and inquiry.

[2] Tesauro, *op. cit.*, pp. 110–13, 450–52.

[3] *Ibid.*, pp. 451 and 445; Croce, *Problemi*, p. 330.

[4] Tesauro, *op. cit.*, p. 450.

[5] Tesauro, *op. cit.*, p. 451; Croce, *Problemi*, p. 341.

metaphorical speech leads to an inadequate conception of the truth by identifying it with plain expression; the inevitable conclusion from this is that poetry is either the embellished 'truth' or a pleasant but total 'lie,' both of which opinions Tesauro held at different times. In practice his distinctions became two purely empirical distinctions between plain and dialectical expression and ornate or witty expression. Thus in the final analysis, he returned to the conventional enthymeme and syllogism.[1] The adherence to the conventional divisions of grammar, rhetoric, and logic always interfered with the conception of poetry as a unique form of statement.[2]

For Croce the theorists are especially important in the history of thought because of their effect on the philosophy of Vico. He finds that Vico invigorated the theory of Pallavicino concerning 'first apprehension' (a notion Croce believes similar to his 'aesthetic intuition') and changed the Tesaurian interpretation of the rhetorical syllogism, analogous to the logical syllogism, into the conception of a 'poetic logic' prior and analogous to a logic of 'developed mind' (*mente spiegata*).[3] This concept of Vico later formed the basis for the aesthetic of Baumgarten.[4] Tesauro also extended the categories of rhetoric to pictorial and sculptural forms of expression, as well as to drama and pantomime, in which expression is accomplished by means of gestures. These various types of expression are extensively discussed in the *Cannochiale*, and Tesauro carefully explained the various sensible modes by which an interior image may be externalized.[5] There are (1) the signs of speech, (2) mute signs, as in sculpture or painting, or (3) mixed signs, by which he meant the drama (gestures and words) and the emblem and *impresa* (picture with accompanying motto). A second classification is into (1) spoken and written expression (*acutezze verbali*); (2) the emblem, *impresa* or other pictorial and sculptural forms (*acutezze simboliche o figurative*); and (3) a classification which refers to the drama and pantomime, called that of *acutezze sensibili*. Tesauro was able to classify

---

[1] Croce, *Storia dell'età barocca*, 2nd ed. (Bari, 1946), p. 188.
[2] Croce, *Problemi*, p. 343, cf. Tesauro, *op. cit.*, pp. 449 and 452.
[3] Croce, *Storia*, p. 288.
[4] Croce *Problemi*, p. 345.
[5] Tesauro, *op. cit.*, pp. 14–54.

any form of expression by means of these two sets of concepts. It is of the greatest importance to observe that all these forms of expression are called *acutezze* or witty metaphorical expressions, and this included the mute forms as well.[1] The implication is clear that all expression, linguistic and symbolic, is basically metaphorical; although Tesauro was working with the conventional categories of rhetoric, in this instance he clearly tried to transcend the old distinctions between rhetoric, grammar, and logic or between plain and metaphorical expression. As far as I know, Tesauro's analysis of the forms of expression constitutes one of the earliest extensive attempts to formulate a unified theory of the arts.

Vico took the interpretation of rhetorical categories that Tesauro made and changed them into the categories by which the imagination states itself. The category of mute signs and mixed types became one of the Viconian *linguaggi mutoli* of the imagination, a faculty which expressed itself not only in words but also in lines and colours.[2] Vico's mute and mixed categories included emblems, impresas, heraldic figures, military ensigns, etc., symbolic modes of expression evidently analogous to Tesauro's *acutezze simboliche o figurate*.[3]

In spite of all this the theorists of the conceit were so bound to the authority of what was conceived to be the Aristotelian theory that when they faced any situation requiring a new definition of metaphor they invariably fell back on ornamental conceptions in spite of their attempt to respond to the theoretical exigencies of their new inquiries. However, when our theorists were free to discuss metaphor without any precision of definition, we find a substantially different conception of metaphor by the side of the old one. This is especially true of Tesauro, and it is in his curious researches on the efficient causes of wit that we find some of his most fruitful ideas about metaphor, ideas which were as much at variance with the traditional conception of metaphor as his analysis and extension of rhetorical categories.

Wit was a topic which the ancients had not exhausted or even investigated thoroughly, and Tesauro's opinions fell freely;

[1] Tesauro, *op. cit.*, pp. 50–53.
[2] Croce, *Estetica*, p. 254.
[3] Croce, *La filosophia di Giambattista Vico*, 4th ed. (Bari, 1947), p. 54.

it is here that we see his link with some of the important currents of Renaissance thought most clearly.

Tesauro maintained that *acutezze* or conceits were not created by men only but by God, his angels, and by animals. The universe was created by a God who was a 'witty creator,' an *arguto favellatore*, a witty writer or talker.[1] The world was a poem made up of conceits. The notion that the world is a poem of God is old enough as a conception and, in various forms, goes back at least to Plotinus.[2] However, the important difference for Tesauro is that the world is a 'metaphysical'poem and God a 'metaphysical' poet. He conceived *ingegno* as the faculty in man analogous to God's creative power. It is a small particle of the divine nature, for it can create 'being' where there was no 'being' before.[3] As God created a 'metaphysical' world, so the poet creates 'metaphysical' poems. God is:

arguto favellatore, mottegiando agli Uomini et agli Angeli, con varie Imprese eroiche e Simboli figurati, gli altissimi suoi concetti.[4]

The sky is

un vasto ceruleo scudo, ove l'ingegnosa Natura disegna ciò che medita: formando eroiche Imprese e Simboli misteriosi e arguti dei suoi segreti.[5]

Thunder is really nothing but an *acutezza* of the mixed type, picture and motto together, and the whole of nature speaks in conceits. They are:

formidabile Argutie et Simboliche
Cifere della natura, mute insieme e vocali;
avendo La Saetta per corpo e il Tuono per motto.[6]

The conventional idea of the book of nature is implied in all of Tesauro's speculation on this matter. This idea is old and

---

[1] Cf. Croce, *Problemi*, 345, where Croce maintains that this concept of nature as made up of *acutezze* prepared the way for the study of the concept of the beautiful in nature.

[2] Rosamund Tuve, *Elizabethan and Metaphysical Imagery* (Chicago, 1946), p. 159. The Stoics also speak of the world-poem or world-drama.

[3] Tesauro, *op. cit.*, p. 76

[4] *Ibid.*, p. 54.

[5] *Ibid.*, p. 68.

[6] *Ibid.*, p. 69.

traditional, but Tesauro sees the book of nature written in conceits, in witty metaphors. This book was read in many ways during the lifetime of the concept. Its most fruitful reading was by Tesauro's contemporary Galileo, who read it mathematically.[1]

Sig. Mario Praz finds Tesauro's conception of the world as *acutezze* bizarre, and it might seem so at first glance. The apparent strangeness of this conception is increased when we are told that angels and demons (identified with pagan deities) all spoke in witty oracles and communicated with men in dreams which themselves were nothing but *acutezze*.[2] The song of the nightingale presented a pattern of verse, revealing one aspect of the rhythmic pulse of the 'world-poem.' The bestiary traditions were made 'metaphysical,' and all animals and plants revealed witty significance to the observer with *ingegno*. As the *acutezze* of poets are called 'flowers,' so flowers are the *acutezze* of nature.[3]

Thus God created a world full of metaphors, analogies and conceits, and so far from being ornamentation, they are the law by which creation was effected. God wrote the book of nature in metaphor, and so it should be read. The arts, the creation of men, are also *acutezze*, and painters are nothing but mute poets.[4] Now the poetic involved in this view of the world is not the poetic of ornamental metaphor, but what I call 'the poetic of correspondences.' When the conceit is said to have those properties which enable it to pierce the intellect or to arouse sensations of marvel and wonder, we do wrong to think, as some critics have, of the more excessive kinds of Baroque art. What is meant is that quality of vision which the discovery of correspondences can bring, the 'thrill' which the awareness of an analogy gives the intellect when it first becomes aware of the identity between things formerly believed unconnected. The universe is a vast net of correspondences which unites the whole multiplicity of being. The poet approaches and creates his reality by a series of more or less elaborate correspondences.

[1] See Galileo Galilei, *I massimi sistemi*, in *Opere*, I (Milan-Rome, 1946).

[2] Tesauro, *op. cit.*, p. 72–75.

[3] *Ibid.*, p. 75.

[4] *Ibid.*, pp. 53 and 306.

Pallavicino, in a very illuminating passage, said that the function of *ingegno*—we must remember that *ingegno* is the poetic faculty *par excellence*—is precisely the power to search out these correspondences. He also speculated upon Homer's 'golden chain,' suggesting that it may have been a mythological representation of this world of correspondences.

Poichè quel dono di natura che si chiama ingegno consiste appunto in congiungere per mezzo di scaltre apprensioni oggetti che pareano affatti sconessi, rintracciando in essi gli occulti vestigi d'amicizia fra la stessa contrarietà, la non avvertita unità di special somiglianza nella somma dissimilitudine, qualche vincolo, qualche parentela, qualche confederazione dove altri non l'avrebbe mai sospettato. Annadò la natura maestrevolmente fra loro tutti i suoi effetti, e ciò fu per avventura il misterio di quell'aurea catena omerica. Nè v'ha nel mondo verun oggetto sì solitario e sì sciolto che frà laberinti della filosofia non somministri qualche aureo filo per giungere alla notizia d'ogni altro oggetto quanto si voglia lontano ed ascoso. Ma queste fila quanto son lucide per la nobiltà del metallo tanto sono invisibili per la sottigliezza della mole. L'arte di ben ravvisarle contiensi principalmente negli otto libri meravigliosi della Topica di Aristotile, in cui si mostra la maniera di indagar le ragioni per disputar probabilmente in ogni maniera ed a favor di ciascuna parte . . . [Ma] che giovano i precetti dell'arte dove manca l'abilita dell'ingegno? Perciò la più vera topica e più sagace è la perspicacia che ne dà la natura.[1]

Nature then was not the object of simple observation and enjoyment; it was the 'matter' in which man discovered and read the metaphors of divine wisdom, for the world itself was a 'metaphysical' poem. God created such a world for the purpose of arousing the wonder of men, and man himself made conceits because he alone of all the creatures of God needed to seek out

[1] Sforza-Pallavicino, *Del Bene* (Milan, 1831), book III, part 2, chapt. 55. 1st ed. (Rome, 1644). This passage suggests a connection between the poetic of correspondences and the renewed importance of the doctrine of the *coincidentia oppositorum* in the Renaissance, although it is an interpretation of the doctrine rather than a restatement of it if, indeed, there is any direct connection.

the variety of the universe and express it. Man cannot remain on the level of plain perception and plain discourse.[1] Wit was, as Mr. Austin Warren states, 'more than an offering,' which is to say more than a technique of ornamentation and decoration:

. . . it was also an instrument of vision. With its occult couplings, it penetrates to the centre of the universe, where, however dissimilar they may appear to the unobservant, all things unite.[2]

The theorists have both these conceptions of wit. Wit is, on the one hand, the exploration of a universe made up of a series of correspondences; and yet there is praise of wit as ornamentation, praise of the kind of wit that is not vision and whose occult couplings do not reveal a higher unity.

The desire to discover cosmic affinities and to draw and develop universal correspondences and analogies indicates an attempt to deepen the value of words; it is a sign of awareness in poets and critics of situations in the multiplicity of being that had not yet been individualized and which they were trying to realize by verbal suggestions and by what seemed to be strange and hybrid analogies. The conceit was the instrument for this poetic exploration of reality. Pallavicino says of the nature of the conceit:

. . . la principal dilettazione dell'intelletto consiste nel meravigliarsi . . . Ma intanto la meraviglia è scaturigine d'un sommo piacere intellettuale, in quanto è sempre congiunta col saper ciò che prima era ignoto; E Quanto più era ignoto, o più eziando contrario alla nostra credenza, tanto è maggior la meraviglia.[3]

The notion of the *mirabile* is in this passage clearly related to the conceit conceived as an instrument of insight, not to the conceit as an ornamentation of knowledge. Tesauro also defined the metaphor as a means of vision:

La metafora tutti [gli obietti] a stretta li rinzeppa in un Vocabulo: e quasi in miraculoso modo gli ti fa travedere l'uno dentro all'altro. Onde maggiore è il tuo diletto: nella maniera,

---

[1] Tesauro, *op. cit.*, pp. 54 and 111.

[2] Austin Warren, *Richard Crashaw: A Study in Baroque Sensibility* (University, La., 1939), p. 75.

[3] Sforza-Pallavicino, *Trattato*, pp. 77–78.

che più curiosa e piacevol cosa e mirar molti obietti per un istraforo di perspettiva, che se gli originali medesimi successivamente ti venisser passando dinanzi agli occhi.[1]

This statement is buttressed elsewhere when Tesauro says that any obscurity in the conceit is justified only as the revelation of a little mystery (*un piccolo mistero*). After all, the whole of reality for Tesauro made up of *acutezze* or the revelation of little mysteries, of which his work treats only those *acutezze* which deal with words and figures.[2]

Thus, by seeking out and establishing correspondences, the *ingegno* makes order out of disorder and brings clarity where there had been only darkness and mystery. Nature to those of little *ingegno* seemed like an obvious thing, but to the man of *ingegno* it was a mystery to be investigated, an obstacle to be overcome. Nature really worked against art, for our theorists, and it had to be probed to reveal Pallavicino's 'golden thread.'

Two conceptions of metaphor, and therefore two poetics, existed side by side in the work of our theorists, and we see them shifting from one to the other, a sign that the problems they raised were not capable of full solution in the terms in which they were stated. One of these poetics, the one built on metaphor as ornament, is negative; the other, which I call the 'poetic of correspondences,' is positive. This does not imply that one theory was responsible for bad and the other for good poetry, for a theory of poetry never creates works of art. A poetic is only the theoretical expression of a living art, of a concrete poetic reality found in the work of the poets whose art elicits observations from critics and aestheticians. What I mean by the terms 'positive' and 'negative' is that the theory of the conceit as ornament was not capable of further development, while the theory of universal correspondences, conceived as a poetic, was revived and culminated in the poetic of Baudelaire. In his essay on Victor Hugo he clearly defined this position:

Chez les excellents poètes il n'y a pas de métaphore de comparaison ou d'épithète qui ne soit d'une adaptation mathématiquement exacte dans la circonstance actuelle, parce que ces comparaisons, ces métaphores et ces épithètes sont puisées

[1] Tesauro, *op. cit.*, p. 276.
[2] *Ibid.*, p. 53.

dans l'inépuisable fonds de l'universelle analogie, et qu'elles ne peuvent être puisées ailleurs.[1]

Although the treatises on the conceit appear to have been little read after the seventeenth century, the theory of metaphor which they developed was kept alive through the occult tradition, and reached Baudelaire through the agency of Swedenborg. It is not an accident that the great analogical complexity of much modern poetry should have been largely the work of Yeats and Baudelaire, two poets who studied the occult sciences and who revived the conception of the poet as one who approaches reality through the discovery of the analogies latent in nature.

If, as Cassirer maintains, the Renaissance theory of mathematical physics is linked to the Renaissance theory of art by the formulation of the problem of form, the positive aspects of the theory of the conceit are linked to Renaissance science by the theories of correspondence and universal analogy. There is then a parallelism between Renaissance scientific and philosophical thought on the one hand, and the theory of the conceit on the other, which helps to account for the way in which 'metaphysical' poetry was able to digest so much scientific and technical imagery.[2] The poetic of correspondences implies an underlying belief in the unity and connection of all things. Such a view simplifies the assimilation of all kinds of unusual images in poetry, for such a universe—unlike the universe of Samuel Johnson and other neo-classical critics—has no class of objects which can be considered 'unpoetic.'

The negative notion of metaphor stated by these theorists is closely allied to the general change in ways of feeling that accompanied the change from 'Renaissance' to 'Baroque.' Many theories have been advanced to explain the emphasis on the Baroque in the seventeenth century, but there is little doubt that, from the point of view of the historian of culture, it may

---

[1] Charles Baudelaire, Essay on 'Victor Hugo,' in *Oeuvres*, 2 vols. (Paris, 1938), vol. II.

[2] Mario Praz, *Studi sul Concettismo* (Florence, 1946), p. 136. This aspect of metaphysical poetry has often been noticed. Sig. Praz attributes the prevalence of scientific imagery in metaphysical poetry to a shift in taste. For Ernst Cassirer's thesis see *Individuum und Kosmos in der Philosophie der Renaissance* (Leipzig, 1927), especially ch. 4.

best be understood as the exaggeration of tendencies already present in the Renaissance. Croce suggests that the Renaissance preoccupation with form became the Baroque preoccupation with ornament.

The critics of the eighteenth and nineteenth centuries often ignored the literary productions of *Concettismo*, or, as it was called in England, the 'metaphysical' school. When they read them, it was usually to hold them up as warnings and examples of what poets should avoid. The most important single objection levelled against the 'metaphysicals' and the *concettisti* was that they were unfaithful to nature. In the light of the *Weltanschaung* implied by the poetic of correspondences, this particular objection has less foundation than it might seem to have. The metaphysical poets of the seventeenth century may have been unfaithful to the eighteenth-century Lockean or Cartesian nature, but not to the nature of their own times. I do not mean to imply that *Concettismo* did not display exaggerations. Even the greatest writers have written inferior works, and every literary movement becomes mannered and exaggerated, in time. The best poets of this kind, a Marvell or a Donne, occasionally strained after a figure of speech. But this seems to be the exception rather than the rule. Many images we today would call 'artificial conceits'—in Dr. Johnson's meaning of the term—were really faithful and accurate images. This universe contained relationships which no longer exist for us; they have been eliminated from our perception by Baconianism and Cartesianism. What may seem to us strange and far-fetched similitudes were often truths, even commonplaces, in their world of insight. The theorists of the conceit envisaged the poet's universe as a complex system of universal analogical relationships which the poets expressed and revealed. The critics of subsequent times no longer understood this view of the world. Although we may, if we choose, agree with Johnson's conclusion about the 'metaphysicals,' we cannot accept his basis for that judgment. This truth by no means reflects on Johnson's critical powers. Bradley's Pickwickian definition of metaphysics might be applied in the same sense to literary criticism; both fields of endeavour are at least partially concerned with inventing 'bad reasons for what we believe upon instinct.'

CHAPTER IV

Notes on John Donne's
Alchemical Imagery

No student of the work of Donne can fail to be impressed by the extent to which alchemical and scientific images and references appear in it. However, few are aware of the skill and precision with which he adapted these ideas to his own use. Although previous studies of his alchemical imagery have not displayed an awareness of the complex implications of alchemical ideas, Donne was nevertheless acquainted with alchemy in its broader aspects, since many of his figures refer to the philosophical, occult, and mystical doctrines associated with alchemical practices and theories.

Although Donne could have learned alchemy from any of the numerous treatises and handbooks of his time, and no doubt did, Paracelsus is the only great alchemist frequently referred to in Donne's works whose theories seem to have captivated his imagination. His treatment of alchemical images and ideas reveals a strong Paracelsian influence, although my citations from this author are not intended as 'sources' but rather as explanatory analogues.[1]

[1] In the course of this study I have documented the various statements on alchemy with the best available English sources, although I have not been unmindful of the fact that the most comprehensive works on the subject are for the most part in German and French. In doing this I have been motivated by what I believe will be to the best interest of the literary student who may want to know more about the subject without necessarily attempting to acquire more than general information about

Whatever the degree of direct Paracelsian influence Donne was no thorough disciple of the great Swiss physician and occasionally referred to Paracelsus in somewhat derogatory terms.

On the whole, Donne most often speaks well of Paracelsus and openly praised him in the *Biathanatos*. There is also more praise than blame underneath the playful satire *Ignatius, His Conclave*, in which Paracelsus is tried in hell along with Copernicus and other distinguished company. It is interesting to observe that Donne placed Paracelsus and Copernicus on the same level. In his opinion they were both equally important and equally revolutionary, a judgment posterity has not confirmed. Although he never proclaimed his complete allegiance to either, his work gives ample evidence of serious consideration of their ideas.

Donne may have vacillated in his attitude toward Paracelsus, but his knowledge of Paracelsian medical alchemy and general alchemical theory was comprehensive. Indeed, some of his poetry is virtually incomprehensible without a knowledge of alchemical theory. Of no single poem is this more true than

---

it. I have not always been able to do this but I have tried to follow this practice as consistently as I could. The select bibliography in F. Sherwood Taylor's *The Alchemists*, Henry Schuman (New York, 1949), is a good guide through the standard literature.

In regard to Paracelsus, I have cited wherever possible the version of A. E. Waite (Arthur Edward Waite, *Hermetic and Alchemical Writings of Paracelsus*, 2 vols. (London, 1894)). Although Waite was an occultist his version of Paracelsus is excellent and as accurate as any translation of such an author can be. However, not all that he translates is definitely to be attributed to Paracelsus himself. Wherever Waite did not translate a necessary work or was inaccurate I have cited either the Basle edition or the *Sämtliche Werke*, which is the critical, standard edition and is divided into two parts.

Abt. I Medizinische, naturwissenschaftliche und philosophische Schriften, ed. Karl Sudhoff, 14 vols., O. W. Bante (Munich, 1922–1933).

Abt. II Theologische und religionsphilosophische Schriften, ed. W. Matthiessen, 1 vol.

These works are cited as ed. Waite, ed. Huser, ed. Sudhoff, and ed. Matthiessen, respectively. Mr. Henry M. Pachter's recent book on Paracelsus (*Paracelsus: Magic into Science* (Henry Schuman, New York, 1951)) finally makes available to the English reader an accurate presentation of the life and work of this unusual and important figure. His short bibliography will guide the student further.

of *A Nocturnall Upon S. Lucies Day*, almost completely written in alchemical metaphor. I will give a further analysis of this poem later in the study.

Imagery Derived from General Hermetic Theory and Alchemical Processes

The ordering of Donne's alchemical imagery for the purposes of analysis presents certain problems. Alchemy was a complex subject and had at least the two distinct aspects: the spiritual and the material. The same alchemical allusion, the elixir or the limbeck, may refer to material or spiritual alchemy alone or to both at the same time. The reader must be aware of this fact if a correct interpretation of the image is to be made. I have therefore analysed Donne's alchemical imagery in two general sections. In the first, I emphasize that imagery which is derived from basic Hermetic theory and from the equipment and stages of the alchemical process. Such imagery is primarily, although not entirely, 'material' in reference. The imagery of the second part is primarily 'spiritual' in emphasis; however, as in the first part, there is a mixture of the 'spiritual' and 'material' themes. In this classification I have also been guided by what I believe was Donne's own emphasis.[1]

The theories of the four elements, the four humours, and of primary matter were part of the generally accepted cosmological and physiological theories derived from antiquity and along with other philosophical concepts were used by the alchemists as the basis of their art. A mastery of its philosophical basis was essential for a mastery of the Hermetic art.[2]

References to these theories abound in Renaissance literature and they seem to have been the common property of many educated men of the period. Donne merely illustrates a com-

---

[1] On spiritual alchemy, perhaps the best introduction is in Evelyn Underhill's *Mysticism*, 16th ed. (New York, E. P. Dutton & Co., 1948), pp. 140 *et seq.*

See respectively, Hitchcock, *Remarks on Alchemy and the Alchemists* (Boston, 1865); *A Suggestive Inquiry into the Hermetic Mystery* (London, 1850), *passim*; Waite, *Lives of the Alchemystical Philosophers* (London, 1888). On the intimate connection between religion and Hermetic science see F. E. Hutchinson, *Henry Vaughn* (Oxford, at the Clarendon Press, 1947), pp. 184–85 and p. 148.

[2] Ed. Waite, vol. II, p. 249.

mon practice and stated a 'scientific' truth of his age when in the fifth of the *Holy Sonnets* he says:

> I am a little world made cunningly
> Of Elements, and an Angellike spright[1]

This statement was not simply a poetic metaphor; man literally was a 'little world,' the microcosm made up of four elements and possessing an immortal soul.

Donne seems to refer to the Paracelsian attack on the four elements and four humours in the following passage from the first *Anniversary*:

> Have not all soules thought
> For many ages, that our body is wrought
> Of Ayre, and Fire, and other Elements?
> And now they thinke of new ingredients
> And one Soule thinkes one, and another way,
> Another thinkes, and 'tis an even lay.[2]

It is interesting to observe that in the *Anniversary* poems Donne was as disturbed over the Paracelsian substitution of the *tria*

---

[1] Donne, *Holy Sonnets* V, ll. 1–2, *The Complete Poetry and Selected Prose of John Donne*, the text of the Nonesuch Edition edited by John Hayward, New York, 1941. Although Grierson's edition is standard (Oxford, 1912), Hayward incorporates the corrections of subsequent scholarship. Pages are given only to avoid confusion between poems with similar or identical titles.

[2] Donne, *The Progresse of the Soule*, ll, 264–68.
The Paracelsian theory of the *tria prima*, a development of the medieval sulphur-mercury theory of metals, was also given a mystical interpretation. The physical theory of the *tria prima* postulated that mercury, sulphur, and salt were the ultimate constituents of matter, not merely of metals. Paracelsus defined salt as a fixed principle which in another form was the element earth. Mercury was the volatile principle and was equivalent to elementary water. Sulphur, also the element air, perhaps fire, united salt and mercury. The classical element of fire was identified with the 'Quintessence,' the element of which the heavens were made (Cf. ed. Waite, vol. I, p. 68). To the mystical interpreters of the *tria prima* mercury became the human spiritual principle and sulphur and salt corresponded to the human body and its soul. On this question see Taylor, *op. cit.*, ch. 7 on Islamic Alchemy; A. J. Hopkins, *Alchemy, Child of Greek Philosophy* (New York, Columbia U.P., 1934), p. 139 *et seq.*; and E. J. Holmyard, *The Works of Geber, translated by Richard Russell 1678* (London, J. M. Dent and Sons, 1928), the introduction. The Sulphur-Mercury theory of metals was of Arabic origin.

prima, sulphur, mercury and salt, for the old theories as he was about the truly revolutionary astronomical discoveries of his time.

The theory of the interconvertibility of the elements is used in a passage in which air is described as being drawn from water.

> Else, being alike pure, wee should neither see;
>   As, water being into ayre rarify'd,
> Neither appears, till in one cloud they bee,
>   So, for our sakes you do low names abide;[1]

The interconvertibility of the elements was linked to a theory of a primary matter from which the elements were derived, and in which all things were latent.

Of all created things the condition whereof is transitory and frail, there is only one single principle. Included herein were latent all created things which the aether embraces in its scope. This is as much as to say that all created things proceeded from one matter, not each one separately from its own peculiar matter.[2]

The creation of the world, referred to as the 'separation,' was brought about by bringing into action all the potentialities latent in the primary matter.

But in the beginning of the Great Mystery of the separation of all things were went forth first the separation of the elements so that before all else those elements broke into action, and each in its own essence. Fire became heaven and the chest of the firmament.[3]

This identical view of the creation of the world appears in Donne's epistle to the Countesse of Huntingdon. Here the elements are depicted as separating from the 'raw disordered heape,' each one finding its place by a kind of gravity, with fire rising up to become the heavens.

[1] Donne, *Verse Letter to the Countesse of Huntingdon*, ll. 33–36, p. 145.
[2] Ed. Waite, vol. I, p. 248.
[3] *Ibid.*, vol. II, p. 253.

Until this raw disordered heape did breake,
And severall desires led parts away,
Water declined with earth, the ayre did stay
Fire rose, and each from other but unty'd
Themselves imprisoned were and purify'd[1]

Another widely accepted philosophical theory, common to alchemy, which is to be found in the work of Donne is the microcosm-macrocosm idea. This notion was a universally drawn consequence of the principle of universal analogy, and entered into much of the speculation of the Hermetic philosophers. Paracelsus explained the whole of creation with this analogy.

The first Separation of which we speak should begin from man, since he is the Microcosm, the lesser, and for his sake the Macrocosm, the greater world, was founded, that he might be its Separator.[2]

Donne frequently used this ubiquitous analogy and in the 'Devotions' he illustrates the cosmos from his own body. In his verse, we encounter the microcosm idea in an epistle to the Countess of Bedford:

What ere the world hath bad, or precious,
Man's body can produce, hence hath it beene
That stones, wormes, frogges, and snakes in man are seen:
But who ere saw, though nature can worke soe,
That pearle, or gold, or corne in man did grow.[3]

The microcosm-macrocosm analogy, so important in the general theory of Renaissance natural philosophy, was for Paracelsus the foundation of medicine.

The subject of the Microcosm is bound up with Medicine and ruled by it, following it none otherwise than a bridled horse follows him who leads it, or a mad dog bound up with chains.[4] The microcosm, man, contained everything which existed in the macrocosm. At times the macrocosm meant the planet earth; at other times it was the whole universe. However, the

---

[1] Donne, *Verse Letter to the Countesse of Huntingdon*, ll. 38–42, p. 127.
[2] Ed. Waite, vol. I, p. 161.
[3] Donne, *Verse Letter to the Countesse of Bedford*, ll. 62–67, pp. 141–42.
[4] Ed. Waite, vol. II, p. 5.

idea that the microcosm contained the objects of the macrocosm was not merely meant in a literal sense but was to be understood in some occult or mystical fashion as well.

You call man a microcosmos and that is right. But you don't know how to interpret it and we shall do it for you . . . Thus you shall understand that man has in himself his firmament, his planets, conjunctions, constellations, aspects, sidera, and the like.[1]

We discover the microcosm idea again in Donne when, in the *Anatomie of the World*, he uses it to eulogize Elizabeth Drury. This idea is cleverly inverted so that the world becomes the microcosm of Elizabeth Drury instead of her macrocosm.

> She to whom this world must it selfe refer,
> As Suburbs, or the Microcosm of her.[2]

In *Satire V* written to Sir Thomas Egerton it becomes the vehicle for some cynical observations about courtiers and their suitors who become part of the microcosm of the courtly world.

> If all things be in all,
> As I thinke, since all, which were, are, and shall,
> Bee, be made of the same elements:
> Each thing, each thing implyes or represents.
> Then man is a world; in which Officers
> Are, the vast ravishing seas; and Suiters,
> Springs; now full, now shallow, now dry;[3]

Astrology—another branch of Renaissance natural philosophy based on the microcosm-macrocosm analogy—was also important in alchemical processes in so far as the proportions of the limbeck could bring astral powers into play.

All things were affected by the powers of the heavenly bodies by virtue of a series of occult correspondences of each object with some heavenly counterpart. Paracelsus even maintained that the stars governed all animal intelligence.[4]

---

[1] Cited in Pachter, *op. cit.*, p. 138.

[2] Donne, *An Anatomie of the World*, ll. 235–36.

[3] Donne, *Satire V*, To Sir Thomas Egerton, ll. 9–15.

[4] Ed. Waite, vol. II, pp. 284 *et seq.* Cf. Thomas Vaughn in *Lumen de Lumine* (*Works*, ed. A. E. Waite, (London, 1919), p. 88): 'There is not an *Herb* here *below*, but hath a *star* in *Heaven above*, and the *star* strikes him with her *Beame*, and says to him, *Grow.*'

The astrological version of the microcosm-macrocosm analogy was so important that Paracelsus was led to find stars in the microcosm to complete the universal analogy and to explain the effects of the heavenly bodies upon man.

Hence it is clear that there is some star in man (if the heavenly bodies are to act on man), in birds, and in all animals; and whatever these do, they do by impulse of the higher influence which is received from the constellation, and regulates the unequal concordance.[1]

In *A Feaver* Donne, employing this same analogy, finds meteors in the 'little world' of the human body and an 'unchangeable firmament' as well.

> These burning fits but meteors bee,
> Whose matter in thee is soone spent.
> Thy beauty; and all parts, which are thee,
> Are unchangeable firmament.[2]

In the *Second Anniversary*, the body-microcosm of Elizabeth Drury is compared to electrum, which Paracelsus calls 'sometimes an alloy of gold and silver, or often a near gold which nature has not brought to perfection.'[3]

> Shee whose complexion was so even made
> That which of her ingredients should invade
> The other three, no Fears, no Art could guesse:
> So far were all removed from more or lesse.
> Shee, of whose soule, if we may say 'twas Golde,
> Her body was th'Electrum, and did hold
> Many degrees of that . . .[4]

The alchemical doctrine of the generation of gold from the baser metals over long periods of growth, and of the striving of nature to produce gold, finds expression in the work of Donne. In the *Eclogue, December 26, 1613,* introductory to the

---

[1] Ed. Waite, vol. II, p. 285.
[2] Donne, *A Feaver*, ll. 21–24.
[3] Ed. Waite, vol. II, p. 364.
[4] Donne, *The Second Anniversarie: The Progresse of the Soule*, ll. 123–36, 241–43.

Epithalamion on the marriage of Lady Frances Howard and the Earl of Somerset, he writes:

> The earth doth in her inward bowels hold
> Stuffe well dispos'd, and which would faine be gold,
> But never shall except it chance to lye,
> So upward, that heaven gild it with his eye;
> As for divine things faith comes from above,
> So for best civil use all tinctures move
> From higher powers; from God religion springs
> Wisdom and honour from the use of kings.[1]

The Paracelsian theory of a natural balm or Balsamum Suum which preserves and heals the body occurs frequently in Donne's writings. In one of the *Whitsuntide Sermons* we read:

. . . everything hath in it, as physicians used to call it, Naturale Balsamum, A natural balsamum, which if any wound or hurt which that creature hath received be kept clean from extrinsic putrefaction will heal of itself. We are so far from that we have a natural poison in us, original sin: for that original sin (as it hath relation to God, as all sin is a violating of God) God being the God of mercy, and the God of life, because it deprives us of both those, of mercy and of life, in opposition to mercy it is called anger and wrath, (We are all by nature the children of wrath) and in opposition to life it is called death, Death enters by sin and death is gone over all men . . .[2]

In the foregoing passage the balsam theory refers to a state of grace, and a body without the natural balsam is, as it were, a man in original sin. We find this theory in another sermon where it is again used to refer to a religious truth, this time to point out the virtues of the soul.

Now physicians say, That man hath in his constitution, in his complexion a natural virtue, which they call Balsamum Suum, His own balsamum, by which any wound which a man could receive in his body would cure itself, if it could be kept clean from the annoyances of the air, and all intrinsic incumbrances. Something that hath some proportion and analogy to this

---

[1] Donne, *Eclogue December 26. 1613*, ll. 61–66.
[2] Edmund Gosse, *The Life and Letters of John Donne*, London, 1899, vol. I, pp. 174–75.

balsamum of the body, There is in the soul of man too: the soul hath nardum suum, her spikenard, as the spouse says, Nardus mea dedit oderem suum, She has a Spikenard, a perfume, a fragrancy, a sweet savour in herself.[1]

Judging by the continual references to this theory in the works of Paracelsus, it is a keystone in his concept of medicine. In some instances he attributes life itself to its activity.

The life, then, of all men is none other than a certain astral balsam, a balsamic impression, a celestial and invisible fire, an included air, and a spirit of salt which tinges. I am unable to name it more clearly, although it could be put forward under many distinctive titles.[2]

The theory of the balsamum also seems to have led to the practice of using biological drugs or serums extracted from a dead body and giving them to the living. Donne writes to Sir H[enry] G[oodyere]:

The late Physician says, that when our natural inborn preservation is corrupted or wasted, it must be restored by a like extracted from other bodies; the chief care is that the Mummy have in it no exceeding quality, but an equally digested temper; And such is virtue.[3]

These particular examples of Hermetic science are drawn from medicine. It is only in the seventeenth and eighteenth centuries, however, that the process of separating the sciences proceeded very far, and the more recent scientific discoveries tend to make the modern distinctions between the sciences less and less absolute. We must remember that, for the Hermeticists, alchemy was the great science of helping nature in any way whatsoever. Regeneration was their watchword and it was unimportant whether it was the regeneration of minerals, sick bodies, or sick souls. All types of regeneration were essentially similar from the Hermetic point of view, and Paracelsus continually reiterates this extended view of alchemy.

The third part, or pillar of true medicine is Alchemy. Unless

---

[1] Alford, *The Works of Donne*, 6 vols., London, 1839, vol. II, p. 406.
[2] Ed. Waite, vol. I, p. 136.
[3] Donne, *Letters to Severall Persons of Honour*, pp. 84–85.

the physician be perfectly acquainted with and experienced in this art, everything that he devotes to the rest of his art will be vain and useless. Nature is so keen and subtle in her operations that she cannot be dealt with except by a sublime and accurate mode of treatment. She brings nothing to light that is at once perfect in itself, but leaves it to be perfected by man. This method of perfection is called alchemy. . . . So, whatever is poured forth from the bosom of nature, he who adapts it to that purpose for which it is destined is an Alchemist.[1]

It is obvious even from the few illustrations I have given that Donne often used scientific fact or theory as an analogue for some spiritual or ethical truth. It was not only valid to make analogies within the sciences themselves, but also to morals. This was not a rhetorical adjunct to style but a concept basic to much of the speculation of the age. Physical facts could, in truth, shadow metaphysical or spiritual ones.

Donne pressed the Paracelsian balsam theory—the commonplace theory Dr. Johnson thought abstruse—to his use in his poems as well as in his sermons. In a *Verse Letter to the Countesse of Bedford* he compared her qualities of birth and beauty to the activity of the balsam.

> In everything there naturally growes
> A Balsamum to keep it fresh, and new,
> If 'twere not injur'd by extrinsique blowes;
> Your birth and beauty are this Balme in you.[2]

In *The Extasie* he refers to a balm but it is not quite certain that this is the balm of Paracelsus' theory. He probably simply means sweat. However, the mystical mixture of the souls of the lovers is partly described in chemical terms.

> Our hands were firmly cimented
>   With a fast balme, which thence did spring
>
>   . . . . .
>
> He (though he knew not which soul spake
>   Because both meant, both spake the same)
> Might thence a new concoction take,
>   And part farre purer than he came.[3]

[1] Ed. Waite, vol. II, p. 148.
[2] Donne, *Verse Letter to the Countesse of Bedford*, ll, 21–24, p. 136.
[3] Donne, *The Extasie*, ll. 4–5, 25–28.

The balm theory reappears in *An Anatomie of the World* in a very effective image in which the decayed world is pictured as having lost its intrinsic balm and being ill in consequence.

> Sicke world, yea, dead, yea putrified, since shee
> Thy' intrinsique balme, and thy preservative,
> Can never be renewed.[1]

In the same poem there is a reference to the Hermetic notion that alchemical methods of perfection would be able to give man a physical well-being far transcending his ordinary state of health.

> There is no health; Physitians say that wee,
> At best, enjoy but a neutralitie.[2]

It was also a property of the quintessence to impart this wonderful health. The 'purest' of substances, it could cure all diseases and induce the most remarkable changes in all living and non-living matter. In a typical panegyric on the virtues of the quintessence, Paracelsus says:

Now the fact that the quintessence cures all diseases does not arise from the temperature, but from an innate property, namely, its great cleanliness and purity, by which after a wonderful manner, it greatly alters the body into its own purity, and entirely changes it.[3]

Several of Donne's figures drawn from alchemy depend upon a knowledge of laboratory equipment and processes. The piece of equipment which most captivated the imagination of John Donne was the limbeck, or alchemical still. In 'spiritual alchemy' the tortuous curving of the retort tube was analogous to the hard path travelled by the soul in the process of its purification.

> Lett not your soule (at first with graces fill'd
> And since, and thorough crooked lymbecks, still'd
> In many schools and courts, which quicken it,)
> Itself unto the Irish negligence submit.[4]

---

[1] Donne, *An Anatomie of the World*, ll. 56–58.
[2] *Ibid.*, ll. 91–92.
[3] Ed. Waite, vol. II, p. 23.
[4] Donne, *Henrico Wottoni in Hibernia Belligeranti*, ll. 13–16.

The limbeck was also the symbol for a regenerating purgation. In the *Satire of Religion* the wars with Spain are considered as vehicles for the purgation of the body.

> and thrise
> Colder than Salamanders, like divine
> Children in th'oven, fires of Spaine, and the line,
> Whose countries limbecks to our bodies bee.[1]

Death was also likened to a limbeck which refined our bodies in preparation for the resurrection. In the *Elegie on the Lady Markham* there is an interesting combination of this limbeck image with the microcosm-macrocosm analogy.

> So at this grave, her limbecke, which refines
>   The Diamonds, Rubies, Sapphires, Pearles, and Mines,
> Of which this flesh was, her soule shall inspire
>   Flesh of such stuffs, as God, when his last fire
> Annuls this world, to recommence it, shall
>   Make and name then, th'Elixir of this All.[2]

In *An Anatomie of the World* the poet used the limbeck figure indirectly when he referred to the bygone silver age and to the fact that people of his own time had not 'changed to gold their silver';

> or dispos'd into lesse glasse
> Spirits of vertue, which then scattered was.[3]

In the *Metempsychosis* there is a curious speculation on the process of respiration in a fish and one of the two explanations Donne gives of this phenomenon is that the fish converts the element of water into the element of air by a process similar to distillation.

> And whether she leaps up sometimes to breath
> And suck in aire, or find it underneath,
> Or working parts like mills or limbecks hath
> To make the water thinne and airlike[4]

---

[1] Donne, *Satire III, Of Religion*, ll. 22–25. Cf. H. Brémond, *Histoire littéraire du sentiment religieux en France* (Paris, 1925), vol. VII, 2nd part, ch. 5.
[2] Donne, *Elegie on the Lady Markham*, ll 24–28.
[3] Donne, *An Anatomie of the World*, ll, 149–150.
[4] Donne, *Metempsychosis*, ll. 264–67.

The limbeck figure is also used in *Elegie VIII* with a reference to the occult fire of the alchemists.

> Then like the Chymicks masculine equall fire
> Which in the Lymbecks warme womb doth inspire
> Into th'earths worthlesse dust a soule of gold.[1]

Certain varieties of fire were held to possess a generative principle and it was important to obtain the right kind of 'fire.' Any substance possessing an active generative principle was called masculine, and the passive substances, acted upon by the active ones, were called feminine.[2]

It must be remembered that this division between active and passive, or male and female, was extended to all natural phenomena. It therefore included fire as well as other substances or phenomena. Donne attributed generative powers to the sun's fire.

> See, Sir, how as the Suns hot Masculine flame
> Begets strange creatures on the Niles durty slime[3]

The growth of the foetus in the womb was thought to be controlled by certain occult kinds of heat present in the human body. These human generative fires had to be of just the right intensity, like 'chymiques equall fires.'

> Adam and Eve had mingled fires, and now
> Like Chimiques equall fires, her temperate wombe
> Had stewed and formed it.[4]

The same concept of proper heat intensities was extended by an analogy to alchemical processes. A fire of too little or too great intensity would prevent alchemical processes from being completed.

In the very first place, therefore, it is Necessary to build the fire for this work in just proportion, neither too large or too small; otherwise this work will never be carried on to its desired end.[5]

---

[1] Donne, *Elegie VIII, The Comparison*, ll. 35–37.
[2] *Ibid.*, vol. I, p. 289.
[3] Donne, *To the E. of D. with Six Holy Sonnets*, ll. 1–12.
[4] Donne, *Metempsychosis*, ll. 493–95.
[5] Ed. Waite, vol. I, p. 83.

There are several references to the specular stone in the work of John Donne, and this prism seems to have been part of the standard equipment of every practising alchemist. Chambers believes that Donne's references are to the magic mirror or showstone used by Dr. Dee and demonstrated by him at the court of Queen Elizabeth.[1] Whether Dr. Dee is to be called famous or notorious is a debatable question, but his story is one of the most interesting in the annals of alchemy.[2] After alchemy was banned in England in the fifteenth century, Dee was one of the few men able to obtain a licence.

The specular stone seems to have been the same piece of apparatus that Paracelsus called the crystal and which he maintained was very important in the process of conjuring.

To conjure is nothing else than to observe anything rightly, to know and understand what it is. The crystall is a figure of the air. Whatever appears in the air, movable or immovable, the same appears also in the speculum or crystal as a wave. For the air, the water, and the crystal, so far as vision is concerned, are one, like a mirror in which an inverted copy of an object is seen.[3]

In a *Verse Letter to the Countesse of Bedford*, Donne refers to the specular stone as if it were a piece of apparatus requiring a high degree of skill to operate.

> You teach (though wee learne not) a thing unknowne
> To our late times, the use of specular stone,
> Through which all things within without were shown;[4]

This same idea about the difficulty of using the stone appears again in *The Undertaking*.

[1] Donne, *Poems of John Donne*, edited by E. K. Chambers (London, 1896), vol. I, pp. 223–24.

[2] Waite, *Lives of the Alchemistical Philosophers* (London, 1888), pp. 153–59.

[3] Ed. Waite, vol. I, p. 14.

[4] Donne, *Verse Letter to the Countesse of Bedford*, ll. 28–30, p. 158. See Donne, Sermon XXVII in *Fifty Sermons* (1649), p. 231, where Donne refers to pagan temples made of Specular Stone but seems to mean merely some kind of transparent mineral.

> It were but madnes now t'impart
> The skill of specular stone,
> When he which can have learned the art
> To cut it can find none.[1]

The use of the specular stone seems to have been abandoned by the time Donne reached manhood. Exactly what this optical device or lens was used for is not clear, but Paracelsus implies that the crystal showed things 'rightly.' This would seem to indicate that the optical effects created by the stone were identified with the occult properties of things, since occult properties were the important ones for alchemical purposes.

The alchemical process had several distinct steps and Donne discovered an interesting analogy between the various steps in the alchemical process and the various steps in the process of salvation, the chemical order reflecting the spiritual as all the orders in his universe reflected each other.

Therefore David who was metal tried seven times in the fire, and desired to be such gold as might be laid up in God's treasury, might consider, that in the transmutation of metals, it is not enough to come to a calcination or a liquefaction of the metal . . . nor to an ablution, to sever dross from pure, nor to a transmutation, to make it a better metal, but there must be a fixion, a settling thereof, so that it shall not evaporate into nothing, nor return to his former state. Therefore he saw that he needed not only a liquefaction, a melting into tears, not only an ablution and a transmutation, those he had by this purging and this washing . . . but he needed fixionem, and establishment.[2]

Although sublimation was the most important alchemical process,[3] it is interesting to observe that, for Donne, the most important process was fixation. His general religious attitude indicated that his faith was a 'fugitive' thing and that it was

---

[1] Donne, *The Undertaking*, ll. 4–8.

[2] Alford, *op. cit.*, vol. III, pp. 100–01.

[3] Read, *A Prelude to Chemistry* (New York, Macmillan, 1937), p. 50. Descriptions of the various alchemical processes will be found in Read, pp. 50–51, and in Taylor in ch. 11. The Taylor analysis is especially good for its thorough study of the numerous analogical extensions made from the alchemical process to other processes and fields of knowledge (esp. pp. 151 *et seq.*).

difficult to make it abide the fire. Although this passage indicated a rather exact knowledge of the alchemical process there is no reason to believe that Donne ever performed alchemical experiments. There is, however, a striking figure in *The Anatomie of the World* which clearly indicates that he at least witnessed some laboratory experiments. Anyone who has watched the formation of the mercury-gold amalgam will recall the quick spread of a dull lustre over the previously shining metal.

> As gold falls sicke being stung with Mercury
> All the words parts of such complexion bee.[1]

One of the strangest claims that Paracelsus ever made was that he could manufacture an artificial man, the Homunculus, in his laboratory.

But there are many kinds of putrefaction and one produces it generation better than another, one more quickly than another . . . For you must know that in this men can be generated without natural father and mother; that is to say, not in the natural way from the woman, but by the art and industry of a skilled Spagyrist a man can be born and grow, as will hereafter be described.[2]

Donne seized upon this idea and used it in a sermon to show the insignificance of man before God. He does not seem to believe such an operation to be impossible nor does the question of its possibility seem to be of major interest. It is simply a case of using the most convenient illustration to make a religious point. If the idea is interesting and illustrative of a spiritual truth its scientific or philosophical truth can be considered as of secondary importance. Donne says:

How poor and inconsiderable a thing is man. Man, whom Paracelsus would have undertaken to make, in a Limbeck, in a furnace . . .[3]

[1] Donne, *An Anatomie of the World*, ll. 345–46.
[2] Ed. Waite, vol. I, p. 121.
[3] Donne, *LXXX Sermons* (London, 1640), no. VII, pp. 64–65. Donne in *LXXX Sermons* (London, 1640), sermon XXIII, p. 226, refers to the 'killing eye' of the Basilisk, another alchemical creature, to be produced without conjunction, whose glance was lethal.

The Quintessence, Spiritual Alchemy, and the Alchemical Quest

Several of Donne's alchemical images are concerned with the properties and powers of transmuting elixirs, or with the 'Quintessence,' the most common name for the great transmuting agent which the alchemists sought. The possibility of finding or creating a transmuting agent was bound up with the notion of the unity of all things. In pursuing this latter notion further, the alchemists came to regard the 'medicine of the metals' as a medicine for man as well. Under its medicinal aspect the stone was called the 'Elixir of Life,' or simply, the 'Elixir.'

In general, the philosopher's stone was said to possess four major properties: it brought metals to perfection, it healed diseases and prolonged life, it could change all base stones into precious ones, and it could soften any kind of glass.[1] The elixir, stone, or quintessence, was the 'purest' of substances and was not of the four elements but was, as its name implies, a fifth element, perfect and incorruptible and the substance from which the heavens were made.

The quintessence then, is a certain matter extracted from all things which nature has produced, and from everything which has life corporally in itself, a matter most subtly purged of all impurities and mortality, and separated from all elements. . . . It is a spirit like the spirit of life but with this difference, that the life spirit of a thing is permanent but that of man is mortal. Whence it may be inferred that the quintessence cannot be extracted from the flesh or the blood of man: for this reason, that the spirit of life, which is also the spirit of virtue, dies, and life exists in the soul, not in the material substance.[2]

The quintessence was believed to reside, somewhat like a seed, at the 'core' of things.[3]

Donne uses the elixir figure as the symbol of virtue and compares the ennobling and purifying power of virtue to the curative power of the elixir.

[1] Read, *op. cit.*, pp. 125–26.
[2] Ed. Waite, vol. II, p. 22.
[3] *Ibid.*, vol. II, p. 290.

> She guilded us: But you are gold, and Shee;
> Us she informed but transubstantiates you;
> Soft dispositions which ductile bee
> Elixarlike, she makes not cleane but new.[1]

She, virtue in the abstract, only affected the males in a superficial manner, as an imperfect elixir would only change the appearance of the base metal without changing its essence. However, the 'projection' was very successful with the Countess of Huntingdon, for she was good material to begin with, and, since she had a soft disposition, she was more susceptible to virtue.

In *An Anatomie of the World*, the transmuting elixir is employed to indicate the superlative merits of Elizabeth Drury and the great and beneficial influence of her character.

> She, from whose influence all Impressions came,
> But, by Receivers impotences, lame,
> Who though she could not transubstantiate
> All states to gold, yet guilded every state,
> So that some Princes have some temperance;
> Some counsellors some purpose to advance
> The common profit; and some people have
> Some state, no more than kings should give, to crave;
> Some women, have some taciturnity,
> Some nunneries some grains of chastitie
> She that did this much, and much more could doe,
> But that our age was Iron and rustie too,
> Shee, shee is dead . . .[2]

One of the important theories in alchemy was that the success of an attempted transmutation depended on the purity of the body to be transformed as well as on the efficacy of the transmuting agent. The importance of securing the proper first matter of the work and the necessity of working with 'pure' materials in every phase of the alchemical process is clearly implied in this passage. What is to be transmuted or healed must be 'pure' or 'She,' otherwise virtue as the elixir will only be able to gild and not transform it. Elsewhere, the alleged purity of the quintessence is made the core of an

---

[1] Donne, *Verse Letter to the Countesse of Huntingdon*, ll. 25–28, p. 145.
[2] Donne, *An Anatomie of the World*, ll. 415–27.

alchemical figure in a cynical reference to love 'being no quintessence.'

> But if this medicine, love, which cures all sorrow
> With more, not only bee no quintessence
> But mixed of all stuffs, paining soul or sense,
> And of the Sunne his working vigor borrow
> Love's not so pure, and abstract, as they use
> To say [1]

We also find a reference to the elixir, or virtue, residing in the Earl of Dorset, and purifying the poet's rhymes.

> As fire these drossie Rymes to purifie
> Or as Elixir, to change them to gold;
> You are that Alchimist which alwaies had
> Wit, whose one spark could make good things of bad. [2]

The analogy between the operation of virtue and the operation of the elixir was not as far-fetched as it might seem to modern readers because the seemingly mysterious acquisition of virtue in a human being, and the mysterious perfection brought about in the sick body or base metal, were believed to be similar phenomena from a philosophical point of view.

A Nocturnall Upon S. Lucies Day is rich in Hermetic imagery. Paracelsus' balm appears in an image of the world as an organism which has lost the health-preserving substance. It has retreated to the earth's centre and its preservative influence is no longer felt.

> The generall balme th'hydroptique earth hath drunk
> Wither, as to the beds-feet, life is shrunke,
> Dead and enterr'd; [3]

In this poem, the quintessence idea is curiously reversed. Instead of being the quintessence of all things, or rather their active principle, the poet, through the effects of his unfortunate love, has been made the quintessence of nothing.

> For I am every dead thing
> In whom love wrought new Alchimie

---

[1] Donne, *Loves Growth*, ll. 7–12.
[2] Donne, *To E. of D. with Six Holy Sonnets*, ll. 11–14.
[3] Donne, *A Nocturnall Upon S. Lucies Day*, ll. 6–8.

> For his love did expresse
> A quintessence even from nothingnesse,
> From dull privations, and leane emptinesse:
> He ruines mee, and I am re-begot
> Of absence, darknesse, death; things which are not.[1]

Love appears as the limbeck in which this transmutation was performed.

> All others, from all things, draw all that's good,
> Life, soule, forme, spirit, whence they beeing have;
>   I, by loves limbecke am the grave
>   Of all, that's nothing. Oft a flood
>   Have wee two wept, and so
> Drownd the world, us two; oft did we grow
> To be two Chaosses, when we did show
> Care to ought else; and often absences
> Withdrew our soules, and made us carcasses.
> But I am by her death, (which word wrongs her)
> Of the first nothing, the Elixir grown;
>   Were I a man, that I were one,
>   I needs must know; I should preferre
>   If I were any beast,
> Some ends, some means; Yea plants, yea stones detest,
> And love; All, some properties invest;
> If I an ordinary nothing were,
> As shadow, a light, and body must be here.[2]

The word 'chaos' probably has an alchemical reference in this poem, although it may very well be used in its conventional meaning alone and still be of significance. The meanings of chaos vary, but Mr. Edgar Hill Duncan seems to think that Donne probably meant a generalized expression for all 'aerial matter.'[3] What is also of interest in this poem is the passage referring to the Hermetic doctrine of Hylozoism. This idea is not exclusively Hermetic but in the light of the abundant alchemical imagery of the poem it is not unlikely that this particular form of the doctrine was extracted from a Hermetic context. Mr. Duncan holds that the term 'flood' in this poem

---

[1] Donne, *A Nocturnall upon S. Lucies Day*, ll. 12–18.
[2] *Ibid.*, ll. 19–36.
[3] Edgar Hill Duncan, 'Donne's Alchemical Figures,' *Journal of English Literary History* (1942), 9, 283.

is of Hermetic origin. A 'flood' seems to have been a phenomenon or situation to be avoided in the preparation of the stone, and Mr. Duncan supports this view with a quotation from Ashmole's *Theatrum Chemicum Brittanicum.*

> Let him drinke noe more than will suffice
> Beware of Floods I you advise.[1]

I have found no reference to floods in Paracelsus, and Ashmole is not at all clear about what happens during a 'flood.'

Red was the colour of the matter in the last phase of the work and symbolized resurrection or immortality. In *The Anatomie of the World*, there is a reference to red which I believe implies the Hermetic symbolism.

> Our blushing red, which us'd in cheekes to spread
> Is inward sunke, and only our soules are red.[2]

Given a Hermetic interpretation, this passage would mean that we lost our immortal bodies after the fall of man and only our souls remain immortal and incorruptible now. One of the *Holy Sonnets* seems to use the complete tricolour Hermetic symbolism.

> Oh make thyselfe with holy mourning blacks
> And red with blushing, as thou are with sinne;
> Or wash thee in Christs blood, which hath this might
> That being red, it dyes red soules to white.[3]

Here, black is used in a symbolic significance for the state of penitential purification. Red is used in three senses, two of them diametrically opposed, once as symbolic of both remorse and sin, and a second time as descriptive of Christ's blood which acts like the tincture, purifying remorseful and sinful souls to white. We find the Hermetic progression from black to white, but red, for human beings, is not the highest state of perfection. Red in this instance corresponds to Christ's grace, whose operation was compared to that of the elixir. Instead of completing the analogy Donne has made a conceit of the term 'red'

---

[1] Edgar Hill Duncan, 'Donne's Alchemical Figures,' *Journal of English Literary History* (1942), 9, 407.

[2] Donne, *An Anatomie of the World*, ll. 57–58. On colour symbolism see Read, pp. 26–29, and Thomas Norton's *The Ordinall of Alchemy*, ch. 5, pp. 63 ff. in Ashmole's *Theatrum Chemicum Brittanicum.*

[3] Donne, *Holy Sonnets IV*, ll. 11–14.

and developed it in the poem in at least three of its possible symbolic meanings.

The possibility of the Hermetic interpretation of this poem does not rest only on Donne's extensive knowledge of empirical alchemy. In at least one passage he mentions a transcendental alchemy, and this fact, taken in conjunction with numerous other references to alchemical theory and processes, gives further evidence that Donne was well acquainted with the larger implications of Hermetic theories.[1]

> She in whom vertue was so much refin'd
> That for Allay unto so pure a minde
> She took the weaker Sex; shee that could drive
> The poysonous tincture, and the stain of Eve . . .
> Out of her thoughts, and deeds; and purifie
> All, by a true religious Alchymie;
> Shee, shee is dead.[2]

It is interesting to compare this question from Donne with a passage from Thomas Vaughn, which seems to disclaim any validity for the material alchemy, since the end of the great work is described as a mystical experience.

Such is the power he shall receive, who from the clamorous tumults of this world ascends to the supernatural still voice, from this base earth and mind which to his body is allyed, to the spirituall invisible elements of his Soul.[3]

The element of fire also had a spiritual significance. When Donne says, 'The Element of Fire is quite put out' he may be making the Paracelsian identification of fire with the heavenly substance.[4] According to the microcosm-macrocosm analogy, fire, the earthly analogue of heaven's substance, would enable the beneficial influences of heaven to be felt. If it is put out, that influence is lost.

[1] Another reference to a transcendental alchemy occurs in the *Essays in Divinity*, p. 122, where Donne says that the Cabalists possessed a 'theological alchymy to draw sovereign tinctures and spirits from plain and gross literal matter.' See *Essays in Divinity*, ed. by Augustus Jessop (London, 1885).

[2] Donne, *An Anatomie of the World*, ll. 177–82.

[3] Cited in Waite, *Lives of Alchemistical Philosophers* (London, 1888), p. 22.

[4] Donne, *An Anatomie of the World*, l. 206.

In *The Crosse*, a distinction is made between material and spiritual crosses, and the healing power of the healing cross is likened to 'extracted chimique medicine.'

> Materiall Crosses then, good physique bee,
> But yet spirituall have chiefe dignity.
> These for extracted chimique medicine serve
> And cure much better, and as well preserve;[1]

In *The Litanie* Donne makes a curious reversal of the usual properties of the tincture and we find a reference to 'vicious tinctures.'

> From this red earth, O Father, purge away
> All vicious tinctures, that new fashioned
> I may rise up from death, before I'm dead [2]

This is analogous to a similar reversal of the chemical properties of the quintessence as in the *Nocturnall Upon S. Lucies Night*.

Resurrection Imperfect is rich in the imagery of the spiritual alchemists.

> Whose body having walk'd on earth, and now
> Hasting to Heaven, would, that he might allow
> Himselfe unto all stations, and fill all,
> For these three daies become a minerall;
> Hee was all gold when he lay downe, but rose
> All tincture, and doth not alone dispose
> Leaden and iron wills to good but is
> Of power to make even sinfull flesh like his.
> Had one of those, whose credulous pietie
> Thought, that a Soule one might descerne and see
> Goe from a body, at this sepulcher been,
> And, issuing from a sheet, this body seen,
> He would have justly thought this body a soule
> If not of any man, yet of the whole.[3]

In this poem, Donne draws an analogy between the reduction of a substance to its 'Minerall' or remote matter from which

---

[1] Donne, *The Crosse*, ll. 25-28.

[2] Donne, *The Litanie, I, The Father*, ll. 7-9. Compare this inversion of the tincture idea with a similar inversion in the *Nocturnall Upon S. Lucies Day*. 'Red Earth' is also a pun on Adam, which means 'red earth' in Hebrew. See H. J. C. Grierson, *Poems of John Donne* (Oxford, Oxford U.P., 1912), 2 vols., vol. I, p. 338.

[3] Donne, *Resurrection Imperfect*, ll. 9-22.

metals and minerals are derived, and death, which precedes a resurrection. The reduction of a metal is followed by a synthesis of the original constituents but in such a manner that the final product is 'perfect.' Gold, the most perfect metal in nature, is, by alchemical means, transmuted to tincture, which is more than perfect in possessing the power to transmute base metals into gold. Similarly, Christ, the perfect man, is crucified and becomes 'tincture' which can transmute 'Leaden and iron wills to good' through the grace which all mankind receives from his sacrifice. A similar analogy between gold as the symbol of natural Christian perfection and its perfection as a metal, occurs in Donne's *Epitaph on Himselfe*.

> Parents make us earth, and souls dignifie
> Us to be glasse; here to grow gold we lie.[1]

Earth is the body which, by the action of the divine tincture, can be made to generate 'gold' or Christian perfection. Since it was also the property of the tincture to soften glass, there may be a remote allusion to grace softening our souls to receive virtue. To 'grow gold' alludes to the theory of the generation of metals, in order to suggest that the duty of every Christian is to perfect himself in the virtues of his faith during his life.

The name of the Countesse of Bedford is on one occasion compared to a 'tincture' which affects the longevity of the poet's verses.

> Verse embalmes virtue; and Tombs, or Thrones or rimes,
> Preserve fraile transitory fame, as much
> As spice doth bodies from corrupt aires touch,
>
> Mine are short-lived; the tincture of your name
> Creates in them but dissipates as fast,
> New spirits: for, strong agents with the same
> Force that doth warme and cherish, us doe wast;
> Kept hot with strong extracts, no bodies last:[2]

One of the most fanciful varieties of symbolism employed by the alchemists was derived from the realm of zoology and

[1] Donne, *Epitaphe on Himself*, ll. 7–8.
[2] Donne, *Verse Letter to the Countesse of Bedford*, ll. 13–20, p. 143.

natural history. Mr. Duncan maintains that Donne's *Canonization* is an example of the use of alchemico-zoological symbolism.[1]

> Call us what you will, wee are made such by love;
> Call her one, mee another flye,
> We're tapers too; and at our own cost die,
> And wee in us find th'Eagle and the Dove
> The Phoenix ridle hath more wit
> By us, we two being one are it.
> So to one neutrall thing both sexes fit,
> Wee dye and rise the same, and prove
> Mysterious by this love.[2]

Paracelsus describes the end-product of the alchemical process as the phoenix.[3] The eagle and the dove symbolize intermediate stages in the production of the phoenix. Death, or dissolution, is followed by a regeneration, producing the eagle and the dove, both instrumental in the creation of the phoenix, which in turn symbolizes the 'mystical' union of the sexes.

The alchemists used the dragon and the serpent as symbols for mercury and sulphur, although they were not by any means exclusively alchemical symbols. Donne applies one of these symbols to the use of Christian doctrine. The serpent is alternately used, both for Satan and for Christ.

That creeping Serpent, Satan, is at war and should be so; the crucified Serpent, Christ Jesus, is peace, and shall be so for ever. The creeping Serpent eats our dust, the strength of our bodies, in sicknesses, and our glory in dust, the dust of the grave: The crucified Serpent hath taken our flesh, and our blood, and given us his flesh and his blood for it.[4]

The unusual use of the serpent to symbolize both Satan, the giver of death, and Jesus, the giver of life, may have been suggested by an alchemical reference to the end of the 'great work'; it is symbolized by a serpent that dies, breaks into

[1] Duncan, *op. cit.*, pp. 269–71.
[2] Donne, *The Canonization*, ll. 19–27.
[3] Ed. Waite, vol. I, p. 40.
[4] Donne, *L Sermons*, London, 1648, p. 445, quoted in Elizabeth Holmes, *Henry Vaughn and The Hermetic Philosophy* (Oxford, Oxford U.P., 1932), p. 29. For a discussion of the alchemical Dragon see Read, *op. cit.*, p. 272, and for the Serpent see *ibid.*, pp. 106 *et seq.*

pieces and is then rejoined. However, this relationship is conjectural.

Donne's Attitude Toward Hermetic Philosophy

An examination of alchemical imagery as John Donne used it reveals the extraordinary skill and precision with which he adapted these figures to the use of his art, and his work demonstrates an exact knowledge of all the ideas involved. It is difficult for us to perceive the precise usage Donne accords Hermetic ideas, not simply because this kind of inquiry is now defunct, but more important still because it was based upon a mode of thought which no longer plays an important part in modern science. The principle of universal analogy was frequently applied as an almost unconscious habit of thought by many thinkers of Donne's time. All branches of knowledge were related to one another by analogy, and it was virtually impossible to say where one branch of knowledge ended and the other began. Not only were intricate analogies made between the various classes of physical beings, but physical truths shadowed truths of the metaphysical and spiritual order. Donne's age accepted the belief in the unity of knowledge and being without much question. Indeed, these concepts were believed to be indispensable to the human intellect in its quest for knowledge. In the light both of the nature of alchemy and Donne's intellectual curiosity and mental habits, there is no reason why he should not have been able to accept the theory and practice of alchemy without any qualms. However, there are passages in his work in which he satirizes alchemy and the alchemists.[1]

In *Loves Alchymie* the discovering of the centric happiness of love is compared to the continual and repeated round of experiments that the alchemist performs in order to achieve his goal. Both the lover and the alchemists are chasing a will-o'-the-wisp and only succeed in finding a substitute with which they must content themselves.

> Some that have deeper digg'd loves Myne than I
> Say, where this centrique happiness doth lie:
> I have lov'd, and got, and told,

[1] Donne, *The Sunne Rising*, ll. 23–24; *The Crosse*, ll. 37–38; *A Valediction: Of the Book*, ll. 53–54.

> But should I love, get, tell, till I were old,
> I should not find that hidden mysterie;
>   Oh, 'tis imposture all:
> And as no chymique yet th'elixir got,
>   But glorifies his pregnant pot,
>   If by the way to him befall
> Some odoriferous thing, or medicinall
>   So, lovers dreame a rich and long delight,
>   But get a winter-seeming night.

and in conclusion we read:

> Our ease, our thrift, our honor, and our day
> Shall we for this vaine Bubles shadow pay?[1]

Some instances of satiric references toward alchemy occur in the earlier poems when Donne was a courtier and writing his poetry for an audience that expected wit and cynicism. Other satiric references, fewer and less extended, are to be found in poems written after his conversion. However, he was always able to use alchemical references without any expressed attitude. As an example, in *The Bracelet* he simply accepts and uses certain alchemical notion without any implications as to what he thought of alchemy.

> Gold being the heaviest metal amongst all
> May my most heavy curse upon thee fall.[2]

We also find, especially in the later poems, that Donne used alchemical figures frequently, and often in the extended meanings imputed to them by the Hermeticists and occultists. We have sufficiently reiterated the legitimacy of alchemy as a science to know that when Donne says 'oft Alchimists doe coyners prove' he does not necessarily mean that the science of alchemy was erroneous. The extent of the scientific knowledge of his own day and the frequent failures of the alchemists could only warrant the simple statement that alchemists were often counterfeiters. The great alchemists themselves were as well aware of this fact as John Donne himself. It was only in the sixteenth and seventeenth centuries that the gold-making aspects of the art became prominent. To the adept, his work was rather a philosophical and religious activity than a scientific or commercial one.

[1] Donne, *Loves Alchymie*, ll. 1–12, 13–14.
[2] *Ibid.*, ll. 93–94.

For they being lovers of Wisdome more than Worldly Wealth drove at higher and more excellent Operations: And certainly He to whom the whole Course of Nature lyes open, rejoyceth not so much that he can make Gold or Silver . . . as that he sees the Heavens open, the Angells of God Ascending and Descending, and that his own name is fairly written in the book of life.[1]

There is no statement in Donne's work giving a definite opinion of the Hermetic Art, but the internal evidence of his work can only point to a strong interest in alchemy and a good understanding of its content. It is obvious that he recognized the elements of charlatanry in the contemporary practice of alchemy and he rightly satirized them. Those of the 'puffers' who were charlatans provided excellent material for the satirists by the manner in which they duped their gullible victims. The rest of the 'puffers,' honest but deluded and greedy, presented a rather ludicrous and amusing spectacle. These men who lived among the most unpleasant odours and performed experiment after experiment, hoping constantly that the next one would make their fortune, were ideal subjects for the clever wits of the day to satirize.[2]

The Hermetic philosophy, with its elaborate system of correspondences, spiritual and material, and its claims for changing men as well as metals into pure 'gold,' was one of the systems which were attempting to unite the natural to the supernatural order. Further, it was unique among rival systems in having an empirical aspect, alchemy. With the publication of the Hermes Trismegistus and the extension of alchemy, the ideas of regeneration and spiritual alchemy became the common domain of the cultured. The man who cast off orthodoxy found himself face to face with a heterogeneous mass of ideas, all of them moving toward the reconciliation of matter and spirit.[3] No one like Donne, who was caught in the spiritual and intellectual confusion of his times, would have ignored this great and influential tradition of his age.

[1] Ashmole, *Theatrum Chemicum Brittanicum* (London, 1652), p. 368.

[2] See Read, *op. cit.*, pp. 126, 161, for further information about the 'puffers.'

[3] For an interesting study of the effect of Renaissance occultism on English literature, see Denis Saurat, *Literature and Occult Tradition* (London, 1930).

'An hydrotique and immoderate desire for humane learning' led him to the study of the major intellectual systems of his time. He eventually rejected them all qua systems, but he did press many ideas from them to the service of his art and made use of incomplete, disjointed fragments of philosophical systems as vehicles for his emotions.

Ideas from alchemy, astronomy, medicine, philosophy, and theology appear and reappear throughout the body of his work, and often in such curious juxtaposition as to seem to justify the strictures of those critics who have accused him of a lack of intellectual responsibility. But Donne as a true poet has an aesthetic rather than an intellectual interest in ideas. He used ideas without much regard for what we would call their truth value but for whatever value they may have had for evoking emotions, expressing attitudes and states of mind, and illustrating the moral truths revealed to faith.

Even Donne the preacher was, in fact, working in the tradition of the Baroque or 'metaphysical' sermon. Such sermons were built upon a system of 'preachable conceits' which correspond closely to the extensively elaborated metaphors characteristic of 'metaphysical' poetry and 'spiritual alchemy.' The 'preachable conceit' was a pedagogical device whereby the truths of faith were inculcated by showing how the particular truth was contained symbolically or analogically in a fact, a word or phrase of Scripture, an historical event, or in a phenomenon of nature. The points of departure did not matter nor their relationship to each other. What did matter was that the preacher, by the exercise of his learning and ingenuity, showed how all or any of seemingly heterogeneous loci converged on the same moral truth. One author had written two books, the Bible and the book of nature and human experience. Both books, in effect, had been written in 'preachable conceits,' and it was the duty of the preacher gracefully to perfect and reveal in their fullness the preachable conceits which God had lightly hinted,[1] just as the alchemist was to unfold and perfect the divine 'gold' hidden in the dross of reality.

[1] Benedetto Croce wrote an interesting essay on the Baroque sermon, 'I predicatori italiani del seicento e il gusto spagnuolo,' in *Saggi sulla letteratura italiana del seicento* (Bari, 1924). The essay is fully annotated with bibliographical notes.

CHAPTER V

Hell vs. Hell : From Dante
to Machiavelli

MACHIAVELLI might, at first glance, seem to stand looking out into chaos from the circumference of a circle in which
Dante occupies the centre, the perspective of perfect order.
Where Dante finds symmetry and coherence, Machiavelli
would appear to find only fragmentary and tenuous relations.
Dante was able finally to time all of his encounters and experi-
ences so as to lead to one another, to be exhaustively usable,
while Machiavelli often found his ambiguous even if he never
failed to learn something from each of them. For Dante all
experience was finally mediation, while, for Machiavelli, each
experience could only, with certainty, illuminate its own
immediate context and not point very far beyond itself.

Perhaps another way of stating all this is that Dante can
imagine a *Purgatory* or a *Paradise* but Machiavelli can only
imagine a *Hell*. This would seem to place them at opposite
ends of the spectrum of moral and imaginative possibilities,
but the category of hell in fact unites the two great Florentines,
for Machiavelli's analysis of experience is made entirely in
terms of incontinence, force, and fraud, Dante's three categories
of sin. In Machiavelli we find them not as three great stages in
a descent to the abyss but as the three terms of a dynamic
system in terms of which life is lived, a system which is not a
pure Dantesque hell but which includes some purgatorial

possibilities and perhaps even a few momentary paradisiacal ones. Machiavelli, like Dante, sees men as driven by infinite desire, but the infinite goal and the ladder to it has, for all practical purposes, disappeared. The enormous energies which Dante had seen as focussed on the infinite Machiavelli sees as unleashed in the world, in a world which has no object that can bind them. In Machiavelli, man appears in fundamental contradiction with his universe, for he is hopelessly incontinent, infinitely desirous, endlessly ambitious, yet his survival depends on some degree of renunciation and restraint. Because of this situation, Machiavelli tells us, force, whether as violence or as the power of law, must come into operation to check incontinence, and, if force is not available in sufficient quantity, then fraud must make up the difference. Fraud, in Machiavelli's context, is by no means always deliberate deception but includes a good many of the conventions, fictions and illusions that society requires for its self-regulation. Biological survival as well as culture rest on this system of thrust and counterthrust.

Before confronting the Dantesque and Machiavellian hells let us try to measure the cultural distance between them and see how Dante's Hell was both preserved and transformed in a different cosmological structure.

The Breakdown of Hierarchy and the Emergence of Fortune and Virtue

Dante lived in a hierarchical order, cosmologically as well as morally, and his universe contained a fundamental distinction between a perfect 'higher' world of circular motion and incorruptible quintessential bodies, and an imperfect 'lower' world of changing elements and linear motion. Machiavelli's statecraft, like Galileo's natural science, starts from the principle of the uniformity and homogenity of nature, the obedience of all events to invariable laws which are everywhere the same. All periods of history, like all segments of nature, possess the same fundamental structure, so that a contemporary event will find its analogue in the past. Machiavelli utterly rejected the medieval concept of correspondence between political, moral, cosmological, ecclesiastical, and celestial orders, the notion of the divine source of power, indeed, the whole metaphysical rationalization of feudalism.[1]

The universe for Machiavelli no longer possessed the extraordinary degree of symmetrical and rational order that the scholastics had conferred upon it. Its outlines had become indefinite, its consistency uniform. It had become in one respect much simpler and in another more complex and ambiguous, for chance had replaced providence as the ruling principle. *Fortuna* again received her due in her old pagan form, wily, capricious and unpredictable. The old, highly specified, supernatural had become irrelevant and had been replaced with an indefinite natural world, imperfectly knowable, but certainly knowable in some sufficient degree to permit successful action, at least at times. Indeed, the problem of action is at the heart of Machiavelli's thought, and it would be an error to dwell too much on the relation of his thought to scientific and cultural changes. Machiavelli is first and foremost a political thinker and man of letters, and his vague cosmology is not an end in itself but the most appropriate frame for containing a universe of discourse about action which will be true to all of the ambiguities inherent in it. He is concerned with those questions about human action which involve consideration of what can be deliberately planned as an end and what cannot, what goals of desire disappear precisely because they are desired, what goals of planning disappear precisely because they are planned. He knows that action with chaotic and ruinous consequences can first appear as rationality and morality. So he, along with his contemporaries and Renaissance predecessors, revived the old deities of *fortuna* and *virtus* because their very indefiniteness permitted greater fidelity to the problematic character of both personal and political affairs.

The revival of the old concepts in the Renaissance was not unique to Machiavelli. The problem of fortune and virtue, chance and ability, was much discussed from Petrarch to Bruno and beyond. Before Machiavelli, however, the emphasis had been placed on personal fortune or the rôle of chance in private

[1] See Ernst Cassirer's penetrating chapters on Machiavelli in his *The Myth of the State* (New York, 1955). For a study of the medieval concept of hierarchy see the first chapter of my *Medieval Cultural Tradition in Dante's Comedy* (Ithaca, 1960).

affairs.[1] Machiavelli, however, applied the concept, like Polybius, to public rather than private life. It seemed to him the best expression of what he had learned from long experience of public life, that the whole problem of politics can be summed up in one platitude: the best advice and the most exact implementation of it cannot always succeed. Therefore all attempts at rational prediction must take account of what we might call an irreducible element of chaos, fatality, necessity or ignorance, a realm of darkness whose boundary, however, can never be clearly defined. It may appear as chance or fate, only apparently opposites, and it can only be discovered in action itself. When action succeeds we have experienced freedom and created order, when it fails we have experienced fate or malevolent chance. Historical experience teaches us, according to Machiavelli, that it is possible for will to overcome fate or chance about half of the time, and, unlike many fatalists in the Renaissance who toyed with similar ideas, Machiavelli strikes a new note in giving man a fifty-fifty chance against the malice of the inanimate as well as against the malice and irrationality of the animate.[2]

Machiavelli follows Polybius in using two concepts of historical explanation, one in terms of chance or fortune, the other in terms of cause and ability. Thus Polybius says that the Romans, to be sure, gained their empire by ability, caused it to come into being, but that they should have been able to do this at a time and place when their abilities, their causal power, could succeed, *that* must be attributed to fortune. Similarly, Cesare Borgia succeeded by his ability, his *virtù*, and only failed at the end because of the sudden death of his father and his own

---

[1] Felix Gilbert, 'Bernardo Rucellai and the Orti Oricellari: A Study on the Origin of Modern Political Thought,' *Journal of the Warburg and Courtauld Institutes*, XII (1949), 101–31, 103; Ernst Cassirer, *Individuum and Kosmos in der Renaissance* (Leipzig, 1927), pp. 77–129, for the history of the concept; Giovanni Gentile, *Il pensiero italiano del Rinascimento* (Firenze, 1940), 3rd ed. ch. 3: 'Il concetto dell'uomo nel Rinascimento,' pp. 47–114. There is extant a correspondence between Giovanni Rucellai and Ficino on the subject of personal *virtù* and *fortuna*, of great interest in view of the fact that the subject was still discussed years later in the group which frequented the Rucellai gardens. On these concepts in Petrarch we now possess the thorough study of Klaus Heitmann, *Fotuna und Virtus: Eine Studie zu Petrarchas Lebensweisheit*, Köln (1958).

[2] Cassirer, *The Myth of the State*, pp. 196–97.

simultaneous illness. This outcome was the work of a truly malignant fortune, since, great as his abilities were, they did not come into play at the right time.[1]

As we examine the use of the concept of fortune in Machiavelli or Polybius we gradually become aware that it simultaneously refers to a cluster of related ideas of causality and limit from which we might, for example, abstract three categories among others which, singly or in combination, enter into a description of action: determinism or fatality, chance and intentionality. To describe all of the real world of action in terms of any single one of these categories would result in a drastic simplification

[1] It might here be well to consider briefly some of the peripheral meanings of *fortuna* and *virtù*. In the Livian connotation *virtù* is the opposite of barbaric *furor*, the savagery of the semi-civilized which can hardly be called courage or ability but which is rather like animal instinct. Such *virtù* is the possession of peoples as well as individuals, although primarily of the latter. Machiavelli, however, sometimes uses the term *virtù* in quite its conventional ethical sense, meaning a good disposition toward correct ethical behaviour, or a good moral quality in a person. There are also times when we find it with what would seem to be a medical connotation, as a power of performing some action or function, a *potestas quadam efficiendi*. On this, see Felix Gilbert, 'On Machiavelli's Idea of Virtue,' *Renaissance News*, IV (1951), 53–55 who stresses the medical origin of the term and a rejoinder to the above by Loren C. Mackinnon, 'Discussion,' *Renaissance News*, V (1952), 21–23 who claims an essentially non-medical meaning and origin of the word. Leo Olschki points out that Leonardo was apparently the first to use the work *virtù* to mean physical motive power (*Machiavelli the Scientist* (Berkeley, 1945), pp. 39–40). Polybius's concept of *fortuna* or *tyche* of course goes back to Thucydides and on this the reader should consult the penetrating study of J. H. Finley, *Thucydides*, Cambridge, Mass., 1952, esp. 314. On the more pessimistically conceived remedies for fortune before Machiavelli see D. C. Allen, 'Renaissance Remedies for Fortune: Marlowe and the Fortunate,' *Studies in Philology*, XXXVIII (1941), 188–97. Mr. Allen maintains that Machiavelli enlarged the popular Roman stoic hypothesis that fortune aided the brave but suppressed the stoic view that fortune was essentially unreasonable and applied only to externals, the true stoic man of virtue being internally free from the blows of fortune.

In the middle ages and later the term *fortuna* had reference to the agent of action as well as to the external conditions of action, although the orthodox carefully distinguished the good of the body from the good of the soul, only the former being subject to the fatalistic influences of the stars or to the operations of chance. Machiavelli makes no distinction of this kind. Cf. Vincenzo Cioffari, 'The Function of Fortune in Dante, Boccaccio and Machiavelli,' *Italica*, XXIV (1947), 1–13, 35.

of the character of experience, and the gain in consistency would be more than offset by the loss of a genuine grasp of reality. The ambiguities of *fortuna* do not stem from confusion of thought. Rather the term contains within itself the necessary categories for grasping the conditions of action and the nature of events, in spite of the fact that these categories logically exclude one another when we abstract them from their position as nuances of a symbol. In fact, these categories may all be applied at once to the same event, depending on who is viewing it.

To use the term *fortuna* permits us to see that action is always ironic, that it may be fate to a victim, freedom for a victor, chance to a bystander, that a man's ability may be his fortune, that his intentions may be necessitated. Machiavelli's *fortuna* is indeed, the old, powerful pagan goddess come alive again in all her richness and power. We have only to turn to Dante's image of fortune in the seventh canto of the *Inferno* to grasp what a tremendous act of the historical imagination Machiavelli's *fortuna* represents, how she restores to human action in time and space all of the ironies that Dante confines to the dynamic of sin when it ends in eternal damnation.

For Dante, fortune is purely an arm of providence, of divine intentionality, and the poet's possession of a highly specified hierarchical and supernatural order permits him finally to transcend all antinomies and all conflict. His is a world in which chance is merely an appearance, after all, and ability of any kind may finally be merely a charismatic event, generated or negated by grace. It is, I think, irrelevant to talk, as T. S. Eliot[1] has done, of Machiavelli's honest, realistic but 'graceless' view of the world if only because Machiavelli does not define himself in terms of the Christian anthropology of grace whether negatively or positively. Grace after all is a very personal matter and involves a single individual's relation to his God. At least St. Augustine, among Christian thinkers, to whose pessimism Machiavelli would appear to be most nearly related, did not believe that the Holy Spirit was a God of Battles and indeed affirmed that God gave Empire to the good and bad alike. With this judgment Machiavelli would have heartily agreed, and yet St. Augustine thought the same thing

---

[1] T. S. Eliot, 'Niccolò' Machiavelli' in *For Launcelot Andrews* (N.Y., 1929).

in a 'graceful' world that Machiavelli thought in a 'graceless' one. Both in effect agreed that grace is politically irrelevant.[1]

While Machiavelli does not define human nature in terms of sin and grace he does define it in terms of an anthropology of desire which has much in common with both Christian and pre-Christian thought. His great figures—in a different context to be sure— strive after their goals as hard as Plato's wakened lovers, are as infatuated by great hopes and endless desires as the actors in Thucydides' great narrative. They live in a universe in which human desire is infinite but in which all human acts are finite and, since Machiavelli's universe is neither Christian nor Platonic, there exists no act, natural or supernatural, which encompasses an infinite object.

We shall return to this question but first let us turn briefly to Dante's Hell and then proceed to that greater Hell of Machiavelli's, a hell expanded to include all the space which had once been occupied by *Purgatory* and *Paradise*.

Dante's Hell

In Canto XI of the *Inferno* there is a pause in the journey of the pilgrim through the society of the damned while his guide explains the structure of this part of the moral universe. Before we briefly describe that structure let us remind ourselves of what we have already learned of the infernal society. It is a place where men live in desire but without hope, where they have lost the good of the intellect, its infinite goal, without having lost the correspondingly infinite desire for that good. Here the will is incessantly active but never free, for its only freedom is to conform to the will of Him in whose will is our

---

[1] Lauri Huovinen, in his interesting book *Das Bild Vom Menschen im Politischen Denken Niccolo Machiavellis* (Helsinki, 1951), rightly, I think, argues that Machiavelli's thought is not to be defined in terms of Christianity and maintains that Machiavelli's anthropology is based on an original concept of man as the limitlessly ambitious creature rather than a creature suffering from *concupiscentia* as a result of original sin. I agree that these Christian concepts have a different dynamic function in their proper context and that Machiavelli's pessimism is of a more radical and hopeless kind than Christian pessimism, but I do not think that there is, from a psychological point of view, any great difference between a concept like 'ambizione' and one like *concupiscentia*. They both unite in the concept of the limitless will whether that will is held to be corrupted through a fall or defined as naturally and, as it were, properly limitless.

peace. The will in this realm is in bondage to an incessant repetition of its own slavery to finite objectives.

At this point in the narrative we learn that there are three broad divisions of the *Inferno*. The region that Dante has just traversed is the region in which the incontinent, like all the damned, eternalize the sinful state of being which defined them at the moment of their death. In the journey that lies ahead the pilgrim will encounter those whose primary sin has been force or violence, the second great division and, last, those who have been guilty of fraud, whether of the simple or treacherous variety.

The scheme, as we know, is partly Aristotelian and partly Ciceronian, adapted to the needs of contemporary Christian dogma by the provision of Limbo and of a place for heretics. Dante works in a tradition which made Aristotle's 'mad brutishness' the equivalent of Cicero's 'force' or violence and Aristotle's 'malice' the equivalent of Cicero's 'fraud.' Unlike Aristotle, Cicero does not mention incontinence.[1] Fraud is, of course, the worst of three great classes of sin because it is the peculiar sin of a rational animal, and incontinence is the lightest because it involves the misuse of essentially good and purposeful appetites and potentialities. In a broad meaning we might give to incontinence it is, of course, a part of all sin, for sin begins in some kind of corruption of desire, whether in its perversion or its excess or defect. This way of looking at moral evil is, of course, the one that Dante makes his own in the *Purgatorio* where all sin is viewed as a disordering of love. The element of incontinence in any sin is dramatically rendered for us in the *Inferno* by the restlessness of so many of the damned, whether their activity is turbulent or apparently tranquil, by the meaninglessness of whatever activity or state of being has now become their eternal condition. Even the treacherous, entirely embedded in ice, should perhaps be seen as restlessly seeking to escape and simultaneously perpetuating their condition by the very desire to escape it. Everyone in hell is the eternal resident of those limiting states of human experience, like despair, which perpetuate and intensify themselves as the very attempt to escape them.

[1] For an exhaustive analysis of the scheme see W. H. V. Reade, *The Moral System of Dante's Inferno* (Oxford, 1909).

Dante, fortunately, has two other societies, *Purgatory*, where hope is certain of its aim and where desire is being trained to attain that aim, and *Paradise* where hope and desire are subsumed into the category which includes and transcends them, that of ever-increasing bliss. I might point out that none of Dante's three realms corresponds, as such, to life, in which hope is never either certainly gained or lost, where desire is never wholly certain of its fulfillment of its frustration and where bliss is always momentary. The moral distance of each of the three realms from life as we live it is, in this case, also the aesthetic distance which the poem requires to illuminate our own experience. His universe is sufficiently 'other' for us to judge it and sufficiently like our own so that it judges us. Dante's moral systems, his philosophical discourses are in the service of engendering vision and of containing the rich variety of dramatic possibilities which the pilgrim generates on his journey. From this point of view Dante's cosmology serves no lesser and no greater a function than that of Machiavelli. It provides a frame for insight.

Machiavelli's Hell

Let us now turn to Machiavelli and consider a few crucial passages on which he builds the structure of his infernal cosmology.

I wish first to cite a brief passage from the *Discourses* on the nature of man which is the underlying principle of all of Machiavelli's thinking. Early in the *Discourses* (I, 3) he tells us:

All those who have written upon civil institutions demonstrate (and history is full of examples to support them) that whosoever desires to found a state and give it laws must start by assuming that all men are bad and ever ready to display their vicious nature, whenever they may find an occasion for it. If their evil disposition remains concealed for a time, it must be attributed to some unknown reason; and we must assume that it lacked occasion to show itself; but time, which has been said to be the father of all truth, does not fail to bring it to light.[1]

It would seem that Machiavelli's pessimism about human

---

[1] C. E. Detmold's translation is the one cited for all quotations from the *Discourses* (New York, 1940). The most elaborate edition of the *Discourses* in a fresh translation and an indispensable apparatus of notes and tables is that of L. J. Walker, 2 vols., London, 1950.

nature is the flat assertion of an historian who, surveying the wreckage of history, simply points to the abundant evidence which the records of the past provide for this stern conclusion. But Machiavelli also passes from history to psychology and deepens this assertion later on in the *Discourses* (I, 37). There we find the analysis of human nature which our first statement seemed to require.

It was a saying of ancient writers, that men afflict themselves in evil, and become weary of the good, and that both these dispositions produce the same effects. For when men are no longer obliged to fight from necessity, they fight from ambition, which passion is so powerful in the hearts of men that it never leaves them, no matter to what height they may rise. The reason of this is that nature has created men so that they desire everything, but are unable to attain it; desire being thus always greater than the faculty of acquiring, discontent with what they have and dissatisfaction with themselves result from it. This causes the changes in their fortunes; for as some men desire to have more, whilst others fear to lose what they have, enmities and war are the consequences; and this brings about the ruin of one province and the elevation of another.

The central thought of this passage is that human desire is infinite but lacks an infinite object. Man stands in a state of continual striving, continual tension and frustration. Each conquest of desire is accompanied by a dissatisfaction so great that it demands a new and fresh object. This dissatisfaction of fruition is both with the self and with the object which that self has just possessed or enjoyed.

As a starting-point, this view of man can lead in various directions. As in Plato's *Phaedrus* and Dante's *Comedy* it leads along a hierarchy of all value and being to an infinite object placed outside of space and time. In St. Augustine's *City of God* insatiable cupidity explains why states pass from external wars to internal ones and why there can really be no true justice in a temporal condition. Death will release the elect from this bondage and we can perhaps assume that the damned will go on living a kind of intensified earthly life. In Goethe's *Faust* the striving itself of infinite desire seems, to some interpreters at least, to be posited as a form of ultimate value. Machiavelli's view is different from all of these. Desire, for him, is not intrinsically valuable nor does it point to a realm outside of space and time. It is simply and fully there. Life *is* incontinence. Church and State are not pedogogical institutions but restrictive ones, using force or myth which serve to protect men, at best, from the most extreme consequences of their own nature.

Let us now consider what great devices can be used against incontinence. Two passages are most germane to our discussion at this point, one from the *Discourses* and one from the *Prince*. In chapter 13 of the second book of the *Discourses* Machiavelli maintains that cunning and deceit will serve a man better than force to rise from a base condition to great fortune:

I believe it to be most true that it seldom happens that men rise from low condition to high rank without employing either force or fraud, unless that rank should be attained either by gift or by inheritance. Nor do I believe that force alone will ever be found to suffice, whilst it will often be the case that cunning alone serves the purpose; as is clearly seen by whoever reads the life of Philip of Macedon, or that of Agathocles the Sicilian, and many others, who from the lowest or most moderate condition have achieved thrones and great empires. Xenophon shows in his Life of Cyrus the necessity of deception to success: the first expedition of Cyrus against the king of Armenia is replete with fraud, and it was deceit alone, and not force, that enabled him to seize that kingdom. And Xenophon draws no other conclusion from it than that a prince who wishes to achieve great things must learn to deceive. . . . Nor do I believe that there was ever a man who from obscure condition arrived at great power by merely employing open force; but there are many who have succeeded by fraud alone. . . . And that which princes are obliged to do in the beginning of their rise, republics are equally obliged to practise until they have become powerful enough so that force suffices them.

Let us note here that Machiavelli devalues brute force as an instrument for the acquisition of political power or for the aggrandisement of the state. Force is indispensable, of course, and almost every page of Machiavelli calls our attention to that fact. But fraud is often better, and it is the indispensable supplement to force until such an internal equilibrium obtains that force alone will suffice for perpetuating and increasing the power and safety of the state.

The Symbol of the Man-Beast

Machiavelli usually provides us with the best commentaries on his own work and we will now gloss this text with a very famous one from the *Prince*, from the eighteenth chapter on how rulers must keep faith. There he tells us, in virtually the identical words of Cicero, that there are only two methods of fighting, one by means of law and the other by means of force.[1] The first is proper to men, the other to beasts. However, he continues, the method of law is not always effective and then one must have recourse to force. It is therefore necessary that rulers know how to use both the beast and the man. Machiavelli then tells us that this doctrine was the secret meaning of the ancient story of Chiron, the semi-human and semi-animal tutor of princes such as Achilles.[2]

Machiavelli then subdivides the beast element into two separate qualities, symbolized respectively by the lion and the fox, again adapting some remarks of Cicero to his own purpose.[3] The lion cannot protect himself from traps and the fox cannot defend himself from wolves. The ruler therefore has to be a fox in order to recognize traps and a lion to frighten the wolves.

---

[1] Cf. *De officiis*, I, 9, 34.

[2] No one has yet turned up an ancient reference to the figure of Chiron with this allegorical interpretation. It would seem to be original with Machiavelli, and in this he follows the practice of many mythographers of the Renaissance in feeling little constrained by historical considerations in interpreting ancient texts. The English reader might wish to compare the practice of Francis Bacon who, by the way, refers to this passage of Machiavelli saying that his interpretation is ingenious but corrupt (*De Aug. Scient.*, II).

[3] Cf. *De Officiis*, I, 13, 41 and also the seventh chapter of Plutarch's *Lysander*, who quotes him as saying 'For where the lion's skin will not reach you must patch it out with that of the fox.' In Pindar's *Fourth Isthmian Ode* (Loeb Classical Library edition by J. E. Sandys (London, 1915), ll. 45 ff.) Melissus, the wrestler, is praised because he displays the spirit of the loudly roaring lion in his boldness and is like the fox in his craft, who lies on her back when attacked by the eagle. Sandys (*op. cit.*, p. 465) explains the behaviour of the fox in throwing itself on its back when attacked as an attempt to defend itself with its feet and also suggests that the lighter colour of the fur on the belly may confuse the eagle.

Princes who wish to be nothing but lions do not understand the necessity of also being foxes, that is the necessity of breaking faith when it is no longer to their interest.

It is most important to observe here that Machiavelli first described the beast nature of the prince entirely with the category of force but then metaphorically subdivided this category into that of the lion, 'force' in some more restricted sense, and into that of the fox or fraud. As his Ciceronian source tells us, the qualities of the fox are precisely those of fraud (*fraus*) while the qualities of the lion are those of violence (*vis*). Thus Machiavelli first used the word *forza* to mean power in its widest sense and then, implicitly and through symbol, subdivided it into *forza* meaning the exercise of violence or brute force and—that which he usually explicitly calls *frode*—other means of exercising power which involve dissimulation. Let us note that this defence of dissimulation as an art of government is simultaneously an attack on those princes who place all their trust in being lions, in the use of violence. This chapter is therefore also an acute critique of the simple-minded militarist who simplifies the complex structure of power into that of brute force.

Princes are urged to break faith because all men are not good. If all men were good this precept would not be a good one and it is precisely those princes who have behaved most like foxes who have succeeded best. To act like a fox, however, requires great powers of simulation and dissimulation, requires a great capacity to be one thing and to seem another. Machiavelli gives us only one example, a contemporary one, of the ruler as a fox, the example of Pope Alexander the sixth Borgia, and what a perfect example it is! All of his seeming, his appearances, were those of the Vicar of Christ on earth but no man was a greater master of the arts of deception. Machiavelli does not draw the conclusion from this that Alexander was a hypocrite or that traditional moral values are not good. He simply says that the ruler, although he should display all the moral virtues and act on them whenever it is possible, must also be able to do evil if constrained. Indeed, to possess the traditional moral virtues and always act on them is dangerous while to appear to possess them and know when to break them is useful. The tension between appearance and reality, 'ought' and 'must' which, in the private citizen, at peace, is small enough to be ignored is immeasurably intensified in the ruler. Let us not forget also that Machiavelli does not say that the ruler is all beast. The human half of the symbol of Chiron is the law but, as Machiavelli never tires of telling us, the law depends on good custom or the willingness of the ruled to respect it.

It is interesting to compare this symbol of the man-beast with those we find in the *Inferno*. One of them, Minos, stands at the entrance to the circle of the lustful, the first place in Hell in which there is a kind of active punishment. The dignified judge of the Tartarus of Virgil's *Aeneid* has here decayed, if only by possession of a tail which he uses to dispatch the active sinners to their various proper places. He is human in that he judges and judges correctly, but he is bestial in the implacable nature of that judgment. He symbolizes what judgment is to those who are beyond repentence and who are caught in despair. Cerberus who presides over the gluttonous is almost pure beast, a bearded 'great worm' with red eyes and three throats who barks like a dog. Plutus, the enraged god of wealth, stands at the entrance to the circle where both the avaricious and prodigal and the angry are punished. We are not told exactly what he looks like but he talks incoherently and is referred to as having a bloated visage, as an accursed wolf and a cruel beast. I believe that Dante's deliberate obscurity in delineating whatever human features these demonic figures may possess is in the service of the imaginative representation of the sins of incontinence, which proceed from the levels of human nature below the rational one.

Dante is more specific when we encounter the Minotaur, who symbolizes the sins of force or violence for, although he doesn't describe him he tells us of his half-human and half-bestial parentage (*Inf.*, XII, 12 ff.) and in so doing asks us to conceive him in the lineaments he possessed in classical tradition. The 'mad brutishness' he represents is the specific human form in which men exercise violence, whether against others, themselves, nature, art, or God. For Dante, thus, violence is not simply the coercion of others but, so to speak, the coercion of natural law, of the proper nature and use of artifacts and of God himself. From this point of view suicide, blasphemy, sodomy, usury, can all be comprehended as forms of violence.

The last figure, Geryon, the image of fraud, has a real face, indeed the face of a just man, but the body of a serpent, and on his back the poets descend to the realm of fraud, simple and treacherous.

It is important to note that the most sinister of these symbols of evil is the one who has the most explicitly mentioned human features. The imagery of the human in these figures is in the service of deepening the significance of the evil they represent. It stands for nothing positive but for the greater and greater use of the higher powers in the service of the lower ones. The greatest evils are precisely those which engage what is most significantly human in the service of what is most distinctively bestial and thereby greatly multiply the evil of the bestial itself.

In Machiavelli the composite figure stands for two discontinuous but not unrelated moral realms or scenes of action. In an ironic way Sir Thomas Browne's definition of man can be applied to Machiavelli's ruler. He is a great Amphibium who lives in divided and distinguished worlds. But each world relates to the other. The threat of the beast can help preserve the rule of law and the action of the beast may create the condition for its institution if it does not exist. Behind all forms of the legitimation of power lies power itself whether as the naked power of coercion, the ideologically and publicly constituted power of authority or the unscrupulous secret manipulation by rulers of the ruled. It is precisely because new rulers have so little claim to legitimacy that they must be fully aware of their 'chironic' nature.

Machiavelli, in fact, uses the man-beast to symbolize his opposition in political life to an ethic of principles so rigidly held that it would lead to destruction. The statesman who acts unconditionally by moral maxims, who justifies his actions, whatever the consequences, simply by congratulating himself for his good intentions, who, as it were, trusts in God for the outcome of his action, such a man is really immoral. There is no doubt that the ethic of concern for consequences can be so formulated that it is subject to distorted, capricious, and grossly immoral use. Nevertheless with all its risks, this must be the statesman's ethic. His unpardonable sin is to deploy himself so that he is a prey to the wickedness of others, and his fault is even more serious if he does so out of rigid adherence to an ethical maxim no matter how valid that maxim might be in its own sphere of operation. The statesman who does not recognize the existence of a plurality of ethical spheres, of levels of validity for ethical precepts, dooms himself to failure.

It would be instructive here to see what Dante makes of the figure of Chiron—indeed, of a whole group of famous centaurs in the *Inferno*.

In the *Inferno* we encounter Chiron who, Dante reminds us, brought up Achilles, right after the Minotaur, among those centaurs who are the custodians of the souls of the violent against others, and who, with their arrows, keep the damned immersed to the proper degree in the river of boiling blood whenever they try to emerge from it. It has been remarked about this canto that, although the centaurs are both representatives and punishers of violence in its crudest forms, they behave like responsible people and display a high degree of dignity and courtesy. Unlike the demons Dante will meet in the barratry cantos, they prove to be trustworthy.

The tradition of Dante commentary from the earliest period has customarily identified the figures of the centaurs with the *condottieri* of the Italian courts of the fourteenth century. Dante would thus have portrayed the professional hired military leader as a semi-human figure dignified by his qualities of military leadership but as semi-human because unhallowed by the spirit of sacrifice and dedication engendered by commitment to some exalted ideal. We have only to think of the martial saints in the heaven of Mars to understand what a proper military mode of life would be, one whose violence is controlled by and subordinated to the goals of universality. The violence of the *condottieri* is really an end in itself and is all the more crude and blatant because it is for sale to the highest bidder.

Another remarkable feature of the encounter with the centaurs is that we find Dante the pilgrim remarkably detached about both the souls of the violent and those agents of the infernal machinery who guard them. It is the only serene part of the whole of the *Inferno*. J. D. Sinclair suggested that the serenity amid the symbols of bloodshed and the centauric symbols of the *condottieri* constitutes an ironic commentary on the 'ordered anarchy' of the Italian political situation in Dante's time.

Dante, knowing the refinement, in many respects, of many of the petty Italian courts, in some of which he had been a familiar guest, and the personal dignity of many such military employees, makes here, perhaps, his ironical comment on that whole situation of ordered anarchy, in the dignified half-brute forms of the Centaurs. However dignified and friendly and, on occasion, serviceable, they are also, like the rest, representative of the sins they punish, as were the tyrants and their mercenaries . . . (p. 164).[1]

That these centaurs have no fraud in them is further emphasized by the face that one of their number, Cacus, turns up among the thieves in Canto XXV specifically separated from his brothers, Dante tells us, for his fraud. They thus might appear to symbolize the military ethos, its combination of chivalry, honour, and straightforwardness with violence, when that ethos has become, as it does in the mercenary soldier and sometimes even in the professional soldier, an end in itself, a complete mode of life. Then violence is not in the service of true order, of law which by its own nature moves towards universality, but in the service of only as much order as is compatible with their own self-perpetuation. Their human aspect does not stand for law in any true sense of the word, for the freedom and reason that law embodies, simply because they are in the service of those who pay them regardless of who or what they might be.

If this line of interpretation be true then Machiavelli and Dante would have agreed pretty well about what to think of the *condottieri*. But the symbol of Chiron in Machiavelli is much more complex, as we have seen, and is an entirely fresh act of the imagination in the service of a different moral situation.

The Meaning of Fraud

We might at this point ask ourselves what, more exactly, does Machiavelli mean by fraud? Certainly one of the meanings is just plain and simply trickery. Cesare Borgia invites his enemies to a parley and kills them. A ruler promises peace and makes war. And so on *ad nauseam*. All these are certainly instances of fraud. But Machiavelli gives a much wider meaning to fraud, as any careful reader of his work will grasp. I will call in the

---

[1] J. D. Sinclair, *The Divine Comedy of Dante Alighieri*, 3 vols. (London, 1939), vol. I, p. 164.

authority of the most careful reader he ever possessed, Francesco Guicciardini his contemporary, whose comment on the very passage of the *Discourses* I quoted will be illuminating. Guicciardini says that he agrees in general with Machiavelli that pure force seldom raises political figures from low to high estate, although with his customary distrust of too universal a principle Guicciardini will not go as far as to say that pure force never can do so or that pure fraud can. It all depends, he continues, on what Machiavelli means by fraud. Guicciardini is prepared to agree with Machiavelli if the latter means to extend the word fraud to include all kinds of shrewd actions (*ogni astuzia*) or dissimulation. However, if Machiavelli means to confine the meaning of fraud to that which really is fraud, such as breaking faith, then many can be found who achieved great realms without fraud in this narrower and more immoral sense.[1]

When Machiavelli talks of force he means coercion, the explicit and ultimate form of power. When he talks of fraud he is also talking of power but in its covert forms, the forms it takes when it is either insufficient to reveal itself nakedly or when it can afford to dissimulate its appearance because of a voluntary obedience of its subjects. Fraud includes the power and genuine authority Numa gained when he fraudulently founded a religion which the Romans believed in and which justified in their eyes the power he claimed but did not safely possess until he gained it in this fraudulent way. Fraud also includes the secret, gross forms of connivance, deception, treachery, and manipulation in which the people are not even presented with a pious fraud or fiction but where they are the ignorant and unknowing objects of the power operations of the apparatus of state. Power thus can wear many faces and Machiavelli saw them all. This is what some of his students have meant when they refer to his creation of a 'grammar of power,' a 'physics of politics' or to his isolation of politics as an autonomous activity. Machiavelli's important words and concepts have to be studied in terms of what we can grasp as the total intention of his thought if we are not to restrict their meaning or misunderstand what varied meanings they are intended to carry.

[1] Francesco Guicciardini, *Considerazioni sopra i Discorsi del Machiavelli*, Bk. III, ch. 40, in *Scritti politici e Ricordi* ed. R. Palmarocchi, Bari, 1933.

We should also bear in mind one other thing when Machiavelli talks of fraud, that he esteems other values besides success. For example, in chapter 40 of Book III of the *Discourses* he tells us that we must not confuse the employment of deceit and strategems in war with perfidy. The latter is dishonourable and should be avoided. This is only one example of many. Again and again Machiavelli talks of the ideal of liberty under law, praises the value of glory which is, or should be, some sort of limit on the agent of action. Nevertheless, Machiavelli has no sooner condemned perfidy in war than he begins the chapter immediately following that one with the following title: 'One's country must be defended, whether with glory or with shame; it must be defended anyhow.' I cite this not as an example of inconsistency, for it is not. It is rather an example of the way in which Machiavelli refuses all absolutes as guides to action and how his acute awareness of the problematic conditions of action leads him not only to give some words like 'fraud' a wider extension than we would give it but also leads him to restrict the meaning of perfidy to a considerably narrower range than we would give it.

The relative fluidity of the meanings of such key words in his writing reflects the shifting values which stern necessity commands that we adopt in different circumstances. If no one principle of political action is always good then, under some tragic circumstances, we may be forced to acknowledge that no one principle of political action is always necessarily bad.

If we briefly examine some of the central passages in which Machiavelli discusses religion we will grasp that he includes under the term fraud a good deal of what Guicciardini thought he included. Where we today talk about myth, convention, social fictions and the like, Machiavelli used the single term 'fraud.'

Let us now turn to some crucial passages on religion in Machiavelli's works and see what valuable and complex meanings the word 'fraud' can assume.

Machiavelli on Religion

In chapter 11 of Book I of the *Discourses*, Machiavelli discusses the Roman religion. Numa, he tells us, found the Romans a very savage people and wished to reduce them to civil obedience.

This he wished to do, not by the use of naked violence or coercion, but by the arts of peace. He therefore had recourse to religion, for he realized that it was the most necessary and reliable support of a civil society, and the religion he founded was of such a character that it facilitated the great Roman enterprises of conquest. By introducing discipline, religion served to create good armies, something difficult to do where religion does not exist. But Numa had to convince the Roman people of his authority to give them a religion and to assume this authority he had recourse to a fiction, what we would call a pious fraud. He pretended that he received it from a nymph. In this deception he was successful, and Numa was able to employ the new religion not only to create good armies but also to create good laws. This is an even more important achievement for a ruler than governing well in his own lifetime, for good laws perpetuate the safety of the state beyond the lifetime of any single ruler. Such good laws bring good fortune and good fortune results in happy success in all undertakings.

In this last remark we seem to catch Machiavelli in one of his more sanguine moments, for he virtually claims that good laws, a disciplined people, can reduce the element of chance in political action to the vanishing point. Let us remember, however, that the meaning of fortune varies for Machiavelli from context to context and that he is discussing an actual instance of what he considered such a reduction. As we know from other instances of the use of the term fortune, especially in *The Prince*, chance will on the average allow us a fifty-fifty possibility of success.

Machiavelli then turns from Numa to Savonarola and, with a fine irony and some circumspection and indirection, indicates to the reader that his contemporaries have not outgrown this susceptibility to pious frauds.

And although untutored and ignorant men are more easily persuaded to adopt new laws or new opinions, yet that does not make it impossible to persuade civilized men who claim to be enlightened. The people of Florence are far from considering themselves ignorant and benighted, and yet Brother Girolamo Savonarola succeeded in persuading them that he held converse with God. I will not pretend to judge whether it was true or not, for we must speak with all respect of so great a man; but I may well say that an immense number believed it, without having seen any extraordinary manifestations that should have made them believe it; but it was the purity of his life, the doctrines he preached, and the subjects he selected for his discourses, that sufficed to make the people have faith in him. Let no one, then, fear not to be able to accomplish what others have done, for all men (as we have said in our Preface) are born and live and die in the same way, and therefore resemble each other.

We know from *The Prince* that Savonarola is a perfect example of the unarmed prophet who always fails. Whether his claims were fraudulent or not, he did not use the authority derived from supernatural claims to establish stable power through belief, and use that power to create a good army and good laws.

Was Savonarola one of those who, in a sense, was used by his religion through too much conviction instead of being able to use it? Was he one of those who destroyed the political efficacy he tried to exercise through his religion by not realizing the irreducible political claims of force and fraud? This possibility suggests itself when we turn to chapter 14 of the first book of the *Discourses*. There we learn that the Romans knew how to use their religion flexibly. They were able to interpret the auspices they took before any important action 'by necessity,' by the claims of the occasion itself and did not rigidly follow the omens given in whether the sacred fowls ate or not. Nevertheless, they always at least pretended to observe the precepts of their religion even when necessity obliged them to disregard those precepts. Indeed, no careless disparagement of their religion went unpunished.

The Romans thus realized that religion has an important instrumental value as a system of fictions which can create and consolidate power through the belief of the ruled in the fictions offered to them by those who exercise power. While this is true of all religions, different religions vary in the degree of their political utility. In a famous chapter (Bk. II, ch. 12) of the *Discourses* Machiavelli draws a comparison between Christianity and paganism from the point of view of political and civic utility unfavourable to the former. Christianity teaches humility and submission, an other-worldly goal and contempt for worldly ones, whereas paganism taught men to cultivate greatness of soul, the classical *magnanimitas,* and strength of body, values which served to make men formidable. The result of belief in Christianity has been to make men feeble, a prey to evil-minded men who can through its use more easily control the kind of people who believe they gain heaven by enduring injustices.

An interesting gloss on this comparison is provided in chapter 1 of Book III of the *Discourses* where Machiavelli discusses how it is necessary, in order to ensure a long existence to religious sects or republics, to bring them back to their original principles. His example of this return in the case of religion is provided by St. Francis and St. Dominic (Dante's two great *exempla* of reformers, by the way) who by their voluntary poverty and their example of following the life of Christ, revived the sentiment of religion in the hearts of men when it had almost been extinguished. At this point we might expect Machiavelli to conclude that the exalted morality of one or two men can regenerate the moral life of the state and so improve it. His conclusion, however, is quite different. The profound and honest goodness of these men gave them great influence over the people, to be sure. But this influence was used to persuade the people that it was evil even to speak ill of bad rulers, that it was right to render bad rulers obedience, leaving their punishment in the hands of God.

The result, according to Machiavelli, of the moral stature of these two great men is that evil rulers do as much wickedness as they please, especially since, unlike Francis and Dominic, they do not fear a supernatural kind of punishment, the kind which they cannot see and therefore do not believe in. Nevertheless, if the political effects of these two great saints were bad, their incorruptible goodness did in fact preserve the Christian religion into Machiavelli's own time.

With perfect consistency in his estimate of Christianity, Machiavelli shows how the moral goodness of its exemplary figures revived a corrupt religion but he also shows how that same goodness had been in the service of subverting the civic values of magnanimity and strength. The humility of the saints had allowed the wicked to prosper.

Like our own near contemporary, George Santayana, Machiavelli felt that traditional Christianity was a religion of great disillusionments about this world and minute illusions about the other, and he was further aware of just what such a teaching might do to classic political values through the very austerity of its morality, in the form we have just described, when taken seriously. Among the many ironies of history those involved with moral reform are not the least paradoxical.

The general focus for these passing comments on religion and indeed for the whole of Machiavelli's thought can be found in the fifth chapter of Book II of the *Discourses*, close to the centre of the work as it is close to the centre of his thought. There he maintains that changes of religion and language, together with the periodic occurrence of deluges and plagues destroy the record of things. Religions and linguistic changes are the work of men while deluges and pestilences are the work of heaven by which, as we shall see, Machiavelli does not mean Providence but the agencies of cyclical, natural change as manifested in the powers of the celestial bodies. Each new religion that men create attempts to destroy the records and symbols of the preceeding one, just as the Christians tried to destroy every vestige of paganism. Machiavelli does not attribute the Christian failure to destroy entirely 'The glorious deeds of the illustrious men of the ancient creed' to any change of heart on their part or to any kind of genuine respect for pagan achievement. In his eyes it was the unsought result of the fact that they were forced to keep up the Latin language as the instrument for formulating their own new laws. Indeed, he tells us, if we bear in mind their other persecutions, nothing would have been left of antiquity had the Christians been able to employ a different language for the formulation of their new creed.

Whoever reads the proceedings of St. Gregory, and of the other heads of the Christian religion, will see with what obstinacy they persecuted all ancient memorials, burning the works of the historians and poets, destroying the statues and images and despoiling everything else that gave but an indication of antiquity. So that, if they had added a new language to this persecution, everything related to previous events would in a very short time have been sunk in oblivion.

The destruction produced by Heaven, which periodically

reduces the inhabitants in some parts of the world to a very small number, are pestilence, famine and flood. Famine and flood are the most important of the three, partly because they are most generally destructive and also because the few that escape their ravages are chiefly barbarous mountaineers, too ignorant to have knowledge to transmit or who, if they have it, pervert it in the process of transmitting it. This they do because such people can only use knowledge to gain influence and reputation, a use of knowledge characteristic of the semi-civilized who are unable to distinguish truthfulness and self-interest.

Machiavelli conceives of this periodic destruction as a natural process which corresponds in the cosmic or social order to the spontaneous and health-preserving purgation of the individual, or so-called 'simple' body.

And so it is with that compound body, the human race; when countries become over-populated and there is no longer any room for all the inhabitants to live, nor any other places for them to go to, these being likewise all fully occupied,—and when human cunning and wickedness have gone as far as they can go, —then of necessity the world must relieve itself of this excess of population by one of these three causes; so that mankind, having been chastised and reduced in numbers, may become better and live with more convenience.

Language and religion, that is the world of culture, are man-made. They come into being and pass away as men make and unmake them. Dante, we may recall, when he meets Adam in Paradise, learns that language is an everchanging creation. It is one measure of the distance we traverse between the two great Florentines that Machiavelli extends convention to include religion.

For Machiavelli, men act out the process of creating language and religion on the universal stage of nature, a nature which purges—by necessity—overpopulation and, be it noted, excessive cunning and wickedness. This it does through periodic catastrophes in which cycles of cultural change are counter-pointed, so to speak, against cycles of natural change. At times these cycles, as it were, will coincide when the trough of one meets the trough of the other. Some such pattern would seem to account for Machiavelli's claim that overpopulation and corruption of a moral sort are one and the same or, at least, prerequisites of one another. Nature or Heaven—the celestial instruments of the natural process of generation and corruption —brings the human race and its cultural potential back to a new beginning in one and the same process. Nature's destructive processes are periodically the necessary prerequisite of new points of departure for mankind.

It is most important that we recognize the way in which Machiavelli both distinguished the biological from the cultural and related them. The race and its cultural artifacts, like the organism, like nature itself, of which they are all finally parts, all are governed by the eternal cyclical rhythm of destruction-purgation on the one hand, generation-health on the other. That languages and religions are man-made and continually changing or decaying, being reborn and growing, means that there is no utopianism in Machiavelli, if that obvious truth really needs to be mentioned. It is clear that, for Machiavelli, culture is necessary if men are to survive in the world, but it is also clear that culture is inevitably the realm of the operation of force and fraud as well as the realm of freedom, glory and reason. Man is a part of nature, a biological organism, but he is an organism whose health and vitality depend on culture with its illusions and opportunities as the necessary condition for his biological survival. But when men have become too numerous and culture has become so much the arena for cunning and wickedness that life becomes too corrupt and too uncomfortable, then nature itself in its catastrophic and destructive upheavals prepares the conditions simultaneously for a new biological and cultural beginning.

Machiavelli offers no eschatology which would permit us to transcend this eternal situation, nor does he try to celebrate it by elevating it into an exact, comprehensive, rigid system of thought. He rejects both of these tendencies and does so, I believe, because he would have thought them finally dishonest. Life, for him, is neither rational enough nor irrational enough for either possibility. The system of political and social appearances of any society is a form of fraud precisely to the extent that those appearances obscure the true nature of decision and status. The claims of the great human institutions are, in a sense, always partly true and partly false. The cause of freedom and reason is always imbedded, so to speak, in the struggle for power within the state and also between states. Furthermore, power and forceful leadership are the indispensable prerequisites for freedom and the exercise of reason. This truth leads us to the paradox that, although reason and freedom are intrinsically realized by individuals and not by institutions, special collective structures of power are necessary for the exercise of freedom and reason. They therefore exist in a continual dialogue with force and fraud and this is the eternal condition of their existence.

The purpose of historical or philosophical studies for Machiavelli is not that we may learn about objects of facts. Rather such studies should alter consciousness in such a way that we will be better able to cognize situations, should transform our attitude to experience so that we can grasp it as the scene of action. It is clear that effective action or the decision which leads to such action is never derivable from some universally valid abstract principle but by an original act, so to speak, grounded in the history and awareness of the agent of action. Moreover this agent acts in a temporal hell, a community in which none can do without the other and where each cannot really accept the other. It is a world in which men may make their plans but in which half of the time, at least, something emerges which no one willed. It is a world in which new situations demand incessant adjustments of thought and perception and in which the process of interpretation as preparation for action can really reach no end. It is a world unified only partially, and usually by danger, a world in which leaders must be understood but can only be understood by all to the extent that they deal in some form of fraud, benign or not. His intellectual posture is his greatest achievement and a difficult one it is to maintain: incessant flexibility with incessant decisiveness, acute awareness with readiness for action, a cautious attitude with a readiness to take risks. This I think is his legacy as artist and statesman and this is the way in which, I believe, he would want posterity to follow him.

Machiavelli orients thought towards a world which is indefinite, various, a world which cannot be made completely or consistently luminous. There is no transcendence in reality, that is to say, reality is not hierarchical. If Machiavelli has any possibility for transcendence in his universe it is given in the work of reason as it continually penetrates reality and in the act of reason when it recognizes the fact that force and fraud, power and illusion, in one form or another, in one degree or another, will always be there. They are in fact the precondition for existence in the world of culture and they are precisely what calls forth the work of reason. To worship force and fraud is just as simple-minded as to abdicate from them altogether. A naive trust in coercion, ideology or trickery can be just as catastrophic and irresponsible as a naive belief that conflict can be entirely avoided.

Freedom, reason, glory, law, ability are embedded in force, fraud, desire, chance, natural and cultural necessity. While these polarities may at times overcome one another we must also grasp the fact that they create each other. Life presents us with the opportunities for the realization of order and value, what Machiavelli calls 'occasions,' and we must learn to grasp them before they lapse back into the chaos from which they emerged.

CHAPTER VI

Machiavelli: The Effective Reality of Things

Machiavelli's Relevance

NICCOLÒ DI BERNARDO DEI MACHIAVELLI was born in Florence in 1469 and died there in 1527. He held high office during the restored Florentine Republic under Piero Soderini and was sent on important missions not only within Italy but also to France and Germany. The reports which he sent back to his government from these diplomatic journeys are a significant fraction of Machiavelli's literary work and, although he did not then think of them in this light, they became the indispensable preparation for the great works of his later life. The restoration of the Medici terminated his active political career and he was even briefly imprisoned and tortured as a suspected anti-Medicean. He was, however, soon released and exiled to his estate near Florence. During this long period of enforced inactivity he wrote his most important works, *The Prince* in 1513 and the *Discourses on the First Decade of Livy*, probably between 1513 and 1517. He was a prolific writer and late in his life, after he had been restored in some small measure to the good graces of the Medici, he wrote his *Florentine History* at the request of Cosimo. His works include, in addition to diplomatic, historical, and political writings, several literary works, including the brilliant comedy *Mandragola*, perhaps the greatest comedy of the Italian Renaissance.[1]

[1] The dating and order of composition of some of Machiavelli's major works presents some problems. For a review of the question see Federico

Oddly enough, although it was widely read, *The Prince* did not provoke any great cry of moral indignation at first. The Pope authorized its publication on August 23rd, 1531, and the first two editions appeared in 1532. These first editions were followed by another twenty-five in just the next twenty years alone. With its diffusion, however, the revolutionary character of the work was perceived and in 1559 the Inquisition condemned it along with all of Machiavelli's works, a decision which was upheld by the Council of Trent in 1564.

Thus within thirty-three years the black reputation of our author was established, with the help of violent attacks by Cardinal Pole, Ambrogio Caterino, Paulus Jovius, and prominent spokesmen of the Jesuit order among others. In part these men were guilty of misrepresenting Machiavelli's thought but not entirely, for Machiavelli certainly offended orthodox sensibility and those consciences moulded entirely by traditional ethical principles. Very few of his critics were prepared to con-

---

Chabod, *Machiavelli and the Renaissance*, trans. David Moore (London, 1958), 30 ff. This collection of Chabod's most important studies on Machiavelli exists only in the English translation. The book contains a very useful bibliography.

It is probable that *The Prince* was composed in instalments as Friedrich Meinecke thought. See the section on Machiavelli in his *Die Idee der Staatsrason in der neuren Geschichte*, 3rd ed. (Munchen, 1929), and the introduction to his edition of *The Prince*, *Der Fuerst*, in *Klassiker der Politik*, VIII (Berlin, 1923). I might mention in passing that Meinecke distorts a valid point when he takes the view that Machiavelli's thought is situated entirely outside of the universe of ethics. Machiavelli has his normative side.

Felix Gilbert's reconstruction of the composition of *The Prince* suggests the following formal organization:

The first eleven chapters are the original draft and the work would thus have begun as a brief essay on the problems of the new ruler. To this original draft Machiavelli added an 'art of war' and a polemical reply to the traditional catalogue of princely virtues of the 'Handbook of Princes' literature. The additions are loosely composed and the final chapter exhorting the expulsion of the invaders from Italian soil is really a rhetorical flourish with little organic relation to the rest of the work. The nationalism of this closing chapter has no real place in Machiavelli's thinking, for his political realism and acute analyses of statecraft were never formulated and elaborated in terms of nationalistic interest (see Gilbert, 'The Humanist Concept of the Prince and *The Prince* of Machiavelli,' *Journal of Modern History*, XI (1939), 449–83, 481 ff.).

sider Moses simply as a secular figure or accept the unflattering comparison in the *Discorsi* (II, 2) between Christianity and paganism.

However, the most extreme and truly gross misrepresentation of Machiavelli's thought came from the pen of a French Huguenot, Innocent Gentillet, who in 1576 wrote his *Discours sur les Moyens de bien gouverner et maintenir en bonne paix un Royaume . . . contre Nicolas Machivel, Florentin* in which, among other things, Machiavelli was accused of atheism and of being responsible for the St. Bartholomew's day massacre. An English version of this work was published in 1602 by Simon Patericke, and it has generally been assumed, probably correctly, that the numerous explicit defamatory references to Machiavelli in Elizabethan drama must have been derived from Gentillet in the original or in translation.

Nevertheless, a more authentic Machiavelli seems to have had a serious influence on men of affairs such as William Thomas, author of the *Historie of Italie* and *Disquisition On Affairs of State*, and on statesmen like Thomas Cromwell, Leicester, and Cecil. Although *The Prince* was not printed in English until 1640, it was available in printed form for the serious reader in, of course, Italian, but also in Latin and three French translations by 1571.[1] Perhaps our awareness of a more authentic, implicit, subtle use of Machiavellian doctrines and perspectives by the great Elizabethan dramatists has been overshadowed by the blatant stage Machiavel or obscured by the quest for crudely direct and explicit influences.

In any case it is clear from this English example that in informed circles, at least, a more accurate knowledge of Machiavelli was available, whatever his popular reputation may have been and that active statesmen found his art of politics useful. In fact he was the first modern author to think of statecraft as an art, not in the sense in which Plato might have used that term,

---

[1] Three different Elizabethan translations in manuscript have come to light, one of which has been published in our time by Hardin Craig, ed. *Machiavelli's The Prince: An Elizabethan Translation* (Chapel Hill, N.C., 1944). For a delightful survey of English interest in the history and art of Renaissance Italy with numerous indications of the influence of 'politick authors' such as Machiavelli and Guicciardini see J. R. Hale, *England and the Italian Renaissance: The Growth of Interest in its History and Art* (London, 1954), esp. chs. 1 and 2.

as knowledge of universal theoretical principles of politics, or as a theory of the legal and ethical state, but statecraft as a body of general principles and maxims concerning particular courses of action in characteristic political situations. His vision of the state also was attractive, whatever its limitations, in an age of growing centralized monarchies in which the main political problems involved the consolidation of power. If Machiavelli saw the state as a dynamic unit with no particular internal goal, a quantity of power awaiting a ruler to achieve direction, so did the great statesmen of the rising sixteenth-century national states. Aristotle's injunction to educate the citizenry because that is the best preservative of the state seemed far less important than subduing the Irish or weakening the Spaniards.

Machiavelli's political examples are types of experience and models of behaviour and, if his theoretical temper made him attribute too great a share in controlling political events to political astuteness, diplomacy or military strength, still he was useful where others were not. In addition, he offered a theory of the rights of nations as such without reference to the various notions of legitimacy tied up with hereditary monarchy, an attractive conception in a Europe in which many revolutionary movements began by raising the question of the legitimacy of the ruler to rule.

Machiavelli on the Origin of the State

Machiavelli's realism and utility rested on a naturalistic conception of the state. In his view, the state began when primitive population increased and men came together to form larger communities. In order to stabilize these new communities they agreed in their own interest to be ruled by the most powerful and courageous men among them. There was thus a surrender and transfer of power at the beginning of political society and this original 'contract' marks the first step in the growth of man's awareness of good and evil. Universal convictions concerning right and wrong grew out of the system of rewards and punishments the newly constituted rulers instituted to govern and organize society. The fact that our ideas of good and evil have such an origin means that right and wrong are not absolute but must be judged in reference to man's original and continuing effort to control forms of activity which he recognizes as inimical to his own well-being.

Machiavelli, in effect, denies the validity of any *lex aeterna* and therefore of natural law itself. Men's intuitions of goodness are not glimpses into a divinely constituted order even though they have come to think so. What is good is that which protects the life, property, and honour of the majority of individuals over the longest period of time. In this denial of natural law Machiavelli is simply following a long Italian tradition of political realism which goes back at least as far as the *Defensor Pacis* and whose roots lie, politically, in the conflict between Empire and Papacy and, intellectually, in the nominalism of the late Middle Ages.[1]

Machiavelli's conception of good as self-interest points to a characteristic tension between the one and the many which we shall find repeated in his conception of the will, and which is formally echoed in those polarities, such as virtue and fortune, in terms of which he organizes his thought. The member of a state, in his own self-interest, wishes his fellow citizens to behave in a way that he will call good. But he and his fellows will in their own individual self-interest be all too ready to behave in ways which contradict their standard of goodness for others. Self-interest, however, is not only society's disease but also its remedy. It certainly marks man as being in some permanent aspect of his nature anarchic or, at least, unsocial. However, as we recall from Machiavelli's myth of the origin of the state, we would not be here at all if man did not have the capacity to be ruled and accept limitations, at least when he becomes aware of the lethal dangers ensuing from rapacious and unlimited pursuit of self-interest. Machiavelli places his conception of self-interest at the very heart of all his political thinking and of his analysis of the main problems of governing and being governed. It accounts for the abiding elements of divisiveness in any society and also explains the conditions necessary for social cohesion.

Machiavelli would have agreed with Hobbes that man is bad

---

[1] J. W. Allen, *A History of Political Thought in the Sixteenth Century*, ed. with revised bibliography (London, 1957), p. 452. 'Machiavelli's realistic mode of thought was only an extreme illustration of a tendency visible in Italian thought since the days of the last Hohenstaufen Emperor.'

and society restrains him, but he is far more dialectical than Hobbes, whose theory of man's radical selfishness leads him to a defence of absolutism simply because he could find little possibility of self-limitation in the very dialectic of self-interest itself. Machiavelli's admiration for the mixed constitution is based on the conviction that areas of freedom and reason can be preserved in a society and interstices created between the one and the many if all conflicting wills in the society are allowed to limit one another through the partial indulgence of each. Men will limit their essentially limitless rapacity if they are allowed to enjoy the fruits of a partially indulged cupidity. Any democratic theory of government which also rests on a pessimistic view of human nature must accept this possibility.[1] In addition, Machiavelli never uses either his theory of the origin of the state or of the nature of man to legitimate society or any particular form of government. Some kinds of order are preferable to others but more than one kind is possible and workable. His myth of a primitive 'contract' is simply in the service of finding an origin for society and for explaining the sources of social order and of morality.

Laws, justice, good customs, institutions, all evolve from the system of rewards and punishments which the strong instituted after the weak agreed to be governed by them. This evolution rests on the fact that the wills of the governed learn to conform to the will of the governors at least to the degree that obedience becomes habitual. It is the growth of habitual obedience that curbs original corruption and lawlessness, lessens the need for the ruler's exercise of incessant coercion, and thereby permits a genuine civil society to exist. While morality may ultimately be derived from fear of force, a state cannot function or endure long by coercion alone. Law and good customs must obtain if a genuine civil society is to exist. Right is the true interest of the majority but they must will and recognize that right.[2]

[1] Cf. the illuminating remarks on psychology and politics, with special reference to Freud, in Philip Rieff, *Freud: The Mind of the Moralist* (New York, 1959), ch. 7, pp. 220 ff.

[2] *Discorsi sopra la prima deca di Livio*, II, 2. All references to the works of Machiavelli are to the edition of Mario Casella and Guido Mazzoni, *Tutte le opere storiche e letterarie di Niccolò Machiavelli* (Florence, 1929). Machiavelli subsumes religion entirely into the category of good customs for the value of any religion resides in the authoritative morality it carries

In the last analysis, Machiavelli's myth of the origin of the state is the presupposition for an analysis of the concept of the state into two categories of coercion: forceful, external coercion, and that form of self-coercion which leads to obedience. The one element grows as the other diminishes, and that society is truly civil in which coercion is reduced to its minimum. As we shall see, myth, convention, religion, pious or even impious frauds, may all be instrumental in reducing the rôle of force.

The Character of Machiavelli's Thought

The first observation we should make of Machiavelli's discussion of the origin of the state is that it shows that he is not a political scientist in the sense that he possesses a system of politics. His political preferences do not follow ineluctably from his assumptions, which could lead in various directions and justify various kinds of political order, as indeed the history of his influence shows they have.

This absence of systematic rigour is a characteristic of all of his thought and it must be understood as deliberate and not as a failure. Machiavelli concerned himself with the effective reality of things, with things as they are. While the phrase may be ambiguous the locus of knowledge concerning the effective reality of things was not. It lay in the history of actual states, judged in the light of his own political experience. That history taught Machiavelli many particular lessons and one big one: the ruler's employment of too rigid or theoretical a system of politics as a guide to action would have disastrous practical consequences. The ambiguity of Machiavelli's thought is deliberate, and his universe of discourse precludes theoretical consistency simply because the prime requisite of effective political action is flexibility.

It is Machiavelli's sense of the prime necessity for flexibility in statecraft, his conviction that no single principle is always under all circumstances good, that leads him to interpret his many specific historical references by means of mythic, poetic,

---

with it. But those religions are best which, like paganism, inculcate martial and civic virtues rather than Christian ones like humility.

and indefinite concepts like *fortuna* and *virtù*. Thus he sometimes reads like a collector of maxims and examples, some of which recur frequently in his writings. Both examples and maxims are generally concrete and vivid, drawn from specific situations and applicable to equally specific ones which recur frequently enough in the course of history to allow for the general utility of what Machiavelli learned from the past.

To the extent that Machiavelli is interested in generalizing from the political records of the past he demonstrates, of course, a theoretical side. He did attempt to introduce some theory and some degree of systematic organization into the art of state-craft and even, on occasion, was rigid in trying to formulate general principles of action on a rather slender basis. He certainly does not confine himself to describing the practices of statesmen but tries to set forth principles of action for his own contemporaries. Nevertheless, we must firmly grasp that his passion for historical analysis was not of an abstract or truly theoretical character. Machiavelli was not interested in under-standing the growth and structure of various kinds of states or, despite his preferences, in classifying them. His great effort and achievement is focussed on the clarification of the manner in which historical conditions may affect political action.[1]

Machiavelli's Relation to his Predecessors

We can perhaps best deepen our understanding of the nature of Machiavelli's thought if we compare him to his predecessors, medieval and humanistic.

The prevailing medieval concept of the ruler was based on the Pauline analogy between the state and the human organism, a convincing image for the feudal ideal of organization. In this view, the ruler's relation to his subjects was understood by analogy with the governing organ of a living body. With the recovery of the Aristotelian corpus, writers of the medieval literature on princes extended their range from more or less exclusive concern with the relationship between ruler and ruled to include the whole field of political institutions, especially military and judicial ones. On the whole, however, this new and rich material was incorporated in the old framework and its

[1] Herbert Butterfield, *The Statecraft of Machiavelli* (London, 1940), pp. 17–25, 80.

interpretation was still governed by the conception of the ruler as the head of a bodily organism.[1]

This conservative tendency in medieval political theory accounts for the fact that the first secular state since antiquity, Frederick II's realm in thirteenth-century Sicily, remained outside the consideration of political theorists. Even those who recognized his greatness, like Dante, had to condemn him on moral grounds, and they did not recognize the originality of his political achievement. Even less would the general run of medieval theorists have attempted to justify it as an attempt to create a truly secular state.[2]

Machiavelli, of course, owed some things to both the medieval and humanistic writers on the art of ruling. However, as we shall see, even where Machiavelli resembles his predecessors the resemblance is frequently formal or verbal. Thus, in the framework of the natural-rights theory of the state, both state and sovereign had been described as 'free from laws' (*legibus solutis*). This might, at first glance, seem to imply some sort of doctrine of reason of state. However, all that the phrase meant was that the state and sovereign could not be legally coerced, not that they were free from accepting moral responsibility for their actions in the sense in which an ordinary citizen holding traditional ethical values might have understood the word 'moral.'

In regard to his humanist predecessors Machiavelli adopted or developed some of their innovations, such as a more secular orientation, the use of historical example, and the positing of worldly fame rather than eternal salvation as the reward for a good ruler. Nevertheless even a superficial examination of his predecessors will demonstrate how much more abstract they were and how strong was their tendency merely to reproduce classical ideas and modes of thought.[3]

---

[1] Felix Gilbert, 'The Humanist Concept of the Prince and *The Prince* of Machiavelli,' *Journal of Modern History*, XI (1939), 449–83, 459. Gilbert points out that the growth of medieval and Renaissance literature on the figure of the ruler has, as one of its causes, the fact that classical antiquity had not left behind an authoritative model for such a figure as it had done for the good citizen or the good state (460).

[2] Ernst Cassirer, *The Myth of the State* (New York, 1955), p. 171.

[3] Gilbert, 'The Humanist Concept of the Prince,' 462–64.

Far more important than Machiavelli's indebtedness to his predecessors was the fact that he was the aware observer of new political phenomena. The contemporary states of Italy were really new, revealed new elements previously unrecognized and old ones in a new light. The new secular states, founded and maintained by the virtually naked use of force, could not be satisfactorily described in terms of classical, medieval, or humanistic theories. Their rulers were frequently 'new men,' men of power who could claim no divine authority and whose rule was unhallowed by tradition, genealogy or, indeed, any of the traditional mythological or ideological apparatus of government. It might seem paradoxical to claim that Machiavelli was the witness of new events when all he claimed was to have rediscovered the timeless effective reality of things, the way things have always been done. Nevertheless, we can claim that never before in history had the mechanics of political power been so starkly disclosed as in Renaissance Italy. There, the difference between civil and external wars had been virtually annihilated, there, he saw the simultaneous successful existence of a number of theoretically incompatible systems and modes of governing, there, new men with no sanction but their own power carved out their realms.

Italy was thus a laboratory of political life. When religious and political mythologies began to lose the important rôle they once had in shaping political life, even if only temporarily and in some places, new ground had to be found for political thought. Machiavelli attempted to meet that need. Traditional political theory also was so tied to the concept of a single natural, theologically or philosophically sanctioned, political order that it could not account for the diversity of viable order that Machiavelli saw before his eyes. Hence his analysis of political life was forced to go below the level of its formal organization or ideological validation, below to the effective reality of things.

Machiavelli's predecessors, for example, tried to express the norm for the perfect ruler in what was at best a very unrealistic way, one especially so in the sixteenth century. For them, the ruler administered justice, preserved the peace and, if he was a good man, would be quite successful in accomplishing these two tasks. They assumed his legitimacy, acceptance of the authority of his person and office and, above all, they assumed that the ideal man, ethically speaking, and the ideal ruler were one.[1]

Machiavelli agreed with the great tradition of political thought that a state governed by evil means or evil men is rarely well governed (*Discorsi*, I, 18). Like his humanistic predecessors he too raised the question concerning what catalogue of virtues applied to the ruler, and whether they were the same as those which applied to the ideal ethical agent. Unlike them, however, he grasped the full significance of the problems this question raised and shattered the identity which had been assumed to exist between the ideal ruler and the ideal human being. In his thinking on the rôle of the prince, Machiavelli conserved the emphasis which his predecessors had laid on the personality and character of the ruler, on his power to manipulate events, but he saw that power as exercised in a completely realistic political universe.[2]

Having seen new and varied political phenomena and having raised new questions, Machiavelli had to find new ground for his inquiry, and he found it in the study of historical examples. For him the great majority of such examples have virtually universal applicability. In this he is perhaps more rigid and

---

[1] Gilbert, 'Humanist Concept of the Prince,' 462–64. Gilbert points out that the humanists introduced a catalogue of princely virtues to the literature on rulers. They included religious ones, so important during the middle ages, but also worldly ones. Their detailed discussion of the virtues was a new interest, and this is what led to the formulation of a new question concerning whether the ordinary ethical norms applied to the prince. They were not aware, however, of the crucial importance of this problem nor of what its implications were. Perhaps this curious lack of realism should not be too surprising. Their models, such as Cicero, recognized the difficulty of distinguishing good from evil in the sphere of political action (*De Officiis*, IV, 3) but did not make this perception the focal point for any protracted discussion of politics. The same is true of other works of ancient political literature in which we find realistic touches but not the realistic perspective.

[2] Gilbert, *Ibid.*, 464–71. Other points of contact between Machiavelli and his humanistic predecessors were: a similar conception of the ruler as a creative force, a discussion of the catalogue of virtues of the ruler in which Machiavelli deliberately refutes his predecessors, and a few formal but not substantive characteristics such as Latin titles to the chapters and the imitation of Isocrates in the dedication (cf. *Ibid.*, 477).

abstract than his great contemporary Francesco Guicciardini. The latter emphasized rational reflection on personal experience rather than imitation of the past—although he also accepted the doctrine of historical recurrence—and was more inclined to note the difference rather than the similarity between past and present, the unique element in every historical event. Guicciardini was convinced that although general principles of statecraft could be derived from the study of history, such principles always had to be applied with full awareness of the differences, sometimes minute but crucial, between events of the past and the present. While I do not wish to suggest that Machiavelli was generally hasty about drawing general principles of action from past events, he certainly was more sanguine than Guicciardini about doing so.[1]

In the last analysis Machiavelli's use of history is a moral and psychological one. He is interested in the conditions under which men have acted politically in success and failure, the motives that have moved them, their awareness of the conditions of action. His history is not, like Dante's or Hegel's, the story of the emergence of great public, universal values and institutions but a collection of finite *exempla* of human action determined by a constant psychological human nature. History is not the process in which the intentions and irrationalities of men are subsumed by grace or a world spirit into great rational structures somehow drawn from that chaos of individual conflicting wills. Machiavelli offers none of the specious consolations of historicism or providentialism, only insight into the nature of human action and the chance of using that insight constructively in the advancement of liberty.

This approach to history was related to a characteristic development in humanist historiography. If the medieval historian wrote universal history, the Renaissance historian wrote civic history. The one was convinced that history was moving toward the creation of a universal community, toward the fulfillment of an eschatology. The other, truly aware of the existence of the new polities which had emerged from the fall of the Empire, classical and medieval, wrote the story of civic

---

[1] *Discorsi*, I, 39 and III, 43; Butterfield, *op. cit.*, p. 39; Cassirer, *op. cit.*, pp. 155–57; Felix Gilbert, 'Machiavelli and Guicciardini,' *Journal of the Warburg Institute*, II (1938), 263–66.

liberty, of its gain and its loss, of the conditions under which it might be reachieved.[1]

Machiavelli's emphasis on the history rather than on the theoretical political treatises of antiquity marks him as a humanist. Just as the artists, lawyers, physicians had all turned to the great achievements of the classical world for guidance so, Machiavelli tells us, the time had come for the statesmen to do the same. Indeed, Machiavelli felt that his great contribution to his time lay in calling the attention of his contemporaries to the political lessons to be imitated and learned from antiquity.[2]

His intense classicism, however, made him sneer at the use of firearms, an error for which the more flexible Guicciardini criticized him. As we shall see, a certain rigidity born of his intense admiration of Rome, occasionally led him into other errors of judgment, in spite of his firm conviction that there are cases for which it is impossible to formulate general rules from historical precedent.[3]

Machiavelli's humanism was in one way or another a constant in his thought. His belief that he was discovering the laws of political behaviour, which the Romans know and which had been forgotten, was a characteristic humanistic approach to the past and is especially conspicuous in the *Discorsi*. Indeed, *The Prince* is the only one of his great works which draws heavily on modern examples and precedent.[4]

In some respects, Machiavelli becomes even more humanistic

---

[1] On this question of humanist historiography see B. L. Ullman, 'Leonardo Bruni and Humanistic Historiography,' 321–44 in *Studies in the Italian Renaissance* (Rome, 1955); T. E. Mommsen, 'Petrarch's Conception of the "Dark Ages",' *Speculum*, XVII (1942), 226–42; Claudio Varese, 'Aspetti e limiti quattrocenteschi della "fiorentina libertas",' *La rassegna della letteratura italiana*, Anno 64-Serie VII (1960), 196–206; Hans Baron, 'Secularization of Wisdom and Political Humanism in the Renaissance,' *JHI*, XXI (1960), 131–50; Hans Baron, 'The *Querelle* of the Ancients and Moderns as a Problem for Renaissance Scholarship,' *JHI*, XX (1959), 3–22; Hans Baron, *The Crisis of the Early Italian Renaissance* (Princeton, 1955), esp. 300–12, 422–29.

[2] *Discorsi*, Introduction, and III, 5; *Il Principe*, ch. 6.

[3] *Il Principe*, chs. 9 and 20; *Discorsi*, I, 18; Butterfield, *op. cit.* 39.

[4] Although the formal structure of *The Prince* is not at first immediately apparent, it is an organized work. Its chapters can be classified into three groups, a first on the form of the state and the acquisition and maintenance of power, a second on military problems and foreign affairs, a third on the

in the later works. From the *Discourses*, he latinizes his style, is more 'idealistic,' and his last major work, the *Florentine History*, is written in the characteristic humanistic mode, using selected historical events and persons as types or *exempla*.[1] Yet he never gets so 'humanistic' as to make historical writing simply the writing of an eloquent narrative. His humanism always remained of the general type of the vernacular humanists, that of an active man who was not a scholar purely for the sake of scholarship.

In the matter of a revival of Roman greatness, an almost obsessive theme among the humanists, Machiavelli was never optimistic. In a letter to his friend Vettori of August 26th, 1513, written while he was at work on *The Prince*, he felt that a little of the old *virtù* of the Romans might still be dormant in the Italian people. Somewhat later, in the *Discourses*, he has completely given up hope in the Italians and other 'Latins,' maintaining that only the northern races have any *virtù* in his world.[2]

[1] Cf. Felix Gilbert, 'Review-Discussion: The Composition and Structure of Machiavelli's *Discorsi*,' *JHI*, XIV (1953), 136–56, esp. 148, 155–56.

[2] *Discorsi*, I, 55.

problems of relations within the state such as the relations of rulers and ruled, rulers and their advisors (Butterfield, *op. cit.*, p. 149).

A more detailed structural analysis could be made as follows: Chapters one to four are concerned with the problems facing new princely governments in the territories they have just acquired; Chapters five to nine deal with the necessary variations in the methods of administering such territories according to whether they were gained by force, favourable circumstances, tricks, or the favour of the citizens; Chapters ten to fourteen deal with the ruler's problem of possessing sufficient power to defend himself whether with his own or foreign forces, or by 'divine protection.' This problem leads to a consideration of different types of armies, mercenary, national and auxiliary: Chapters fifteen to eighteen deal with the ruler's relations with subjects and friends, and further methods of keeping and increasing power, in particular the covert or 'fraudulent' ones such as clever liberality, wise parsimony, cruelty, dissimulation, bad faith as may be required by circumstances or a 'higher' political objective: Chapters nineteen to twenty-three are concerned with how the ruler can save his reputation by avoiding contempt and hatred, how he may maintain his reputation by recourse to armament, resoluteness, prudence in alliances, generous support of artists and men of talent and ability, and by exercising caution in choosing his ministers and in relating himself to his courtiers. The final chapter is an exhortation to free Italy from the barbarians (Leonardo Olschki, *Machiavelli the Scientist* (Berkeley, 1945), ch. 1).

130

In respect to the revival of Roman glory, at least, Machiavelli became less of a humanist as he grew older.

It is probable that Machiavelli's growing concern with antiquity, his adoption of a Latinizing style and the forms of humanistic historiography, were in part the result of his prolonged association with a remarkable group of scholarly men of affairs who met in the famous *Orti Oricellari*, or Rucellai Gardens. Under the sponsorship of Bernardo Rucellai, early in the sixteenth century, the gardens became a place for the discussion of political and humanistic problems. These discussions were continued under Cosimo Rucellai to whom, among others, Machiavelli expounded the *Discourses*.[1]

The particular kind of scholar-statesman or politician-humanist that frequented these meetings undoubtedly influenced Machiavelli in the development of the method we have come to see was his, the emphasis on experience as a guide to the solution of political problems and the study of Roman history in particular as the most extensive and useful record of past political experience.[2]

The flexibility—perhaps inconclusiveness—of this new political 'history' developed in the garden meetings is demonstrated by the fact that, using the same methodology, Bernardo Rucellai came to favour an aristocratic government with an exclusive base of power while Machiavelli came to favour a democratic regime with an inclusive one. Each felt that his choice was best suited to solve the problem of stability and to help man control the inherent tendency of all things to decay. Lest we absorb Machiavelli too much into the traditional connotations of humanism it is necessary to make the observation that Machiavelli also belongs to what has been called the 'Counter-Renaissance,' the pessimistic current of Renaissance thought. Categories such as 'Humanism' or 'Counter-Renaissance' are pretty slippery intellectual coin, but they will serve if

---

[1] Felix Gilbert, 'Bernardo Rucellai and the Orti Oricellari: A Study on the Origin of Modern Political Thought,' *Journal of the Warburg and Courtauld Institutes*, XII (1949), 101–31. Bernardo Rucellai introduced the term 'balance of power' to the political vocabulary in his history of the French invasion of Italy led by Charles VIII, *De bello Italico*. See E. W. Nelson, 'The Origins of Modern Balance-of-Power Politics,' *Medievalia et Humanistica*, I (1943), 129.

[2] Gilbert, 'Bernardo Rucellai, etc.', 123–24.

we apply them to Machiavelli to mean that he shared an enthusiasm for antiquity and a belief in its contemporary utility with
the humanists but tempered his enthusiasm with a pessimistic
view of human nature.

Machiavelli on the Will

The darker, more profound, and perhaps more characteristic
aspect of Machiavelli's thought grows out of his consideration
of the nature of the human will. First and foremost, Machiavelli insists, that will is selfish and limitless and man is, above
all possible definitions, the creature that cares only for himself.
A man will reconcile himself sooner to the murderer of his own
father than to the thief of his property, and gratitude is but the
mask a man wears when he is still in hope of benefits to come.
Men will break the bond of love, of obligation, at the first
opportunity if it comes into conflict with their own self-interest.[1]

This black view of human nature, however, need not lead us
to despair, for the selfishness and greed of men demands at least
sufficient order and security so that they may enjoy the demands
of their own selfishness. To the extent that he must have order
a man must also demand it for others and, therefore, recognize
some degree of coincidence between the general interest and his
own. Nor does man's selfishness generally conduce to rebellion.
On the contrary, as we know from the myth of the origin of the
state, man finds it much more safe and comfortable to conform
to the will of authority than to expose himself to the savage
hardships of anarchic rebellion. Man is, in fact, not eager for
change and, granted a sufficient indulgence of his selfishness,
generally finds it easier and less dangerous to support the
status quo than to change it very radically.[2]

On the other hand few men can learn to disregard their
personal interest and truly labour for the common good. As he
tells us in the preface to the *Discorsi* he is one of the few that can.
What Machiavelli is in effect telling us is that because the
infinite will of man is a selfish one it is therefore in contradiction
with itself. This contradiction acts as a self-limiting element in

[1] *Il Principe*, ch. 17.
[2] Cf. the remarks in Allen, *op. cit.*, pp. 454 ff. The best of Allen's
remarks in an otherwise uneven essay on Machiavelli are those concerning
his concept of the will.

the dynamics of the will. Because the infinite will is a selfish one it must curb its own infinite drive in order to gratify its own cupidity. Men can forgo their unlimited greedy aspirations in order to enjoy limited but actual gratifications. Machiavelli's belief in the genuine possibility of developing public spirit rests on this characteristic of the will.

The nature of man's will never changes. It is the constant which underlies all historical and political events, such as the cyclic changes of the forms of the state from monarchy to tyranny through transitional good and bad forms, aristocracy or oligarchy, 'republicanism' or 'democracy.' All the large public monuments of history and politics may be seen as resulting from the achievement or disturbance of the uneasy equilibrium between infinite desire and actual gratification. The will is constantly the same, but conditions change and the nature of events is given by the interaction of the fixed nature of the will with changing circumstances. The contradictory nature of the will provides the possibility of political order but it also points to that quality in men and their institutions—the instruments of collective acts of self-interested will—which will destroy them. The universe after all offers only partial gratifications, finite goals, and therefore men are always unsatisfied. A society may be satisfied enough not to destroy itself for a time, but no society is ever completely satisfied with its equilibrium. Sooner or later, it seems, men will tire of their current indulgences and demand greater ones, they will forget the terrible conditions which led them to form the state, they will grow soft and 'corrupt,' they will indulge their selfishness too far and become decadent. In their decadence they become too pleasure-loving to meet the stern demands of war and the austerity which changing conditions may demand, or they become too rigid, too inflexible in meeting the demands of chance or fortune. Man's fundamentally changeless will must adapt itself to the continually altering circumstances of life but, all too often, it fails to do this. As Machiavelli in effect tells us in the famous chapter on fortune in *The Prince*, men can meet the caprices of fortune about half the time if they are flexible, but half the time they are not flexible enough. The central tragic contradiction of mankind is the possession of a more or less unalterable volitional nature in a world which demands constant flexibility.

Machiavelli's conception of the will thus accounts for the possibility of political stability and limits its duration, it accounts for the existence of the eternal political problem and points to a more or less temporary solution. The frequent complaints that Machiavelli has no theory of the state are all beside the point. He is serving notice to mankind that all political arrangements are provisional. Some are better than others, no doubt, but all are more or less inadequate. All are equally adequate to the extent that they secure life, property, honour, and rule by law. Political life is *essentially* conflict. A utopia is not only not possible, it would not even contain life at all, because life itself is contradiction and conflict.

Machiavelli thus defines man as the desiring animal, the special quality of whose will leads to a fundamentally self-contradictory mode of existence, and his self-contradictory mode of being manifests itself in the dialectical character of the relation between the infinity of his selfishness and its need for gratification, a relation which both creates and destroys political equilibrium. It further manifests itself in the irony that human desire may be so rapacious in its quest for gratification and security that it loses the very flexibility needed to manipulate reality. A final manifestation of this self-contradictory mode of being reveals itself in the fact that man simultaneously wills obedience and anarchy. Prompted by selfishness and actual gratification, he wills to obey; prompted by the infinity of his selfishness and blind greed for more possessions, he wills anarchy. As we shall see, a ruler exploits fraud, pious or impious, to capture obedience and force to curb anarchy.

This psychology of Machiavelli's is in the service of the clarification of the central problem of politics, that of the stability of the state. Throughout the *Discourses*, he refers again and again to the dependence of political stability on the creation of what we would call 'public spirit.' By this, Machiavelli means nothing more than the recognition on the part of a citizenry that the common welfare and their own selfish interests do in fact overlap sufficiently to justify the restraint and co-operation that society demands. Its growth, of course, depends on the existence of a government which secures life, honour, and property, and which administers the law impartially. This is what Machiavelli means by liberty, not a form of government, and its opposite is the arbitrary action of tyranny and that fearful egocentric state of society which he calls 'corruption.' Religion, especially a good civic religion like that of ancient Rome, fosters public spirit as does strong military force based on the service of the citizenry itself.[1]

The highest form of public spirit, which includes patriotic sentiments such as those which carried Rome on its great career of conquest and glory depends, from the rational point of view, on 'liberty' and the willing, grateful acceptance of restraint. Since relatively few men are as self-disciplined and rational as this, religion performs a great rôle in capturing willing obedience, thereby providing a ground for patriotic love of authority and a consequent readiness for self-sacrifice in the larger number of mankind. Religion helps the believer to reconcile himself to authority, to love what he would normally be tempted to rebel against, to accept present palpable restraints for intangible but psychologically significant rewards. Machiavelli's thought is often misrepresented as a simple analysis of force and fraud, but it is clear that his conception of the will introduces into his political cosmos all the perplexing problems of obedience and rebellion, and the complex interrelations between love, hate, and authority, even though he did not systematically treat these problems.[2]

[1] Cf. Allen, op. cit., pp. 457 ff. Allen remarks that Machiavelli distinguishes liberty quite clearly from patriotism and associates the latter with republican liberty, that is with some share, however small or inconsequential, in governing. He also says that Machiavelli is not clear on this point. But it is surely the case that Machiavelli felt that patriotism grows out of republican liberty when the people, through participating in good government, come to love the symbols of authority because they have identified those symbols with themselves.

[2] Cf. Machiavelli's conception of the will with the perceptive remarks of Rieff on the rôle of aggression in Freud's political thought and its formal resemblance to the rôle of free will in Christian psychology, in op. cit., p. 274:

For Freud, however, freedom of conscience is a contradiction in terms; there are only alternative submissions. In place of such freedom there is the empirical capacity for aggression—a capacity without which Freud cannot explain the moral order and the individual's need for religion. For him the instinct of aggression plays the same rôle, formally, that Christian psychology assigns to free will. Thus aggression is the psychological potency that enables a man to rebel against authority, in the person

It is perhaps time to point out that Machiavelli's brilliant inquiries into history and political action, the profundity of his basic perspectives, the great courage and realism of his conclusions, are not unmixed with some remarkable errors.

First of all the method of historical analogy itself is risky. For example, Rome, which Machiavelli frequently compares with his time, was in many respects a misleading analogy for him to use. The peculiar combination of agrarian and military greatness in ancient Rome was hardly comparable to the commercially based power of the states of Renaissance Europe.

Also, his disparagement of Italian mercenary armies and his attribution of the disasters of Italy primarily to them is by no means correct and derives from his tendency to over-generalize and, sometimes, to over-simplify. There is no doubt that the economic growth of Florence had greatly separated civil and military life. Machiavelli mourned the loss of the old citizen soldiery. They had been the mainstay of Roman power during its most creative period, the republic, and the same institution, he thought, would have served Florence equally well. He did not grasp that the art of warfare had changed so much that no state of his time could have dispensed with mercenary soldiers. All needed to hire outside professionals if they were to have a balanced army and get the proper combination of the various arms, infantry, cavalry, and artillery needed to fight contem-

---

of the primal father (as, in the religious account, free will allows us to rebel against God), and at the same time it supplies the means by which men can end that rebellion. Freud's idea of 'introjection' of aggression formally resembles the religious idea of the free act of faith; it reconciles the subject to authority.

As in Freud's thought aggression is both the cause and cure of the political problem so in Machiavelli's thought selfishness is both the cause and cure of the political problem. Only selfishness enables man to accept as well as reject the restriction of freedom that life in any society or group demands. The selfish will is also, frequently enough, a prudential one which acknowledges the necessity of restraining universal selfishness and self-centredness. On the other hand, men are selfish and irrational enough to destroy any political equilibrium under the right circumstances. Unlike Freud, Machiavelli's psychology does not see political society as basically the manifestation of man's irrational nostalgia for authority, although no earlier political thinker was more aware of the rôle of the irrational and of authority in the phenomena of political life.

porary wars. Thus England hired its cavalry in Burgundy while the Germans and Swiss provided Europe with infantry.

Certainly, the Italian wars were not as bloodless as Machiavelli implied, nor were the *condottieri*, the paid captains of hired troops, necessarily over-cautious or treacherous. The *condottieri* bands frequently settled on their conquests and thus fought for more than a stipend, indeed for new homes. Their commanders were not always adventurers but were often related to the princely families which they served and whose dynastic interests were thus of intimate concern to them. Italian military difficulties came not from such causes but from divided commands, national disunity, and from too much reliance on political action.[1]

The Character of Machiavelli's Nationalism

Nevertheless, although some of Machiavelli's methods and attitudes resulted in certain weaknesses of judgment, others permit us to understand political action with greater clarity. He is, for example, free of the confusions which romantic nationalism introduced into political thinking. He worked and thought before the nation state had come into being and before wars had become mass conflicts fought in the name of the symbols and ideologies of romantic nationalism. His analysis, based on a situation when the old city-state was giving way to the modern nation state, has recovered a great deal of its original relevance in a time in which the traditional classic nation state is no longer a viable unit of political power.

We must not forget in regard to Machiavelli's freedom from nationalistic bias that his great exhortation to free Italy from the barbarian has nothing to do with a nationalistic mystique but is simply the recognition on the part of a passionate Florentine of the need for a large unit of power on the Italian peninsula in order to preserve the freedom of its peoples. These Italian peoples indeed share a common cultural tradition in their Roman past which the course of history has turned into an

---

[1] *The New Cambridge Modern History*, vol. I, *The Renaissance*, pp. 273, 277–80, 285. Machiavelli had also over-estimated the invulnerability of the Swiss when he claimed that they could not be defeated by the French. The battle of Marignano proved him wrong. (*Ibid.*, p. 364) Cf. Chabod, *op. cit.*, pp. 85 ff.

Italian present. They are not, however, in any sense a 'folk' and Machiavelli is never very precise about just how many of the various peoples of the peninsula or adjacent islands would constitute this larger unit of power.[1]

For Machiavelli the nation is not the instrument of progress, much less a divine instrument, for he didn't believe in progress at all. It is a mechanism for achieving security, a quantity of power which unified, or reunified, a group of people who ought to be one. The Italians were simply the descendants of the Romans, whether or not the ancient *virtù* was latent in them, and they ought for their own well being be together. Indeed, whenever Machiavelli wants to express something close to what we might mean by 'nation' he uses the word *provincia*.[2]

The true *patria*, 'fatherland,' or *nazione*, 'place of birth,' is the city-state such as Florence, and most of the deepest patriotic sentiment of the time was directed to this political unit, a phenomenon still persistent in modern Italy with its strong regional loyalties. Yet Machiavelli grasped that the city-state was doomed to instability in his changing world and that the strong regional loyalties were as destructive to peace and order as the ultranationalism of the modern nation state has been.

Yet Machiavelli had no illusions concerning the then emerging nation state, for the state, large or small, is by nature an expansive, aggressive, and energetically active organization. He never lost sight of the fact that Rome itself had grown by absorbing smaller nation states as well as city-states. Whatever the state may be for him, it is certainly not necessarily benevolent or a custodian of popular rights. The same rules of power apply, in his view, to its external as well as internal operations so that he never conceived of an internally ethical state which operates by an entirely different and amoral set of rules externally. The inner logic of power politics—and it is in essence

[1] Felix Gilbert, 'The Concept of Nationalism in Machiavelli's *Prince*,' *Studies in the Renaissance*, I (1954), 38–48.

[2] Machiavelli, *The Prince*, trans. by Luigi Ricci, rev. E. R. P. Vincent with an introduction by Christian Gauss (New York, 1952, Mentor Books), pp. 19, 25. Whitfield, *op. cit.*, p. 65. On these terms see especially Vincent Ilardi, ' "Italianità" Among Some Italian Intellectuals in the Early Sixteenth Century,' *Traditio* XII (1956), 339–67, esp. 343 and 357–69.

a logic of unlimited power—operates in all the activities of the ruler.[1]

Part of the difficulty in assessing the exact nature of Machiavelli's nationalism lies in the fact that he frequently uses the same word to express different ideas, or expresses the same idea with different words. In addition, changes were taking place in the very meanings of the words he used. This is particularly true of the word *stato* or state. *Status, lo stato, l' état*—all of these words did not mean the modern state prior to the seventeenth century. Nor does Machiavelli generally use *stato* to mean the fundamental condition of the realm, the rights and duties of the ruler or his prerogative, both legitimate medieval uses of the term. Rather, he uses it in a restricted political sense to refer to that which the ruler acquires, holds, maintains, loses, or has taken from him, and the term is frequently used with these verbs (i.e. *acquistare, tenere, mantenere, togliere, perdere*). He is no more consistent with this term in its denotations than he is with *fortuna* or *virtù*, but its fundamental connotation is that of *imperium*, command over men. That is why there can be degrees of it, and one can have too little or enough.

Stato is thus not the *patria* or *nazione* or *città*, not the fatherland or the body politic. For the body politic Machiavelli uses terms such as *il vivere libero, il vivere civile* or *il vivere politico*. Thus his statecraft does not involve a theory of right such as 'reason of state,' for there is, as we have seen, no mystique of the state which rationalizes placing it beyond ethical judgments, no sense of an over-riding obligation to the future which positively enjoins on the ruler repugnant actions, no sense of the body politic as transcending its constituent members, and no well-developed theory of the common good.[2]

Power and Legitimacy: Ethics and Politics

For Machiavelli, the state is essentially effective control over men and thereby the instrument of acts of power. These may be ordering or exploitative, politically creative or destructive, but their existence testifies to the existence of the state itself. The

---

[1] Gauss, *op. cit.*, pp. 27–28.

[2] For Machiavelli on the state see the acute analysis by J. H. Hexter, '*Il Principe* and *lo stato*,' *Studies in the Renaissance*, IV (1957), 113–38.

charges of immorality levelled against *The Prince* finally derive from the fact that there Machiavelli's focus is on the substratum of power any state needs in order to exist. He thus largely prescinds from questions concerning the common welfare and even where he refers to such values he does not justify the behaviour of a ruler on that ground but on the ground of pure self-interest.

He does not identify the nation as a group of people autonomously organized in a specified territory with the state as the authoritative structure over them which monopolizes the legitimate use of force. He is free of the confusions concerning the legitimate use of force because he does not identify the state with a particular government or with the bearers of a particular cultural tradition. He faces the problem of the legitimation of power in its starkest terms. Force is legitimate when the people consent to the state's monopoly of it for reasons which to them seem good ones, whether out of religious piety, respect for law, reverence for tradition or some combination of these. But force may also be legitimate when the alternative is wholesale slavery, destruction or chaos, any one or combination of these.

Such claims concerning force must be taken seriously not because they may justify ruthlessly effective ways of guiding political conduct but because it is precisely the state that claims a monopoly of the legitimate use of force over the community and territory which comprises it.[1] Whatever right men may assume they have to use violence either on their co-nationals or on foreign countries in war, they derive from the state, and even internal politics is concerned with the sharing or distribution of the legitimate right to use force. The very skeleton of the state is force and Machiavelli is perhaps inordinately aware of it for very good reasons. Most important perhaps is that almost none of the major Italian states of his time—with the possible exception of the Papacy—possessed any of the usual means through which the rulers could legitimate their rule. They were new men, like the Medici or the Sforzas, without long tradition, who ruled populaces which did not have the habit of conforming. No ruler in Italy had the kind of charismatic domination exer-

[1] See Max Weber's classic essay, 'Politics as a Vocation,' 77–128, in *From Max Weber: Essays in Sociology*, ed. with an introduction by H. H. Gerth and C. Wright Mills (New York, 1946), p. 78.

cised by prophets and demagogues, nor could anyone claim the kind of absolute devotion derived from personal confidence in the leader's ability, his possession of a revelation or his heroism. Nor, finally, was the principle of legality always operative, since the new rulers were often dictators who had usurped the old democratic communes or traditional monarchies after the latter had torn themselves apart through class warfare.

As we have seen, Italy furnished examples of states which lacked all of the customary modes of the legitimation of power. The enormous building programmes of Renaissance despots and their handsome subsidies to artists and scholars can be seen as an attempt to achieve the external appurtenances of grandeur which history had not bequeathed them, and to create new symbols for the old ones, no longer operative but which had served in the past to legitimate enforced obedience.[1]

Like artists, the new princes were often men of talent, not of birth, and they strongly identified themselves with men of artistic ability, so much so that Burckhardt was virtually forced by the evidence to evolve his brilliant concept of the Renaissance artist-prince who considers the state as a work of art, moulding and shaping the inchoate mass of people under his rule into citizens.

Machiavelli was thus able to observe states in, so to speak, their elementary conditions, those conditions in which all the elements which entered political action were simplified and reduced to the absolute essentials—power and the dynamics of power. He simply could not avoid the question as to whether the traditional ethic—or indeed, any ethic—could establish principles of similar content for erotic, familial, commercial, military, and political relations.[2]

He was compelled to recognize that the absolute ethic could be disastrous in politics. The statesman must know how to resist evil by force, must operate in terms of an ethic of responsibility for the actual consequences of his actions. I don't think,

---

[1] The division of legitimation into three types, traditional, charismatic and legal, is from Weber, *op. cit.*, pp. 78–80.

[2] *The Renaissance in Italy* (London, 1944), ch. 1. Cf. Eric Hoffer, *The True Believer* (New York, 1958), p. 132, for some acute comments on the political fanatic as the frustrated artist.

in spite of Machiavelli's bitter irony, that he ever advocated raw opportunism and he certainly did not maintain that an ethic of ultimate ends is *identical* with complete irresponsibility. In his own life and aspirations the two supplement each other, for he sought peace and order for Italy, the ultimate end of all his effort. He simply felt that the statesman is responsible for the disasters that befall his country and its allies no matter how pure his intentions may have been. He must take account of the average morality of the people whom he governs and with whom he deals, and must never presuppose any too sanguine idea of their goodness.[1] He must not dodge the fact that he may be compelled, as ruler, to commit acts which would be culpable in a private person. He must operate in terms of the principle that good may come from evil or evil may come from good.

It would probably be an error to refer to Machiavelli's answer to this whole question of the relation between politics and ethics as an absolute separation of the two. Even where Machiavelli appears to advocate the most unethical courses of action he is guided, implicitly or explicitly, by the welfare or the interest of the individuals in the political community. What is good is what promotes that welfare and what is bad is what destroys the welfare of the whole. Those general principles of conduct which govern the relations between the individuals in a community cannot be applied without residue to politics, simply because the ruler must act for all while the individual is more or less free to pursue his own self-interest. If homicide or deception on the part of a ruler can promote the welfare of the collective then it can be called good even though they are injurious of the common good when practised by private individuals. The important point to grasp here is that the same criterion of good or evil will lead to a different judgment of the same act depending on whether it is in the private or the political sphere. It is not the intention which validates an act but its result. Sentiments, intuitions concerning right and wrong, appeals to an objective absolute moral order—all these are irrelevant.[2]

Machiavelli's view of war must be taken with reference to his thinking on the question of political ethics. Certainly, he was

[1] Cf. Weber, *op. cit.*, p. 119.
[2] Cf. Weber, *op. cit.*, pp. 120–21.

convinced that wars may act as regenerators of the state in so far as they unify it and dispose the people to obedience to the ruler, the fundamental precondition for political order. If war is necessary to make the state cohere then like all measures which contribute to the common welfare, war is good. This is certainly the case when the alternative to order—any viable order —would be chaos. There is, however, no trace in Machiavelli's thought of the romantic glorification of war. It has a strictly political function and even when Machiavelli thought of war as the health of the state and condemned the Latin races for being overcivilized he simply means that any nation must be ready to wage war to protect its own liberty.[1] Both militarism and pacifism would be pathological extremes, both would be unrealistic alternatives and negate the prudential considerations indispensable to successful political action. In a sense, neither the conscience-burdened or the conscienceless belong in politics. Political authority reaches its greatest crisis at the point where it may fail to create, or maintain, the individual's necessity for order, and it may fail in this essential task precisely on the grounds of the exercise of too little or too much conscience. There is a moral pathology of goodness as well as evil, and one can be as perilous as the other.[2]

It is perhaps the greatest strength of Machiavelli that, while he is acutely aware of the limitations of an ethic of good intention or of absolute ends, he is also aware of the limitations of an ethic of results or responsibility. The ethic of result has its own dilemma in that it introduces the dimension of time into the act of ethical judgment so that judgment becomes ambiguous simply because we cannot always determine the farther consequences of any particular result. Which of the many results, predictable or unforeseen of any action, of Alexander Borgia, for example, should be the criterion for judging it? Machiavelli symbolizes this whole area of ambiguity concerning the results of action in that aspect of *fortuna* which defeats or ironically alters the desired results of action. In effect he tells us that we must have

[1] Cf. Allen, *op. cit.*, pp. 471–72.
[2] On war in the Renaissance, with particular reference to Machiavelli's view of it, see the excellent remarks of J. R. Hale 'War and Public Opinion in Renaissance Italy,' 94–122, esp. 116 ff., in *Italian Renaissance Studies*, ed. E. F. Jacob (London, 1960).

our good intentions but that we must understand that they cannot be always agreeably or painlessly implemented and that, even if we appear to have succeeded, the further consequences of apparent success may be failure.

CHAPTER VII

Machiavelli: The Artist as Statesman

I T is as the author of *The Prince* that Machiavelli has received his greatest fame and, to some extent, this is unfortunate, for that brilliant and revolutionary book gives us too limited an impression of the variety of his thought. Nevertheless, any study of Machiavelli must certainly begin with this work and, I think, perhaps even end with it. For *The Prince* was a truly revolutionary book.

It was the first and still is the most imaginative and compelling statement of what we have since come to call the dynamics of power politics, the first in a long line of speculative inquiries into the nature and uses of political power.[1]

Classical and medieval political theory had been subordinated to traditional ethics, and I wish here to stress the word 'theory,' for power politics obviously existed before Machiavelli and continues after him. Although the amoral character of at least some necessary political action did not escape the attention of political theorists before him, they could not help analysing such behaviour and judging it from the traditional ethical point of view. This ambivalence was even stronger in men of affairs, who frequently offered and may even still offer dubious ethical generalizations for their own behaviour. While traditional legal theory before Machiavelli had recognized instances where the force of facts dictated courses of action not entirely justifiable

---

[1] See Friedrich Meinecke, *Die Idee der Staatrason in der neueren Geschichte*, 3rd ed. (Munich, 1929), and the introduction to his edition of *The Prince*, *Der Fuerst* in *Klassiker der Politik* VIII (Berlin, 1923).

from the ethical perspective, political theory continued to keep itself subordinated to ethics in the hierarchy of knowledge.

This cultural situation changed with the writing of *The Prince*. In that book Machiavelli studied politics as an activity with an autonomous aspect and attempted to arrive at the principles of statecraft by inference from actual instances of political success drawn from contemporary and ancient history. Not that *The Prince* is entirely a technical and descriptive work. It is certainly true that Machiavelli sometimes could not help making covert ethical judgments and that he had ideals and goals which he wished realized. Nevertheless, it is certainly the first great work in which divine moral injunctions and traditional ethical authority are in irreconcilable collision with secular human concerns, and this is true precisely to the extent that *The Prince* is in great part a technical treatise. In it the state appears in its simplest and most basic form, essentially although not entirely isolated from all the conditions which Machiavelli considered extraneous, including religious, social, and cultural ones.[1]

A revolutionary departure in thought and feeling is generally associated with profound historical and cultural changes, and *The Prince* is no exception. By 1513, the date of the writing of *The Prince*, political affairs in Italy had reached a point where moral persuasion and ideological abstractions were no longer effective in maintaining order. The French invasion had destroyed the balance of power so carefully maintained by Lorenzo the Magnificent up to his death in 1492, and had turned Italy into a European battleground, for French success had encouraged the Spaniards and the Empire. This situation had been preceded by internal troubles in the major city-states of Italy which, by Machiavelli's time, had led to the surrender of all power to despots, the only authorities, it would seem, able to curb class war and political factionalism. Government had become not only despotic but personal, and affairs were more and more subject to the whims and judgment of single individuals.

Italy had come to such a pass that, to Machiavelli, men seemed even more what they had always seemed—essentially evil, and

[1] L. A. Burd, 'Florence (II): Machiavelli,' *The Cambridge Modern History*, I, *The Renaissance* (Cambridge, 1902), pp. 190–218, 213–14.

history looked more and more like the work of a largely incomprehensible and uncontrollable power, a power which, nevertheless, Machiavelli attempted to understand by trying to learn how much human foresight and prudence could do to mitigate the operations of chance or fortune.

Thus Machiavelli boldly rejected all providential and theological interpretations of the course of history, but his pessimistic view of human nature is traditional and allies him with the Augustinian tradition within Christianity. Both St. Augustine and Machiavelli would have agreed that men are born bad and generally do not do good unless they are forced to do so. Machiavelli was convinced that few men had mastered the art of self-restraint and that coercion and forceful repression were the only means through which the destructive impulses in man could be kept in check and civilization endure. We emphatically should not conclude from this that Machiavelli was a proponent of dictatorship or tyranny. The rule of law and good custom is the best government, but where the political will is corrupt force must be brought into play. It is precisely because men are inordinately self-seeking and rapacious that Machiavelli advocates the mixed constitution of the *Discourses*. In that work he tells us that by distributing power and authority, and giving to each group in the commonwealth something of what it wants, people will check their desires if only to enjoy the fruits of their own cupidity.[1]

Machiavelli and St. Augustine would also have agreed that power seeks more power, that the nature of the state is essentially expansive, and that from its origin to its apogee, the story of the state is the quest for power, first over internal enemies and next over neighbouring states.

While this point of view concerning the nature of man and the state underlies all of Machiavelli's work, it is most dramatically expressed in *The Prince*. Unlike the *Discourses*, in which Machiavelli also studied the state as a going concern, one in

[1] *Il Principe*, Ch. 18: *Discorsi sopra la prima deca di Livio I*, 3. All references to the works of Machiavelli are to the edition of Mario Casella and Guido Mazzoni, *Tutte le opere storiche e letterarie di Niccolò Machiavelli* (Florence, 1929). Cf. also Burd, pp. 202–03, and Federico Chabod, *Machiavelli and the Renaissance*, trans. David Moore (London, 1958), pp. 42–51.

which laws and good customs are at least operative to some degree,[1] *The Prince* is written with one special kind of situation in view, a situation of 'necessity' (*necessità*) in which the general corruption has become so great that laws and custom cannot halt the dissolution of the political structure, a situation in which only a forceful monarch (*mano regia*) can reverse the trend to anarchy or establish a new state out of chaos.[2]

We might add that by 'monarch,' Machiavelli does not mean 'tyrant,' nor does he claim that a true civil society is less stable than absolute rule. Quite the contrary: tyranny and other degenerate forms of true civil governments are the least stable forms.[3] Machiavelli, in fact, is almost obsessed by the problem of political stability. *The Prince* is finally concerned with the problem of how to free Italy from internal anarchy severely aggravated by external interference, but Machiavelli spends the major part of the treatise discussing how states can be formed and made to endure. The verbs 'to maintain' (*mantenere*), 'to endure' (*durare*), appear insistently in his political writing in connection with the state,[4] and he everywhere attempts to offer advice on how men, through the exercise of prudence, can achieve the maximum stability in the political order. If no state is eternal, it can at least last as long as Sparta or Rome, the two longest-lived states Machiavelli knew about.[5]

Stability, longevity, are, in fact, the primary task of each and every state, and survival is something that ethically good or bad governments can achieve. If over the long term a strong civil society of some form has an advantage over degenerate forms such as tyranny or oligarchy, the latter, if they are strong, may have the advantage over divided, vacillating, inconsistent states of any kind.[6]

[1] Burd, *op. cit.*, pp. 206–09; *Discorsi*, II, 2.

[2] *Discorsi*, I, 45, for *mano regia*. The word *necessità* occurs 76 times in *The Prince* and its derivatives would increase the number substantially. See J. H. Whitfield, *Machiavelli* (Oxford, 1947), pp. 67–68. Whitfield also traces (142) the term *mano regia* to Petrarch's *regia manus*.

[3] Cf. *Il Principe*, ch. 9 and the famous chap. 10, Book I of the *Discorsi*, against tyranny, abundant evidence of his dislike of absolutism, although he equally disliked chaos.

[4] Whitfield, p. 76, and F. Colotti, *Machiavelli-Lo Stato* (Messina, 1939), p. 25.

[5] Cf. *Discorsi*, I, 48; Whitfield, pp. 144, 157.

[6] Cf. Whitfield, pp. 104–05.

As we have seen, Italy's political stability had formerly relied on a delicate balance of power, but the French invasion in 1494 had rapidly diminished constructive diplomatic alternatives within the peninsula. New quantities and variables had entered the Italian political equation, and the only possibility for Italian stability and freedom lay in the creation of larger units of power. The inability or unwillingness of the Italian states to achieve greater strength through a permanent coalition left only one alternative, a unification by force. External weakness was matched in many cases by internal instability, so that everywhere he looked Machiavelli found little comfort. The situation in every respect had become one of *necessità* and the only recourse was 'strong medicine.' The patient was in a desperate condition, and the cure, if any, had to be a nasty one.

In addition to this pessimistic view of human nature and of the life-cycle of the state, we find two other broad principles which govern Machiavelli's thought, and they are so closely interrelated in his mind that they are best discussed together: the doctrine of imitation, so important to the whole of Renaissance culture, and the view of history as a perpetual repetition of a finite number of virtually interconvertible events. In Machiavelli's view, the past afforded models of political behaviour which could be imitated in the closest detail, and the finest repository of such models was to be found in the history of Rome. In this respect Machiavelli works in a humanistic version of the medieval literary tradition of *exempla*, of types of virtuous behaviour to be imitated. But his *exempla* are not examples of static virtues, nor of conquering vices, but specimen instances of men coping with typical political situations in circumstances which are particular and, because they will repeat themselves, also general and useful to know about.[1]

Rome was the great state with the longest history and had therefore traversed more of the historical possibilities than any other. Since those possibilities are finite and the essential character of history is to repeat the same events and situations, it is possible to deduce general principles of political behaviour

---

[1] See *Il Principe*, ch. 6 and *Discorsi*, III, 5, on imitation. Cf. also Herbert Butterfield, *The Statecraft of Machiavelli* (London, 1940), 28 ff. and Leonardo Olschki, *Machiavelli the Scientist* (Berkeley, Calif., 1945), pp. 43–44.

from historical evidence, especially Roman evidence. It was because history was potentially so useful that Machiavelli applied to the interpretation of history the same outlook and techniques that he applied to contemporary events, in many of which he had been involved during his active career as a diplomat.

In spite of this contemporary and utilitarian outlook on the past, Machiavelli nevertheless felt that the experience of the more remote ancient world was superior as a guide for action to the experience of the recent past. For this I think we can find two reasons. History, in Machiavelli's view, tends to repeat itself in progressively degenerate form so that Roman experience was better simply by virtue of being ancient. On the other hand, human passions remain the same, causing in every age the same actions, and the Romans, in their long, full political cycle, could be assumed to have very nearly exhausted the possibilities of human behaviour. The men of Machiavelli's own time were in another cycle, which had not yet gone far enough to run through the gamut of types of action.

In a somewhat obscure manner Machiavelli thus blends two views of history, the cyclical and the degenerative. The image for this view of history would therefore be a descending cyclical series. The constancy of human nature and the natural tendency of men to imitate ensure that the same limited number of constant factors will repeat themselves and that there can be no historical evolution. However, the repetition of history will always be retrograde, for all things are equally subject to the law of decay. Any hope of reform lies, analogically, in a retrograde movement to the more vigorous starting-point. For example, any state that wishes to renew itself must return to its old ethos, a return which, Machiavelli says, can only be the work of one powerful man. To an even greater degree must the creation of a new state or institution be the work of a single individual, for it is only a single unusual person who can arrest the natural processes of decay. Machiavelli thus pins all his hopes on one man even though, inconsistently enough, he also believes that *vox populi vox Dei*.[1]

Nevertheless, the possibility of reform is distinctly limited,

[1] *Discorsi*, I, 58 and 44; Burd, 203–05; Ernst Cassirer, *The Myth of the State* (New York, 1955), p. 183.

and even the most remarkable leadership cannot overcome the fact that everything human, men and their institutions, contains the seeds of its own destruction. The life of states or institutions, like human life, can be prolonged or even renewed, but only for a time. When the acme has been reached, the descent inevitably begins. We can recognize in this doctrine an interesting adaptation of Aristotle's theory of generation and corruption applied to historical phenomena. Both Machiavelli and Aristotle hold that decay is indispensable to further growth and all growth feeds on decay. Applied to the moral and political sphere, this physical and biological doctrine means that evil can give rise to good and good to evil, a bold conclusion which Machiavelli does not fail to draw. For him good and evil not only succeed each other but create each other. The relative proportions of growth or decay, good or evil, are constant and only their relations change. While one society is decaying another is coming to birth. Thus political vigour and ability originally belonged to the Assyrians, from whom it passed to the Medes, and finally to the Romans, the quantity of it remaining constant.[1]

While Machiavelli's mixture of a theory of historical decay with one of cyclical returns has little theoretical vigour, its intent is clearly to indicate the limits of human mastery of historical events while at the same time allowing to human prudence, knowledge, and foresight some measure of control over the longevity and vitality of the state. It is true that the destructive and anarchic side of human nature makes it inevitable that a state shall go from political virtue and peace to idleness, disorder, and finally ruin. Yet even if no state is eternal, strong laws and good customs can help to modify and control the process.[2]

It is clear that Machiavelli reserves areas of freedom, of the possibility for successful action, within a total framework which anticipates a far more pessimistic eventual outcome to political efforts. Yet had the great founders and perpetuators of Rome and Sparta been obsessed with the inevitability of the dissolution of all their achievements, their states would either have not come into existence or would soon have perished. Human

[1] *Discorsi*, II, introduction; cf. Burd, p. 204.
[2] Cf. Burd, pp. 205–06.

freedom and creativity operate precisely within limits set by the span of the longest- and shortest-lived states. The knowledge of men is limited and the unknown is immense, but ability counts and may be in your favour as well as against you. You must not try to plot your exact point on the curve of the life of the state.

Machiavelli views political and social events from this complex perspective, in which the fundamental human passions remain the only constants while all action and thought have become problematic and discontinuous. The heroes of many of the dramas which unfold themselves in his universe are endowed with great courage and agitated, restless wills. Although they have, like all men, finite intellects and limited powers of foresight, they are nevertheless driven by boundless desires, desires which outstrip whatever goals and checks their thought can posit. Superficially, this looks like the beginning of certain ruin, of nemesis, and Machiavelli's moral cosmology might, up to this point, suggest the kind of pattern we are familiar with in Boccaccio's *De casibus* or Lydgate's *Fall of Princes*. However, the last acts of Machiavelli's little dramas are seldom so edifying. The good and bad succeed and fail alike; the bad in their success may bring about good consequences, the good may succeed only in bringing about disasters. Like any great artist Machiavelli does not simplify our moral judgments while he helps us to clarify them. On the contrary he complicates our moral vision, making it almost impossible for us to use the various simple categories we often keep ready to receive even some of the more complex characters we come to know.

Machiavelli's hopes for creative political action rested on the course and ability of the single individual. Hence, again and again in his works, historical as well as political and diplomatic, we encounter powerful and fascinating personalities, rapidly drawn and highly individuated through some characteristic act or bold decision which reveals their temper. Although they are presented to us as historical figures, they really belong as much or more to literature than to history. If, for example, the historian were to try to reconstruct the actual life of Castruccio Castracane of Lucca, of whom Machiavelli wrote a short biography, he would discover that Machiavelli chose and suppressed details with the freedom of a novelist. The same would be true, although in lesser degree, of his version of the

characters of some of his own contemporaries such as Julius II
and Cesare Borgia. Rather than actual portraits, such figures
are really types of men whose advent Machiavelli desired,
creations of the wishes of an unarmed prophet disposed to
attribute to his heroes even more of the same abilities that he
detected in them.

The extent to which man can control the inherent tendency
to decay in all things human was, as we have seen, the central
concern of Machiavelli, and it was a problem with which he
struggled all of his life. His favourite way of stating it was
through the use of two polar concepts, or rather symbols, that
of the goddess *fortuna* and that of *virtù*, also an ancient goddess.
Judging from St. Augustine's attack on these two deities in the
City of God, they must have still retained a strong hold on the
imagination of his contemporaries. And we can well understand this, for, in a poetic way, they stood for two compli-
mentary and polar aspects of human experience. The human
power to effect change and control events was subsumed in the
image of *virtù*, not the plural *virtutes* of Christian tradition but
a single quality, which, to the pagan mind, manifested itself as
civic and martial ability. Around the image of *fortuna* there
clustered a host of related concepts—all the impersonal agencies
active in the lives, collective or individual, of men, the force or
logic of history, the frequently mysterious concatenation of
events which can neither be predicted nor understood after
they have come to pass, blind chance, or, at times, an equally
blind fate. It is in this essentially pagan form that Machiavelli
revived the goddesses of antiquity whom St. Augustine had
banished, for they seemed to describe the actual course of history more accurately than Christian theology. The uncertainty
of the concepts only reflects the uncertainty of prediction in the
world, especially one in which the decision of a single powerful
individual may make the best advice and the most complete
knowledge useless.[1]

These terms as terms are indeed rather ambiguous, but they
are really poetic, allegorical symbols pointing to a variety of
related concepts, which taken together are not necessarily
logically coherent. Thus, from one point of view, *fortuna* would

[1] Chabod, pp. 69–70, 189–90; Benedetto Croce, *Teoria e storia della
storiografia* (Bari, 1917), pp. 215–16.

seem to signify the inevitable character of processes of nature, of growth and decay, while *virtù* is the human power which, guided by an understanding of the nature of things, can do what is possible to arrest decline. But it is clear that 'fortune' is also the unknown, and that man cannot completely know or conquer her. Machiavelli tells us that he can only operate with and minimize her bad effects or, if he is very lucky, turn them to advantage. In any case Machiavelli maintains that *fortuna* and *virtù* divide the world between them half and half, so that human effort ought to succeed in about half of the events which occur.

Machiavelli derived these polar deities, like most of his conception of historical causation and recurrence, from Polybius[1] and, like him, used the concepts with the skill and flexibility of a poet rather than the abstract rigour of a philosopher. Thus *fortuna* or *tyche* appears in both authors as a half-personalized and semi-divine power that bends events to her will. In this respect fortune is simply that which the agent of action could not reasonably foresee, including even natural events and events with unknown causes, such as floods, storms, and plagues. Both would consider it illegitimate to attribute to fortune whatever can be understood by humans and concerning

[1] Kurt Von Fritz, *The Theory of the Mixed Constitution in Antiquity: A Critical Analysis of Polybius' Political Ideas* (New York, 1954), appendix II, 'Polybius' Concept of Tyche and the Problem of the Development of His Thought,' pp. 388–97, esp. 389–90. Machiavelli also followed Polybius in his utilitarian view of religion as an instrument for obtaining political order, and, more important, he adopted Polybius' theory of the mixed constitution as the most stable form of government. Aristotle had described the stable constitution as a mixture of oligarchy or aristocracy with democracy, all under legal definition. For Polybius the mixed constitution was made up of monarchy, aristocracy, and democracy as these were represented in the consuls, senate, and people of the Roman constitution. In fact, Aristotle's mixed constitution is not really such at all but the description of a state with mixed principles. Polybius advanced a theory of checks and balances in which all units needed to co-operate to govern and according to which any unit may obstruct the rest. See Von Fritz, pp. 76–95, 396; and C. H. McIlwain, *The Growth of Political Thought in the West* (New York, 1932), pp. 100–01. On the problem of how Machiavelli may have come to know Polybius' doctrine of the mixed constitution, when that part of the latter's work was unknown to him, see J. H. Hexter, 'Seyssel, Machiavelli and Polybius VI: The Mystery of the Missing Translation,' *Studies in the Renaissance*, III (1956), 75–96.

which humans can exercise foresight and control, whether actively, by taking measures, or passively, by avoiding action.

The external circumstances, the particular conditions for action which fortune may give, Machiavelli calls the *occasione* or 'occasion,' and the degree to which a man is aware of and able to take advantage of the occasion is a function of his *virtù*. Yet personal fortune may be said to coincide with or overlap *virtù* in the sense that the mysterious ability to find quickly the successful course of action in a complex situation can sometimes hardly be distinguished from some impetus, internal or external, which virtually impels the agent to act successfully among many imponderables. The terms *virtù* and *fortuna*, while primarily antithetical, sometimes shade into one another. Machiavelli even virtually identifies the two when he says that good laws make good fortune,[1] and it is obvious that the excellence of one individual may play a leading rôle in the fate of another. The rhetorical flourishes which Machiavelli makes—fortune as a turning wheel, as unpredictable as shifting winds, as one who disregards all human feeling and justice, as a capricious woman, as a personified power that wants to raise everything that's down and lower everything that's up—all these are best interpreted as metaphors expressive of how men *feel* about chance and its unfathomable mystery, not of how men ought to *think* about it.[2]

[1] *Discorsi*, I, 2.

[2] See *Istorie Fiorentine*, III, 18; *Il Principe*, ch. 25 and Vincenzo Cioffari, 'The Function of Fortune in Dante, Boccaccio and Machiavelli,' *Italica*, XXIV (1947), 1–13. In stressing the pagan concept of fortune, Machiavelli indirectly attacked the medieval one, which equated it with divine providence or, on a cruder level, simply with the notion that whoever rises must fall. Dante's image of fortune in the *Inferno* is a good example of the former, for he represents her as an angelic intelligence who, under the will of God, redistributes periodically the goods of this world, while Boccaccio's *De casibus* or Lydgate's *Fall of Princes* are good examples of the latter view. Philosophically, the medieval Aristotelians rendered it as the accidental cause, e.g. when looking for water you find gold, or as the *concursus causarum*, the occasional unpredictable concatenation of events which the human intellect finds puzzling. The term *fortuna* was also applied in the Middle Ages and later to the agent of action as well as to the external conditions of action, although the orthodox carefully distinguished between the goods of the body and the goods of the soul, only the former being subject to the influence of the stars or the operations of chance. Machiavelli, obviously, makes no distinction of this kind.

Virtù, the corollary of *fortuna*, is certainly a simpler concept, although at times equally amorphous. Its primary sense is quite classical and means what Livy might have meant by it, military skill and valour and the kind of civic integrity associated with the old Roman republican heroes like Cincinnatus, Horatius, or Mucius Scaevola. Such *virtù* is the possession of peoples as well as individuals, although primarily of the latter.[1]

But in the meaning which interests us most and which is the most singular use of the term, it quite clearly has no conventional ethical connotation and means sheer ability, prudence in the sense of practical insight and the power to act on it, without any ethical meaning attached. It involves an acute understanding of the real nature of things and circumstances as well as the ability to act on that understanding. It points to the obscure and complex realm which the general principle must traverse before it can effectively govern a unique and particular instance. Aristotle's ethical man knew what good to do to the right person, to the right extent, at the right time, with the right motive, and in the right way, something which Aristotle tells us is not for everyone nor easy. If we transpose all of these skills into Machiavelli's world, stripping the term 'right' of its customary ethical values, we will have something very close to what Machiavelli means by *virtù*.[2] It is the power of constant adaptability to circumstances, the power to operate in conditions which men are not responsible for and on realities which they did not bring into being. The exercise of *virtù* requires constant flexibility, knowledge of how circumstances alter cases, and, above all, the knack of always avoiding rigidity. Only by such behaviour can man minimize the effects of fortune.

It is clear from this analysis of some of Machiavelli's leading ideas and presuppositions that he is not a political scientist in the

[1] There was ample classical precedent for the coupling of *virtus* and *fortuna*, e.g. Quintus Curtius, X, 160; Sallust, *Con. Cat.*; Cicero *De officiis*, II, v, 17–18 and II, vi, 19–20, in which Cicero argues that virtue is the basis of co-operation and that the latter is the remedy for fortune. The ally of fortune was, in some versions, necessity (cf. Macrobius, *Sat.*, I, 19, 17, and Horace, *Carm.*, I, 35, 17).

[2] Cf. Whitfield, pp. 95–98, who gathers some of the most important meanings of *virtù*. He points out that only the singular applies to energy of the will or bravery; the plural is referred to moral habits in the more conventional sense.

sense that he possesses a system of politics. On the contrary, his is essentially a literary intelligence, aware that life escapes all the abstract schemes we may construct to control it. He would have said that a systematic approach to experience would have disastrous practical consequences, for no single principle is always, in every instance, good. It is the prime necessity for flexibility in statecraft as well as other spheres of action that leads Machiavelli to organize his thinking around mythic, poetic, and indefinite concepts like *fortuna* and *virtù* in a way that precludes any logically coherent result. Yet the indefiniteness is, in this case, part of the precision, for, like all effective poetic symbols, the realities they capture are themselves indefinite and problematic. Fidelity to the element of risk and chance in all action whatever actually compels Machiavelli to be unsystematic. Avoiding large abstractions, he teaches like an artist, by concrete examples to be applied to specific and typical situations, and by subtle repetitions.

His great words and images—*fortuna, virtù, necessità, occasione*—appear and reappear like expanding figures running through the texture of his work, each new appearance subtly modifying the meaning of the last and all enriching each other. In this sense, Machiavelli's thought is his style and we can no more preserve its variety and subtlety through paraphrase and summary than we can the meaning of a poem.

It is almost impossible to discuss Machiavelli at any length without discussing the traditions of interpretation and the myths associated with his name and work. The first and in some respects still the most vital popular interpretation, little known outside of Italy, is of Machiavelli as the prophet of a strong and united fatherland, the lover of freedom, and the bitter ironist of human depravity in the political sphere.[1]

It was primarily the Elizabethan dramatists who, for the English-speaking world, gave rise to the demonic version of Machiavelli, a version largely inspired by the 'Anti-Machiavel' of the Huguenot writer Gentillet.[2] The references to Machi-

[1] For a brief but excellent discussion of the two myths, see A. Robert Caponigri's introduction to Peter Rodd's translation of Machiavelli's *Il Principe, The Ruler: A Modern Translation of Il Principe* (Chicago, 1955).

[2] See the classic study of Mario Praz, 'Machiavelli and the Elizabethans,' now available in his collection of essays, *The Flaming Heart* (New York, 1958).

avelli in Elizabethan literature are very numerous indeed and by far the most of them support the demonic version of Machiavelli. No one who has read it can ever forget Richard's speech in *Henry VI, Part III*, when he promises to out-dissemble all the dissemblers of history and even 'set the murderous Machiavel to school,' or the prologue of the stage Machiavel himself in Marlowe's *Jew of Malta* who weighs 'not men, and therefore not men's words' and whose followers are given to poisoning their rivals for high office.

Such was the popular Elizabethan version of Machiavelli, and few men were dispassionate enough to declare with Francis Bacon that 'we are much beholden to Machiavelli and other writers of that class who openly and unfeignedly declare or describe what men do, and not what they ought to do.'[1] Time, distance, and erudition have done much to temper the demonic version of Machiavelli, but lingering traces of it remain not only in common allusions to 'Machiavellianism' but even in some of the scholarly literature on him.[2]

The countermyth, or heroic version of Machiavelli, was in part the creation of Rousseau. He read *The Prince* as an ironic *exposé* of the vices inherent in the very occupation of ruling. In this he seems to have followed Spinoza who, in the *Tractatus theologico-politicus* (V, 5), had suggested that Machiavelli's work was intended as a warning to peoples not to entrust their welfare to a single individual. Still later, during the full flowering of the romantic movement, Italian romantic nationalists such as Alfieri and Foscolo greatly fostered the more benign interpretation of Machiavelli. This new reading was supported by the attempt to place his thought in some sort of historical context and by emphasizing the *Discourses* rather than *The Prince*.

There is, of course, a partial truth in each one of these versions of Machiavelli, and certainly far more truth in the later than the earlier one. Yet both are, in very different degrees, too one-

[1] *De augmentis scientiarum*, VII, 2, sec. 10.

[2] L. A. Burd was perhaps the best of an older generation who had to go out of the way not to appear to be endorsing the Florentine's ideas. (See his edition of *Il Principe* (Oxford, 1891), esp. the introduction, but even here and there in the commentary.) More recently, L. J. Walker in his edition of the *Discourses* (2 vols., London, 1950) in the opening pages of his introduction has also felt the need to 'dissociate' himself from Machiavelli's ideas.

sided. Some of Machiavelli's views were, and still are, disturbing, but they were more disturbing than they might have been because Machiavelli did not attempt to exhaust the whole realm of political reality or simplify the kinds of complex interrelations which do in fact obtain between morals and politics. He simply isolated for study what he felt was the most neglected part of political behaviour and refused to rationalize away the bitter realities of power politics. It is a major irony of literary history that a man of great personal integrity who never attacked moral principles should have become the symbol of purely destructive ruthlessness.

On the other hand, to turn Machiavelli into an embittered Italian patriot and a prophet of a new, modern, national state is to be both misleading and anachronistic. His national feeling was not unique in his time nor was his attitude for the most part new. The confusion on this question arises from the fact that, although an Italian national sentiment was operative in Italy on the emotional level during the Renaissance, such sentiment did not actually influence the conduct of diplomatic relations between the various Italian states. Genuine and powerful national interest was invariably subordinated to the interests of the particular states of the peninsula. Where Machiavelli differs from his contemporaries is that—in the famous closing chapter of *The Prince*—he appeals directly to one man to unify the country, bypassing the rulers of the various Italian states and resting his case on the existence of sufficient national feeling for this purpose in the population of all Italy. Previous proposals for a united Italy had been based on the notion of a coalition of Italian rulers or on their co-operation.[1] He was realistic enough to realize that no Italian ruler was voluntarily going to co-operate himself out of a job and that force was the only remedy for the current state of affairs.

We can also isolate a third version of Machiavelli, that of the scientist, which has become fairly current in modern scholarship, and which also has a basis in the truth as long as we are not too rigid or precise in our use of the term 'scientist.' There is no doubt that *The Prince*, for example, has some of the characteristics of a scholarly or scientific work. It is organized

---

[1] Felix Gilbert, 'The Concept of Nationalism in Machiavelli's *Prince*.' *Studies in the Renaissance*, I (1954), 38–48.

with classifications and definitions illustrated by examples. It attempts to set forth principles of some general application based on reason and drawn from personal and historical experience. It has a partly theoretical character in that the author reveals the processes of his reasoning on political behaviour and attempts to define the nature and character of rulers and states, although it also has a practical character in that the rules that Machiavelli sets forth are presented as eminently practical and binding on those rulers who would succeed.[1]

Another argument for Machiavelli as a scientist rests on the fact that he reduces all historical phenomena to two principles, *fortuna* and *virtù*, and that such a reduction is characteristic of the scientific approach to experience. He is also said to be scientific in the 'abstract' and theoretical nature of his approach to the study of politics, in his attempt to discover principles applicable to any place and time, and, most of all, in abandoning occult forces and religious concepts.[2]

It is of course true that Machiavelli, like Leonardo, for example, treats man as an element in nature and attempts to reason inductively about his behaviour. Yet naturalism of this sort is certainly not synonymous with the scientific method, nor is Machiavelli purely descriptive. He certainly has preferences and intentions, advocates certain courses of action as beneficial, and frequently makes normative rather than technical judgments.[3] Further, his inductions are often drawn from rather limited areas and according to rules which were themselves formulated on relatively limited observation. He too often generalizes a little too readily, and his method, particularly of historical analogy, is simply too risky.

[1] Leo Strauss, 'Machiavelli's Intention: The Prince,' *The American Political Science Review*, LI (1957), 13–40, and Leonardo Olschki, 1–23. Strauss's study has been reprinted in his book *Thoughts on Machiavelli* (Glencoe, Ill., 1958).

[2] Olschki, 35–6, 38, 40. Note that Machiavelli has little to say about the *virtù* of institutions. His conviction is that political achievement really depends on individual great men more than on anything else. No reader of *The Prince* can fail to be impressed by the degree of faith Machiavelli seems to have in the ability of a single man to accomplish an enormous amount and how little he seems to be aware of the special cultural and historical contexts often necessary for creative political accomplishment.

[3] See also Aldo Scaglione, 'Machiavelli the Scientist?,' *Symposium*, X (1956), 243–50.

Machiavelli frequently made errors—for example, his underestimation of the importance of artillery, his overestimation of the disadvantages of mercenary armies, his excessive faith in the capacities of the single gifted individual to effect political change. And, in the last analysis, these derive from what we would have to call an unscientific frame of mind. Not that Machiavelli deliberately excluded evidence. He simply was too optimistic at times about how much evidence he needed to make an accurate assessment of conditions and, more important still, to make predictions.

Certainly, the reduction of phenomena to polar opposites or principles like *virtù* and *fortuna* is as such hardly scientific. Lucretius, for example, has Venus and Mars presiding over his universe of swirling atoms, personifications of the forces of creation and of destruction. The history of philosophy presents us with all sorts of pairs like matter-form, active-passive, and the like, concepts often of limited utility, which sometimes served as impediments to discovery. Perhaps the most recent use of such a disjunctive way of organizing phenomena is Freud's polarity of Eros and Thanatos, the anabolic and catabolic aspects of the psychic economy.[1]

If Machiavelli is not a scientist, or a hero, he has his own kind of greatness. In the first place he is a great writer, a matchless ironist, and a master of narrative. The more one reads him the more one is inclined to agree with Foscolo that Machiavelli's is the finest Italian prose. At his best, he writes the flexible, direct language of the so-called vernacular humanists such as Leonardo, close to the rhythms of Tuscan speech and of immediate thought, free from the misunderstood classicism which was to dominate so many writers of the Italian *Cinquecento* and leave the writing of some of the most significant literature to amateurs like Michelangelo or Cellini. The virtual incorruptibility of true genius aside, we might say that Machiavelli was free to be bold in his thinking because he escaped the growing Ciceronianism of the scholarly academies.

Yet he is also of great intellectual interest to us now because his work, especially *The Prince*, is still a powerful statement of the problem of the relationship of conscious intention of the

---

[1] Cf. the sound and penetrating assessment of Machiavelli in Gaetano Mosca's *Storia delle dottrine politiche*, 7th ed. (Bari, 1957), pp. 105 ff.

agent of action to the actual effects achieved in society.[1] On the level of personal interaction this problem is at the heart of literature, and one of the central concerns of both the tragic and comic vision of life. Machiavelli applied this great literary vision to society and, like the artist he was, did not merely study the intention by itself or the result by itself, but focused his awareness on the complex relations between them.

Machiavelli's universe, like that of Montaigne, Shakespeare, and Cervantes, is open at the farther end. It is finally beyond ideology, political or otherwise. Questions are brilliantly illuminated from various points of view and the differing conclusions afforded by various perspectives may all be validated and, as it were, left in suspension. Experience transcends system, and it is for this reason that Machiavelli can maintain that there is something bad about so-called good intentions which produce catastrophes, and that the agent of such results is responsible for them no matter what his intention may have been. Men, especially statesmen, must learn some bitter lessons. Even the best of intentions, and even when coupled with accurate insights into how to bring about a good result, cannot always be effectively realized entirely through the agency of apparently good actions. What appears to be a good means and what, indeed, may be good in itself is frequently so interwoven with other elements that the total result which would flow from using it may not be desirable. The ultimate context in which the affairs of men take place is one with disproportions and incommensurabilities between guilt and retribution, intention and result, known causes and perceived results. Where Machiavelli is truly original is not in his awareness of the difficulty at times in knowing what is a good or bad thing to do, but in the fact that his whole analysis of politics and history is made from a new perspective, that of the ethical irrationality of human experience taken as a whole. Unlike any of his predecessors, he works from the conviction that no set of moral

[1] See Jurgen Ruesch, M.D., *Disturbed Communication* (New York, 1957), p. 9. This problem, as Dr. Ruesch implies, is more familiar to us in the context of present-day psychiatric theory concerning inter-personal communication. According to this view, disordered behaviour is the result of a failure to correct one's technique for realizing intentions in the light of the actual results achieved.

principles of identical content can govern all areas of life, public, private, professional, and personal. In addition he fully grasped the fact that force is not simply a means that the state uses but is a means specific to the state, a part of its very nature.

Why does Machiavelli emphasize this aspect of politics so? There is more to it than force, essential as that may be. We have suggested some answers, but the final answer, I think, lies in the conditions of Italy in his time, in the ruthless and suspicious character of the diplomacy of his era, riddled with treason and betrayal, in which money and threats seemed the only effective instruments. Hence his despair, his irony, and his bitter injunction to be either wholly good or wholly evil.

Machiavelli's final vision is the tragic one, for he places us in a paradoxical realm where chance and ability meet and overlap, where culpability and self-awareness are in an obscure relationship to one another, a world whose 'justice' is not our justice. It is a world in which men must frequently choose between bad alternatives and where even the best choices entail losses. Only in an imaginary world of perfect knaves and fools, such as we find in his *Mandragola,* can everyone come off happily, and then only to the extent that the fools are delusively pleased by the success of the knaves.

The first scene of this great comedy finds Callimaco hopelessly in love with Lucrezia, the beautiful young wife of the aged Messer Nicia, a foolish, pompous know-it-all. Callimaco opens the play with an analysis of his erotic situation which sounds like the syllogistic and disjunctive analyses of *The Prince.* Succinctly and powerfully he sets forth his attitudes and his possible courses of action. Hopeful, although not sanguine, about his chances of success, he realizes that his best course of action lies in exploiting the foolishness of Messer Nicia, foolishness reinforced by Nicia's inordinate desire for a child. In addition he plans to exploit the corrupt character of Nicia's mother-in-law, Sostrata. Later in the play, with the aid of his parasite, Ligurio, Callimaco is also able to use the avarice of Fra Timoteo, a corrupt monk, to his advantage. By deftly playing on the corrupt and restless desires of assorted knaves and fools, Callimaco succeeds in corrupting Lucrezia, who, to her surprise, discovers that corruption is delightful. This play could, of course, have been a tragedy, but the exact mixture and relation of gullibility and knavery leads to the felicity of all.

Indeed, the laws that govern the world of this great comedy are the same as those that govern the tragic universe of actuality. *Mandragola* is the model of what a perfect diplomatic solution would be, a solution which would be painfully realistic yet one in which all sides would get what they want. Since this is impossible in the great political world, a world little tolerant of the deluded, the model must have a different setting. In the microcosm of that play, and in terms of a successful erotic chase, all appearances and realities, intentions and results are harmonized, all losses and gains cancelled, not in reality, but through the power of illusion and deception, the power of seeming rather than of being.

Machiavelli's famous maxim that it is sometimes really better to seem good than to be good has struck some observers as the most cynical of his principles. Perhaps it is, but it is also true that the life of effective action is never merely the immediate expression of a mysterious inner essence but the adoption of means, consciously or unconsciously, for the achievement of particular intentions, and this must be so precisely because the distance between an intention and result may be great and filled with antinomies. Life goes on not only in a system of cause and effect but in a system of action and counteraction simply because the object of personal and political action is not passive but reactive.

Whether in the imaginary world of comedy or the tragic world of political action, the felicitous solution may rest more on appearances than on realities. In the last analysis Machiavelli gives to appearances, conventions, fictions, and manners their proper status as necessary realities. Action demands that we be oblique as well as direct, and right action demands a high degree of awareness of both kinds of discourse. But what is the right course of action in any specific context depends on concrete particulars and they cannot be known before they appear. The agent of action must know very well what seems and what really is if he is to grasp the true particular features of a situation as it emerges from the unknown. Only then, if necessity demands deception, can he hope to make it right.

Perhaps Machiavelli's greatest gift is his ability to clarify the nature of the scene of political action without simplifying it.

As against what Burckhardt would have called the 'terrible simplifiers,' Machiavelli is aware of the complexity of that scene. Moreover, his sense of complexity does not derive from any inadequacy of thought, nor does it paralyse action. Certainly, given enough time, men can identify causes and predict effects. But the scene of action does not always afford enough time for that, and men must therefore act in partial ignorance, an ignorance which can be reduced but never eliminated, and which must be accepted if men are to act at all. The agent of action has already reduced the risks of action when he grasps that he is one among many more or less cloudy centres of consciousness acting in finite intervals of time on concrete situations. He further reduces those risks when, paradoxically, he is prepared to take them armed with a full awareness of 'the effective reality of things.'

If Machiavelli is acutely aware of the ambiguities of action, he is surely equally aware of the necessity of intelligent planning for action. If he is acutely aware of the fact that a grim necessity can drive men to immoral action, he is also aware that an equally grim necessity can save men from taking action which would have catastrophic consequences. Unlike the 'terrible simplifiers,' he does not substitute abstract attitudinizing for concrete thought, nor does he confuse taking risks with being rash. He not only knows what can be gained through bold action but also, and equally important, what can be lost.

CHAPTER VIII

Cromwell as Machiavellian Prince
in Marvell's *An Horatian Ode*

F irst I ought to say that this essay will not be a study of the history of Marvell's political opinions, nor will I attempt to find more consistency in them than they will bear. His elegy on Lord Francis Villiers, the poem to Lovelace, the poems on the death of Hastings and on the death of Tom May, all furnish evidence of Royalist sentiment. The three poems on Cromwell furnish equal evidence of Puritan sentiment. Even if all the problems of dating and attribution of Marvell's poetic corpus could be solved, we would still be faced with understanding the transformations of an almost frighteningly complex mind, one that, as we know from his poetry, is capable of holding in consciousness simultaneously both the playful and serious implications of an analogy, and of surveying experience from multiple perspectives without trying to reduce them to one another. He is a master of the representation of those ranges of experience which are heterogeneous, of a poetry of transformations, each metamorphosis corresponding to a transformation of consciousness. I suspect that even if we knew what went on at various times in Marvell's life, the actual shifts in mood, feeling, and attitude in his unrecorded consciousness, we would still be left with as much of an enigma as confronts the Dante scholar who tries to show a consistent development from the *Vita Nuova* to the *Paradiso*.

The *Horatian Ode* does not give a simple or a ready answer to the question, what did Marvell think of Cromwell when he wrote this poem? Mr. Cleanth Brooks in a well-known essay surveyed various answers and furnished a tentative one of his own. If Pierre Legouis finds an utter impartiality toward both Cromwell and Charles, and Margoliouth a divided sympathy but with a genuine preference for Cromwell as an ideal civic ruler, Mr. Brooks concludes his analysis of the poem with the following summation:

These [i.e. contrasting or contradictory] implications enrich and qualify an insight into Cromwell which is as heavily freighted with admiration as it is with great condemnation. But the admiration and condemnation do not cancel each other. They define each other; and because there is responsible definition, they reinforce each other.[1]

[1] Cleanth Brooks, 'Literary Criticism,' in *English Institute Essays, 1946* (New York, 1947), 127–58. Brooks' comments on other critics are on 132–34, the citation on 153. I take Mr. Brooks' paper as my point of departure since he raised the issues which have since been debated in the interpretation of the *Horatian Ode*. Mr. Douglas Bush answered him in 'Marvell's *Horatian Ode*' (*Sewanee Review* LX (1952), 363–76, esp. 364), contending that Brooks distorts the poem primarily because he forces the view that Marvell could not really have admired Cromwell. Instead, Bush agrees with M. C. Bradbrook and M. G. Lloyd Thomas (*Andrew Marvell* (Cambridge, 1940), pp. 73–76) on a providential interpretation of the poem. Ruth Wallerstein agrees in general with Brooks in so far as she feels that the *Horatian Ode* expresses 'an unresolved conflict of feeling.' She recognizes a 'Machiavellian' atmosphere in the poem but neglects to interpret it in terms of the authentic Machiavellianism it contains (*Studies in Seventeenth Century Poetic* (Madison, Wisconsin, 1950), pp. 278–79). More recently James F. Carens in 'Andrew Marvell's Cromwell Poems' (*Bucknell Review* VII (1957), 41–70) has surveyed the interpretations of the Cromwell poems, concentrating on the *Anniversary*. He has given us a very balanced interpretation of that poem based on a skilful reading of the text and some use of seventeenth-century political and religious doctrine. Recently, L. W. Hyman maintained ('Politics and Poetry in Andrew Marvell,' *PMLA* LXXIII (1958), 475–79) that the *Horatian Ode* rests on a distinction between the government that ought to be (Charles') and the government which had to be (Cromwell's). Unless this is fully amplified and qualified, the statement reduces the tension in the poem to a rather simple antithesis between an ineffective right on the one hand, and an efficient might on the other, plus a pious wish that the latter will eventually be moralized. It is the task of this paper to show that Marvell's viewpoint is substantially richer than that.

I do not disagree with this view of the poem in so far as I too discover in it a double perspective on the events it imagines and interprets for us. Yet I think that the tension in the poem has far less to do with conflict of feeling in the poet (something difficult if not impossible to determine) than with the poet's deliberately maintained intellectual attitude on historical and political events which transcends questions of personal commitment and reveals his full awareness of the ethically irrational and problematic character of human experience.

I believe that fresh light is thrown on the dynamic structure of this poem when considered from the standpoint of Machiavellian political theory, for the *Horatian Ode* is the only literary work of the English Renaissance which is faithful to the authentic Machiavellian vision in all of its antinomies, courage, and complexity. And I would stress the word 'vision,' for the tensions and paradoxes of the *Horatian Ode* and *The Prince* stem not from ambiguity of feeling but from inclusiveness of intellectual insight, from fidelity to all relevant experience whether it can be neatly packaged or not. In neither work are we in a Christian universe; but if God is not present, neither is Satan, for both works move in a realm beyond those antitheses as tradition, at least, defined them. This does not mean that either work is amoral, any more than Freud's *Civilization and Its Discontents* or, for that matter, Montaigne's *Essays*. It simply means that traditional ethics and morality cannot interpret the whole of experience, that no one set of principles of identical ethical content can be applied to all of the disparate activities of life, commercial, military, political, or erotic.[1]

If we try to sum up the originality and greatness of Machiavelli we will find it in two great perspectives from which, as we have seen, he surveyed the world of politics and history, two points of view which also underlie Marvell's vision of Cromwell in the *Horatian Ode*. The first is the recognition of the ethical irrationality of the world, the awareness of the fact that the same

---

[1] See Max Weber's classic essay on the relations between ethics and politics. 'Politics as a Vocation' in *From Max Weber: Essays in Sociology*, edit. and trans. H. H. Gerth and C. Wright Mills (New York, 1946), pp. 77–128. On the relation between conscious intent and achieved result as a guiding principle in interpreting experience see Juergen Ruesch, M.D., *Disturbed Communication* (New York, 1957), pp. 1 ff.

set of rules with exactly the same ethical content cannot govern all the activities of life. Men therefore live in a tragic universe where all choices entail some losses and where an action can never be *au fond* wholly unambiguous. The second principle derives from his awareness of the complex and heterogeneous relation which obtains between conscious intent and actual result achieved. This is surely familiar to us all as one of the central themes of literature, one which lies at the heart of both the tragic and the comic visions of life. What Machiavelli did was to transfer this perspective to the social and political realm, and this is precisely what Marvell did in the *Ode*. It follows from both of these principles that political behaviour cannot be judged entirely on the same principles which govern personal behaviour, and that a man with the best intentions in the world cannot escape responsibility for a catastrophe which he engenders.

Let us now turn to Marvell and apply what we have learned of Machiavelli to his *Horatian Ode*.

The opening of the *Horatian Ode*, as Margoliouth discovered, seems to portray Cromwell as a type of Caesar, Caesar as we find him in Lucan's *Pharsalia*, the young, ambitious, dynamic man of action who crashes like lightning through the opposition of both his party and of the enemy to the position of undisputed leadership.[1] Restless for glory, 'forward' to 'appear,' he forsakes the arts of the Muses practised in retirement and enters precipitously and successfully upon the life of action.

> The forward Youth that would appear
> Must now forsake his *Muses* dear,
>   Nor in the Shadows sing
>   His Numbers languishing.
> 'Tis time to leave the Books in dust,
> And oyl th'unused Armours rust,
>   Removing from the Wall
>   The Corslet of the Hall.

[1] *The Poems and Letters of Andrew Marvell*, ed. H. M. Margoliouth, 2 vols. (Oxford, 1927), I, pp. 237–38. A second edition of this masterly work was published in 1952. I cite, however, the text of Hugh Mac-Donald, *The Poems of Andrew Marvell* (Cambridge, Mass., 1952), since it reproduces the unique copy of Marvell's *Miscellaneous Poems* (1681) containing the Cromwell poems.

So restless *Cromwell* could not cease
In the inglorious Arts of Peace
    But through adventurous War
    Urged his active Star.
And, like the three fork'd Lightning, first
Breaking the Clouds where it was nurst,
    Did through his own Side
    His fiery way divide.
For 'tis all one to Courage high
The Emulous or the Enemy:
    And with such to inclose
    Is more than to oppose.   (1–20)

It is important to observe that Marvell begins the poem, not with Cromwell himself, but with a description of the nature of the times, the 'occasion.' Both Machiavelli and Marvell use the word to mean the particular circumstances and opportunities which condition a particular political action. They are not times when a young man of *virtù* who would make a name for himself can do so through the study of letters, the traditional vehicle for the acquisition of fame and glory in times of peace. The times, on the contrary, are troubled and warlike. Disorder reigns, and Cromwell, restless and ambitous, could not rest content with the arts of peace precisely because they are now inglorious. Both his restlessness, his need to engage in the activity appropriate to the times, and the urging of his 'active Star,' the sheer physical, cosmic power which seeks expression through him, marks him as the true Machiavellian man of *virtù*. He has fortune—here identified with the astrological powers which govern the processes of nature—and he has ability, and the external urgings of his fate are really aspects of one condition. His 'Star' is active in that its influence urges him, while he in turn urges it by grasping actively at the opportunity and power it offers.

The emphasis on youth and rapidity of action in these lines is striking and, in the context, suggests the concluding thoughts of the famous twenty-fifth chapter of Machiavelli's *Il Principe*:

I conclude then that since fortune varies and men remain obstinately fixed in their ways, men will succeed only so long as their ways coincide with those of fortune, but whenever these differ, then they are unsuccessful. In general, I think that it is better to be impetuous than cautious, for fortune is a woman, and it is necessary if you wish to master her, to strike and beat her; and you will see that she lets herself be vanquished more easily by the bold than by those who proceed more slowly and coldly. And therefore she is always a friend to the young, because they are less cautious, more fierce, and master her with greater audacity.

Cromwell's impetuosity, the nature of the times, the very sense of urgency in the rush of the lines, all indicate that he is the child of fortune. Nevertheless, like the successful child of fortune, he does not rely on fortune alone, for he would then seriously risk destruction, but exercises his own 'courage high,' his own *virtù*, in conjunction with it. The element of fortune as a favourable, natural, physical power, is again alluded to in the image of Cromwell as a three-pronged bolt of lightning smashing through the cloud in which it was born, at once the birth-portent and the birth itself, simultaneously overcoming and reconciling all the opposition in his own party, a feat more difficult than merely opposing an enemy.

Thus Marvell wishes us to realize that Cromwell's ability is not merely military and destructive but also political and creative. He further suggests, by making Cromwell himself an omen of the portent of power and ability he embodies, that Cromwell is no passive instrument of fortune but so active and 'virtuous' an agent that he becomes the fortune and the fate of others.

Marvell then continues with the effect of the Cromwellian lightning, which smashed palaces and temples, and finally struck 'Ceasar's head.'

> Then burning through the Air he went,
> And pallaces and Temples rent:
>   And *Caesars* head at last
>   Did through his Laurels blast.   (21-24)

The allusion to both Cromwell and Charles I as 'Caesar,' the first indirect and revealed through the imagery of *Pharsalia*, the other explicit, has been puzzling to some readers of the poem, and the thesis that the poem is a poem of great personal conflict rests in part upon this identification of both Charles I and Cromwell as 'Caesar.' Yet as any student of Roman history knows, the name, after Julius himself, was no more a proper name than 'Kaiser' or 'Tsar.' Much more relevant, however, is the fact that Marvell, like Machiavelli, Guicciardini, and other historians of the Renaissance, uses historical allusions and events in a special way. Cromwell is like the Caesar who won a civil war, Charles I like the Caesar who was assassinated. This mode of exemplarism is no more strange than the fact that, in the fourteenth chapter of Machiavelli's *Prince*, Caesar is offered to rulers as a model to be studied along with Alexander, while in the tenth chapter of the first book of the *Discourses* he is execrated as the founder of a tyranny. Indeed, Machiavelli there reproduces all of the classic arguments in favour of tyrannicide. This is not really a contradiction but a consequence of the practice of reading history in order to seek particular examples from which to derive the norms of behaviour for particular occasions. The life of one man can obviously afford many useful as well as useless *exempla*, many praiseworthy as well as damnable actions. Thus Cromwell is like Caesar in his brilliant success, in his ability to bring order to a nation torn by civil war. In these respects, he is Caesar at that moment when he rose to supreme power in the state. Charles I is like a Caesar at the moment of his destruction.

An analogous instance from Dante's *Divine Comedy* will make the exemplar method still more apparent. On the ledge of sloth in *Purgatory*, Caesar is offered as an example of the virtue of zeal, as a goad to virtue: 'Caesar, to conquer Lerica, thrust at Marseilles and made haste for Spain.' On the ledge where lust is purged Dante tells us that the sodomites being punished there 'offered in that for which Caesar heard himself called *Regina* in a triumph.'[1] Thus Caesar is the example of both a vice and a virtue, and neither use of him cancels the other.

The next two lines have been used to argue that the poem has a religious character and presumably advocates a puzzled submission to the inscrutable will of God:[2]

> 'Tis madness to resist or blame
> The force of angry Heavens flame:

It seems to me, however, that the context of this poem does not

---

[1] *Pur.*, XVIII, 101–02 and XXVI, 76–78.
[2] Cf. Wallerstein, *op. cit.*, p. 281.

give us leave to interpret Heaven in too 'pious' a sense. Cromwell is the flame of heaven, a lightning bolt born in a cloud, but his success is also the work of fate (37), nature (41), and fortune (113). I would suggest that these are all mutually convertible terms. Although Marvell does consider the heavens as instruments of providence in 'The first Anniversary,' the universe of the *Horatian Ode* lacks the providential dimension in any religious sense. The angry heavens of the poem are more like those which rage above the head of King Lear. The difficulty here lies in the fact that the stars and their influence were considered at times to be in part the instruments of providence and at other times to be entirely the instruments of nature, fortune, and fate. Dante, for example, quite bluntly identifies fortune and celestial influence with the workings of a wise providence (*Inf.*, VII). Machiavelli, equally bluntly, does not. While I cannot absolutely prove that Marvell does not mean Christian providence by 'heavens,' the universe of the poem is so exactly that of Machiavelli that the odds seem to me all against our reading a religious dimension into the poem. Indeed, it is precisely the physical, natural fatedness of Cromwell's forceful success that precludes both resistance and blame, a theme which culminates in the image of Cromwell filling a power vacuum.

The next lines delineate Cromwell in terms of another historical type, this time Cincinnatus, the type of old Roman republican integrity of character who left the farm he worked with his own hands to deliver Rome from the Aequians and, after ruling for sixteen days as dictator, returned to his farm. This analogy too suggests a Machiavellian context, his belief that when the state had reached a particularly grave level of disorder only a single individual of high *virtù* could restore it.[1]

> And, if we would speak true
> Much to the Man is due.
> Who, from his private Gardens, where
> He liv'd reserved and austere,
> As if his highest plot
> To plant the Bergamot, . . .   (27–32)

---

[1] Cf. Wallerstein, *op. cit.*, p. 289, who does not, however, identify the notion with Machiavelli.

The covert allusion to Cincinnatus might conceivably be read as a covert hope that Cromwell would soon retire to his estate after settling things, and it is of course true that Cromwell led the country in the name of an impersonal state of government, whatever the realities of his rule were in 1650 or later. However, I think that Marvell here uses an historical parallel in the standard Machiavellian way, for a particular act. Cromwell's emergence into public life, like that of Cincinnatus, is a spectacular manifestation of a *virtù* which displays itself at the right time, for he

> Could by industrious Valour climbe
> To ruine the great Work of Time
>   And cast the Kingdome old
>   Into another Mold.   (33–36)

'Industrious valour' is the active ability and skill—an excellent rendering of one of the important meanings of *virtù*— by which restless Cromwell urges his propitious fortune or 'active Star.' Like the artist-ruler of Machiavelli he creates a new state in very little time out of the old state which was the work of ages. The following lines are the pinnacle of the Machiavellian vision of Cromwell:

> Though Justice against Fate complain,
> And plead the antient Rights in vain:
>   But these do hold or break
>   As Men are strong or weak.
> Nature that hateth emptiness,
> Allows of penetration less:
>   And therefore must make room
>   Where greater Spirits come.
> What Field of all the Civil Wars,
> Where his were not the deepest Scars?   (37–46)

Fortune conquers justice, but it is a justice which is purely abstract, without the force to concretize itself. It is therefore empty and yields to the *virtù*, the martial valour of Cromwell, who, be it noted, does not destroy effective justice but only that impotent justice which pleaded for the Stuart's 'legitimate' rights to rule. If the ruler can't rule he leaves a vacuum which is immediately filled by a capable successor, a law of politics as binding as the law of nature. Beyond all the trappings of tradition lies the irreducible fact of political power, its dynamic and its exercise.

Cromwell not only possesses the martial *virtù* of a successful new prince or usurper, but he possesses the requisite cunning. Marvell accepts as fact the story, quite certainly unfounded, that Cromwell connived at Charles' escape from Hampton Court to Carisbrook in November 1647 in order to trap him and, eventually, to execute him.[1]

It is, as I have tried to indicate, by no means insignificant that the imagery of Cromwell's assumption of power is physical. The king's impotence and Cromwell's power are facts of the natural order. There is for Marvell as for Machiavelli a 'physics' of politics. Nature in its rôle as *fortuna* brings about the revolution as blindly as it fills the vacuum it 'abhors.' This event is outside ethics as the dynamics of political force is outside ethics. Marvell is witness to the moment of force in political activity, has seen the coercive element that underlies all effective rights, and has learned, as did Lear, that much that appears to be nature is in fact convention, and that nature will reassert itself.

This phase of the poem corresponds to the Machiavellian concept of *occasione*, half-way between *fortuna* and *virtù*. This 'opportunity' is more than the favourable operation of fate or fortune when it blindly and accidentally presents the man of *virtù* with *his* opportunity. Just as fate or fortune overcomes the ancient rights and presents Cromwell with the *occasione*, so Cromwell shows his *virtù* by the cunning with which he purportedly trapped the king.

> And *Hampton* shows what part
> He had of wiser Art.
> Where, twining subtile fears with hope,
> He wove a Net of such a scope,
> That *Charles* himself might chase.
> To *Caresbrooks* narrow case.

[1] The view that Cromwell lured Charles to Carisbrook in order to trap him was believed and seen not only by Marvell but also by others such as Flecknoe, Carrington, and the author, Henry Fletcher, of *The Perfect Politician*, as an example of the highest skill in statecraft. Cf. Robert S. Paul, *The Lord Protector: Religion and Politics in the Life of Oliver Cromwell* (London, 1955), pp. 152–53.

That thence the *Royal Actor* born
The *Tragick Scaffold* might adorn
While round the armed Bands
Did clap their bloody hands

(47–56)

If Cromwell is in part the creature of fortune so too is Charles, but negatively. The 'Royal Actor' is an actor precisely because he lacks the force to assert his right, lacks *virtù*, and so becomes the unhappy instrument of the malignant side of the same fortune whose benign aspect Cromwell experienced. Charles I is an actor in that he has only the appearance of a king, but he is a tragic actor because his fated retribution is out of proportion to his guilt. The imagery of the stage is here especially interesting and revealing, and not merely because of the obvious and ancient stoic metaphor for life and history as a drama. Rather, it serves to indicate the particular 'aesthetic' and moral distance from which Marvell views the events of history. They occur on another plane according to a sense of 'justice' which is not ours.

How persistent this perspective on public life and history is with Marvell can be seen from his return to the imagery of the tragic stage at the very beginning of his poem on the death of Oliver Cromwell. There he explains that the 'spectators,' the people, esteem a horrid death a glorious one and, exactly like the audience at a play, actually *want* the 'Prince' to be slain. It is not merely appropriate but actually fitting for a martial prince so to die, a right which fortune should not deny him. But, alas, Cromwell died in bed precisely because his *virtù* was so great, his valour and clemency so enormous, that fortune was, in effect, able to find no one to give him a glorious and fitting closing scene since he had eradicated his enemies and his friends loved him too much.

The People, which what most they fear esteem,
Death when more horrid so more noble deem;
And blame the last *Act*, like *Spectators* vain,
Unless the *Prince* whom they applaud be slain.
Nor Fate indeed can well refuse that right
To those that liv'd in War, to dye in Fight.
But long his *Valour* none had left that could
Indanger him, or *Clemancy* that would.

And he whom Nature all for Peace had made,
But angry Heaven unto War had sway'd,
And so less useful where he most desir'd,
For what he least affected was admir'd,
Deserved yet an End whose ev'ry part
Should speak the wondress softness of his Heart.   (7–20)

The Machiavellian moment in the last poem on Cromwell is there subsumed into a providential conception of his rôle as Davidic king, as instrument of the God of the Bible and history. What is significant here for our understanding of the *Horatian Ode* is Marvell's sense of the typological figure for a valorous prince, his attempt to explain why Cromwell did not follow out some archetypal pattern appropriate to him. It would almost seem as if Marvell lamented the lack of opportunity to match for Cromwell his own magnificent lines upon the death of Charles I in the *Horatian Ode*:

> *He* nothing common did or mean
> Upon that memorable Scene:
>   But with his keener Eye
>   The Axes edge did try:
> Nor call'd the *Gods* with vulgar spight
> To vindicate his helpless Right,
>   But bow'd his comely Head,
>   Down as upon a Bed.
> This was that memorable Hour
> Which first assur'd the forced Pow'r.   (57–66)

These lines are the culmination of the dramatic and tragic dimension of Marvell's political vision, the moment of pity for the king's benign conscious intent, and the moment of terror for the terrible and incommensurable result he achieved. Marvell is faithful to the necessity of what is and must be without trying to rationalize away the pain, suffering, and personal injustice involved. Charles' greatness, indeed, lies in his submission to his fortune, the nobility with which he accepts his fate. The drama of the Civil War is played out on a public stage with different laws than those which regulate ordinary life, laws which are intuitively known and understood by the great figures who act out their parts in the great drama. Cromwell accepts his fortune in leaving retirement to become a 'prince' and Charles accepts his fate on the scaffold. What they are as private individuals is incommensurable with their public selves and their historical destinies. This they seem to understand and accept even if we, as spectators, find a powerful tension in that incommensurability.

The good ruler is not identical with the good private citizen, the ideal ethical agent. The catalogue of his virtues cannot correspond part for part with that of the good retired private man. This was Machiavelli's answer to the question which had been posed in earlier writings and answered in the affirmative, whether the good ruler and the good man were identical.

Marvell then interprets the significance of the regicide by alluding to an event recorded by Pliny. The diggers of the foundations of the ancient Roman Capitol found the head of a man while excavating. This at first frightened them, but it was later correctly interpreted as a good omen for the state. Analogously, the bloody head of Charles I frightened the architects of the new state at first, but in that same frightening symbol the state found the beginning of a fortunate future. Like Machiavelli, Marvell here sees history in terms of the polarities Aristotle found in nature: 'generation and corruption.' The head which the Romans found, and the bloody head which the Puritan party made, coverge into one gory symbol of the interdependence of creation and destruction. Everything decays when it has reached its apogee and there can be no creation without the decay of something else. The death of Charles I was the completion of his already actual death as a king. This concept, so morally acceptable when applied to the natural order, becomes shocking in the political order. Nevertheless, neither Machiavelli nor Marvell is timid on this score. Good and evil eternally succeed each other, but even more, they are here, in a sense, the cause of each other.

> So when they did design
> The *Capitols* first line,
> A bleeding Head where they begun,
> Did fright the Architects to run;
> And yet in that the *State*
> Forsaw it's happy Fate.   (67–72)

The immediate consequence of the successful revolution is the conquest of the Irish, which Cromwell proved could be accomplished in a year by 'one Man. . . . That does both act and know.' Marvell then proceeds to a description of the great prince as Machiavelli defined him in the *Discorsi* (I, 10), the man who seizes power in order to found a republic and not a tyranny, who is self-circumscribed by law and who endeavours to institute rule by law. Cromwell begins in the *Horatian Ode* as the Prince of Machiavelli's *Prince* and ends as the Prince of Machiavelli's *Discorsi*. And this is exactly what Machiavelli hoped such a man as he required for the salvation of Italy would do. Cromwell comes in this poem not as the despoiler of the state but as its reformer, not by authority of ancient rights but by his fortune and virtue as a creative political agent, as one who has effective *imperium* or *stato* over men, an artist who seeks the true and lasting glory which comes to the good prince who could have been a tyrant but refrains from acting as one:

> They can affirm his Praise best,
> And have, though overcome, confest
>   How good he is, how just
>   And fit for highest Trust:
> Nor yet grown stiffer with Command,
> But still in the *Republick's* hand:
>   How fit he is to sway
>   That can so well obey.
> He to the *Commons Feet* presents
> A *Kingdome*, for his first years rents:
>   And, what he may, forbears
>   His Fame to make it theirs:
> And has his Sword and Spoyls ungrit,
> To lay them at the *Publick's* skirt.   (77–90)

Cromwell forgoes his fame, the Renaissance reward for great rulers replacing the promise of eternal glory in heaven which the medieval theorists saw as recompense, and surrenders all to Parliament. Indeed, he is like a falcon, that prince of trained birds who does not wantonly kill, but only at the bidding of the falconer, the bird who does the will of another:

> So when the Falcon high
> Falls heavy from the Sky,
> She, having kill'd, no more does search.
> But on the next green Bow to pearch;
>   Where, when he first does lure,
>   The Falckner has her sure.   (91–96)

The death of the king was, as Machiavelli would have put it, of *necessità*, by which, however, he does not mean physically necessitated. The kind of necessity in question occurs, for example, when a state simply has to undertake a course of action, no matter how risky or immoral, because any other would lead to its own destruction. Like Machiavelli's good prince, however, he performs all necessary cruelties once and keeps them to a minimum, exchanging such measures for those useful to his subjects.[1] The moment of gross unethical necessity is largely confined or perhaps fully revealed in the founding of a new state. Once the state exists as a secure unit of force, as a regime, then the good prince submits to law. There is really far less conflict between the statecraft of *The Prince* and the *Discorsi* than there appeared to be to Taine, for example. Political idealism cannot exist unless the state is a really functioning unit with its substratum of power secured. The state as regime demands something else than the state which is coming into being as a unit of force, for the conditions are different and the 'times' are not the same, although in neither case will politics and morals ever exactly coincide.

Cromwell's success and his submission to law are signs of the future glory of the 'Isle.' He will be, incongruously enough, Caesar to Gaul and Hannibal to Italy (97–102). Again Marvell uses historical examples in the characteristic Renaissance way without any attempt at total integration of those *exemplars*. Not only do France and Italy, the seat of the Papacy, fear Cromwell but Scotland will shrink from the steadfast *virtù*, the 'Valour sad.'

The poem closes with an exhortation to Cromwell, the child of martial valour and of fortune, to remain armed and to maintain his power, as he must, by those same arts with which he won it.

> But thou the Wars and Fortunes Son
> March indefatigably on:
>   And for the last effect
>   Still keep thy sword erect;
> Besides the force it has to fright
> The Spirits of the shady Night,
>   The same *Arts* that did *gain*
>   A *Pow'r* must it *maintain*.   (113–20)

[1] *Il Principe*, ch. 8, 'Of Those who have Attained the Position of Prince by Villainy.' Cf. also ch. 17.

It is important to observe here that although Cromwell must be alert to crush his enemies his sword is also 'moral' in that its cross-hilt can avert the spirits of evil. The exhortation is really one to continue in the rôle of the good prince of the *Discorsi* who seizes and maintains power, but who also submits to law and fights against evil.

The complexity of Marvell's vision and the tensions in the poem are those we feel in the work of Machiavelli. They result from a perspective on politics as an activity which cannot be entirely subsumed in the categories of traditional ethics. In the teleological ethics of Aristotle and of Christianity there are some acts which are just wrong and no goal whatever can give any-one leave to commit them. Machiavelli denied that this was true of political activity, without saying—and this is most import-ant—that white was black and black white. He simply says that the safety of the state, the maintenance of the minimum order and peace necessary for civilized life within the state, may demand that the ruler commit acts which are evil from the strictly moral point of view. Further, there is never any course of action open to a ruler that is always safe or, we might add, always moral. All policies are doubtful, all ambiguous.

Finally, the question becomes basically: Are there particular circumstances in the history of states when whether in external or internal policy, the correct course of action is not a good one from the moral point of view? If we can celebrate revolutions, acknowledge the necessity of a civil war, or reluctantly agree that some executions are necessary, some assassinations desir-able, then we must agree with the basic perspective of Machi-avelli whether or not we follow him elsewhere.

In the last analysis, man is moral but society is not. Any group is such for particular ends, and the only ethically unambiguous sphere is that of individual morality. This is the vision which is expressed in the *Horatian Ode*. The poem does not express unresolved personal feeling any more than *Oedipus Rex* expresses an unresolved personal feeling of Sophocles about whether or not to side with Oedipus or with Fate. We are in a realm analogous to that of Tragedy where we are compelled to recognize that the judgments concerning justice and injustice, good or evil, that we employ in our daily life cannot be easily or unambiguously applied when the context in which we use them is no longer the living-room, but the state, the world, or the universe.

This is the perspective from which Marvell regards the central events of the Great Rebellion. Cromwell is the embodiment of two of the major dimensions of the Machiavellian new ruler, the man of *virtù* who creates a state from chaos, the central figure of *Il Principe*, and the legally self-binding new ruler of the *Discorsi*, who, having consolidated his power tries to establish the rule of good laws and good customs enforced by good arms. It would seem that the 'Prince' for whose arrival Machiavelli yearned, who, like his Moses, would be a new prince in a new state with new laws, finally arrived on the stage of history, but on the English and not the Italian stage. He comes fulfiling the prophecy of that greatest of unarmed prophets, Machiavelli himself, as if in fulfilment of the archetypal model Machiavelli had created. It seems to me that some of the awe and excitement the *Horatian Ode* communicates flows from Marvell's shock at finding this theoretical figure fulfilled in reality, not in distant Italy, but in his own time and country.

CHAPTER IX

Cromwell as Davidic King

BEFORE we can fully understand Marvell's transformation
of Cromwell from a kind of Machiavellian prince in the *Horatian
Ode* into a Davidic king in the later poems we must first consider some aspects of traditional biblical exegesis and the
philosophy of history to which it gave rise.

The allegorical interpretation of Scripture antedates Philo
Judaeus, although he was the major influence on Origen and
other Eastern Fathers who preferred his abstract, moral, and
philosophical reading of Scripture to a more literal one. In the
West, the work, first of Tertullian, and then of Augustine
signalized the triumph of a more concrete and historical way of
interpreting Scripture which has since come to be known as
typological allegory or, as Erich Auerbach called it,
'figuralism.'[1]

This is the method of interpreting Scripture whereby the
persons and events of the Old Testament are seen as 'figures,'
realities which are also simultaneously prophetic signs of the
drama of salvation unfolded in the New Testament. The New

[1] See H. A. Wolfson, *The Philosophy of the Church Fathers*, I (Cam-
bridge, Mass., 1956), pp. 24 ff., for a study of rabbinical, Philonic and
patristic allegory, and Beryl Smalley, *The Study of the Bible in the Middle
Ages* (2nd ed.; Oxford, 1952), for later developments. Auerbach's thesis
is presented in 'Figura,' *Archivum Romanicum*, XXII (1938), 436–89.
Reprinted with minor changes in *Neue Dantestudien* (Istanbul, 1944).
See also his 'Typological Symbolism in Medieval Literature,' *Yale
French Studies*, IX (1952), 3–10, and, more extensively, *Typologische
Motive in der Mittelalterlichen Literatur* (Krefeld, 1953).

Testament in turn is prophetic of the events and realities of the Last Judgment, not only when it is obviously prophetic, but even through the events and personages it describes. The latter, when properly understood, point to further future events of which they are the paradigms.

While the Eastern tradition of allegorical interpretation tended to weaken the literal and historical veracity of the Old Testament, the figural method was based on the literal and historical value of the events recorded in Scripture. It is unlike ordinary allegory or symbolism in that both terms in the analogy are literally and historically true. They are realities and not merely signs. Thus Moses, Adam, Joshua are types of Christ, but they are also Adam, Moses, and Joshua. The Deluge is a type of baptism, but there was a real deluge. The sacrifice of Isaac was a type of the sacrifice of Christ, but there was a real Isaac and a real Abraham. In short, the relationship between the terms of a figural analogy is not that of sign to reality signified, but that of shadow (*umbra*) or *imago* to its fulfilled truth. Both terms are concrete, real and historical realities, and only the link between them is abstract.[1]

This method of interpretation, in the Christian tradition, begins as early as Paul. Thus the Jews in the wilderness are types of the present human situation (I Cor. 10.6, 11). The Jewish law is a shadow of what is to come (Col. 2.16 ff.), and Adam is both the type and the antitype of Christ (Rom. 5.12 ff.; 1 Cor. 15.21). The relations between the law and grace, bondage and freedom are prefigured in the relationship of Hagar and Ishmael or Sarah and Isaac (Gal. 4.21–31). The Pauline method of interpretation was rooted in rabbinical allegorical exegesis, the *Midrash*, but Paul modified it and turned it into a weapon for his attack on the judaizing Christians. His main intention was to deprive Judaism of its normative character because of his profound convictions on the paradoxical and antithetical character of the relations which obtain between law and grace, or between justification by faith and by works. In effect, he tried to reduce the Old Testament to a prediction even in those many parts which were not prophetic in character. In so doing, he made the unfamiliar history and mythology of a particular people accessible—in an enormously altered way, to be sure—

[1] Auerbach, 'Figura,' pp. 454 ff.

to gentiles, but his transformation of Scripture also contained the seeds of a new philosophy of history and a new way of interpreting contemporary events.[1]

Augustine, as in other important matters in the Western Christian tradition, gave definitive shape to figural interpretation and to other exegetical techniques as well.[2] Along with rather abstract moral and philosophical allegories of a more familiar sort we also discover in his writings many typological allegories. Thus Noah's Ark is a figure of the Church, Moses of Christ: the priesthood of Aaron is a shadow and figure of the eternal priesthood, Hagar is a figure of the earthly Jerusalem of the Old Testament, while Sarah is a figure of the New Testament, the heavenly Jerusalem, or of the City of God; Jacob and Esau are figures of Jews and Christians, and so on.[3] Such figuralizations do not serve merely to moralize those parts of Scripture repugnant to a later moral consciousness and reduce them to mere allegory. Indeed, even where the Bible reports immoral acts Augustine insists that they are to be taken literally and historically. However, they are also, like the more edifying episodes, to be taken figuratively as well, although the interpreter should here use the figurative interpretation alone.[4] This is not as arbitrary a procedure as it may seem. The actual polygamy to be found in the Old Testament, for example, is to be understood as a special divine dispensation appropriate to a special time in the historical drama of salvation. Nevertheless, even though such practices are no longer permissible, the now immoral events that Scripture records have an eternal reference, a figurative and moral meaning which is always applicable, and a prophetic meaning which will last until the end of history. This is why the Bible must be read both literally and historically on the one hand, and figuratively and prophetically on the other.[5]

---

[1] Cf. *Ibid.*, pp. 466–68, and Rudolf Bultmann, *History and Eschatology* (Edinburgh, 1957). These brilliant Gifford Lectures survey the field of Christian historiography briefly and lucidly.

[2] For a brief survey of kinds of scriptural and secular medieval allegory see my *Structure and Thought in the Paradiso* (Ithaca, N.Y., 1958), ch. 2.

[3] *De civitate Dei*, XV, 27; X, 6; XVIII, 11; XVII, 6; XVI, 31, XVII. 3, in Migne, *PL*, XLI. Cf. Auerbach, 'Figura,' pp. 456 ff.

[4] *De doctrina Christiana*, III, 12, 20, in Migne, *PL*, XXXIV, col. 73.

[5] *Ibid.*: 'non solum historice et proprie, sed figurate et prophetice.'

We can easily grasp here one of the ideas which, especially after it was secularized and applied to lay figures and the history of 'secular' peoples, could easily lead to the possibility of countenancing apparently or actually immoral actions on the grounds that they were providentially ordered. In its barest form and stripped of some of its complexity, the conception underlies a good deal of Marvell's apologia for Cromwell.

The nature of figural interpretation and its historiographical implications might be further clarified if we compare it to modern historical interpretations. The latter places events in a sequence moving, so to speak, horizontally towards an ever-receding horizon. The meaning of any single event is given in a development to a further event which defines what came before. Hence each generation must write its own history anew, for each event alters the significance of the past. On the other hand, in figuralism, the meaning comes from above. It is given by a vertical dimension, by the operation of divine grace and judgment. The pattern of events is not a uniform series. There are breaks, mistakes, miracles, moral incongruities, and conversions, and this is particularly true of sacred history.[1]

II

The figure of David passed into medieval history and imagination in two modes, as the type of biblical king, anointed of God and an instrument of Providence, and as the moral type who combines the antithetical attributes of humility and sublimity. The first is more strictly the political tradition of David symbolism, the latter was bound to a moral ideal pre-eminently found in moral interpretations of Christ and Francis of Assisi. However, these two modes were closely bound to one another in view of the fact that, until Machiavelli, the ideal ethical man and the ideal ruler were generally assumed to be synonymous, and that all the attributes of the good man were believed to be indispensable to the good ruler.

Let us turn first to the earliest medieval version of the figure of the Davidic king before discussing the 'humble psalmist' and Marvell's effort to place Cromwell in the framework of these traditions.

The crowning of Pepin saw the introduction of the Biblical

[1] Cf. Bultmann, *History and Eschatology*, p. 148.

rite of royal unctions into European history so that, according to the theories of the Franks, his coronation marked a revival of the kingship of David. This revival is simply one symptom of the growth of the use of liturgical formulas and techniques in the secular sphere, in turn a result of the strong tendency to employ theocratic techniques in the political realm. By the time of Charlemagne, it is clearly established that the ruler of the Franks was simply continuing the tradition of Davidic kingship.

Ever since the time of their victory over the Arabs, the Franks had come to consider themselves as a new chosen people, and this they did with full papal approval. They chose to identify themselves with a 'new Israel' which carried on from biblical and ecclesiastical history rather than with a 'new Rome,' although they also claimed descent from the same Trojan stock which founded Rome. Nevertheless, they did not think of their armies as reconstituted Roman legions, but as armies that might have fought under the leadership of David or Gideon.

'Like other nations in revolutionary times, like the English people under Cromwell, the Franks believed themselves to be God's chosen people destined to execute the plans of Divine Providence.' The Frankish kingdom was a *regnum Davidicum*, its king a *novus Moysus* or *novus David*. He was also a priest, a *christus Domini*, anointed of God and the ruler of a new Jerusalem. As Kantorowicz points out, Pepin's anointment as if he were a king of Israel was of great importance for the political evolution of Europe, for it is 'the keystone of this evolution and at the same time the cornerstone of medieval divine right and *Dei gratia* kingship.[1] Not only were the Franks a chosen people and their king a new David, but they were at the centre of the universal *populus christianus* and their king was *Rex Christianissimus*. Indeed, this conviction led them to feel superior to the ancient Romans, for the latter were pagans while the Frankish dominion was Christian.[2]

The liturgical acclamations of the time not only link the king to biblical traditions of kingship, but also to angelic

[1] *Laudes regiae, a Study in Liturgical Acclamations and Medieval Worship* (Berkeley and Los Angeles, 1946), pp. 56, 57. See also Kantorowicz' references there, and cf. his latest book, *The King's Two Bodies: A Study in Medieval Political Theology* (Princeton, 1957), pp. 77, 81, 83.

[2] Kantorowicz, *Laudes regiae*, p. 58.

intercessors who constitute, as it were, a continuation of the hierarchy of which he is the temporal pinnacle and which reflects the hierarchical order of the unseen world. Thus the political as well as the ecclesiastical order is conceived as a temporal imitation of the unseen superhuman order of saints and intelligences, made a part of that 'ladder cosmos' up which men climb to God and down which all divine gifts descend. The political and the secular sphere thus have a likeness to the structure of the City of God and these formulas are among the earliest attempts to posit such a structure.[1] The surrounding of the ceremony of crowning with biblical concepts and ecclesiastical legitimation, with a sacramental and liturgical character, simply reflected this continuity and fundamental unity of the *scala Dei*. What is most important here for our purposes is that the sanction for all this and the type of the inauguration was the anointing of David by Samuel.[2]

This tradition of Davidic kingship as model kingship which started with Pepin persisted through the Middle Ages into the Renaissance. Thomas Aquinas, for example, in *De regimine principum* (ch. 8) gives David as an example of the ideal ruler, one who does what every ruler should and places his reward in God. A good example from the Renaissance is offered by Erasmus, who advances David as certainly one of the best models of kingship, although with the proviso that not even the best are perfect, so that the ideal Christian prince should try to imitate the best actions of all the best princes.[3] The uses of David as a political type were varied, as we can see, although it is a little startling to find Grotius arguing that contemporary rulers could use as a precedent the fact that David rightfully took the spoils of the Amelekites which they had previously taken from others.[4]

[1] Kantorowicz, *Landes regiae*, p. 62. Although in Frankish theory there was a sharp cleavage between the *regnum Davidicum* and *Imperium Romanum*, events and the politics of the Holy See turned the Franks into the heirs of Rome (*ibid.*, pp. 62–63).

[2] *Ibid.*, p. 78.

[3] *The Education of a Christian Prince*, trans. with an intro. by L. K. Born (New York, 1936), pp. 202, 255.

[4] *De iure belli ac pacis*, III, vi, vii, 1, ed. by P. C. Molhuysen (Leyden, 1919). This work is rich in the use of biblical precedents and should be very useful in elucidating politico-literary allusions in Renaissance culture.

The interpretation of David as a 'humble psalmist' which, along with the conception of kingship attached to his name, had such a profound effect on the medieval understanding of the figure of David does not derive from the general delineation of David in Scripture, from David in his providential and historically important rôle, but from a specific text in 2 Samuel. This is the source for Dante's use of him as an example of humility in the *Purgatorio* on the ledge of pride (X, 55–69), in harmony with the moral interpretation of David as a symbol of *humilitas*.[1] The biblical text in question is worth citing at length because of the importance of its details in creating this conception of David, details which do not appear in another report of the same incident in 1 Chronicles 15.16–28.

So David went and brought up the ark of God from the house of Obededom into the city of David with gladness. And it was so that when they that bare the ark of the Lord had gone six paces, he sacrificed oxen and fatlings. And David danced before the Lord with all his might: and David was girded with a linen ephod. So David and all the house of Israel brought up the ark of the Lord with shouting, and with the sound of the trumpet. And as the ark of the Lord came into the city of David, Michal Saul's daughter looked through a window, and saw king David leaping and dancing before the Lord; and she despised him in her heart. . . . And Michal the daughter of Saul came out to meet David, and said, How glorious was the king of Israel today, who uncovered himself today in the eyes of the handmaidens of his servants, as one of the vain fellows shamelessly uncovereth himself! And David said unto Michal, It was before the Lord, which chose me before thy father, and before all his house, to appoint me ruler over the people of the Lord, over Israel: therefore will I play before the Lord. And I will yet be more vile than thus, and will be base in mine own sight: and of the maidservants which thou hast spoken of, of them shall I be had in honour. Therefore Michal the daughter of Saul had no child unto the day of her death.[2]

[1] See Erich Auerbach, 'Figurative Texts Illustrating Certain Passages of Dante's *Commedia*,' *Speculum*, XXI (1946), 474–89, 476–77, section II on David as *humilis psalmista*.

[2] 2 Sam. 6.12–16, 20–23.

The version of this story in Chronicles (*Vulg. Paralipomenon*) places considerable emphasis on the choice of musicians and singers to accompany the ark into the tent David pitched for it in Jerusalem. However, there is no singling out of David as dancing and leaping before the ark. Nor does Michal accuse David directly of disgracing himself and there is no explanation on David's part of his unkingly behaviour. The emphasis on humility is completely missing. Michal simply looks out of the window to see David dancing and leaping 'and she despised him in her heart.'

Dante uses the version from Samuel:

There, carved in the same marble, were the cart and oxen drawing the sacred ark on account of which men fear an office not committed to them. In front people appeared and the whole company, divided into seven choirs, made two of my senses say, the one: 'No,' the other: 'Yes, they sing'; in the same way, at the smoke of the incense that was imaged there, eyes and nose were in contradiction, with *yes* and *no*. There the humble psalmist went before the blessed vessel girt up and dancing, and at that time he was both more and less than king; opposite, figured at the window of a great palace, Michal looked on, like a woman vexed and scornful.

> Era intagliato lì nel marmo stesso
> lo carro e' buoi traendo l'arca santa,
> per che si teme officio non commesso.
> Dinanzi parea gente; e tutta quanta,
> partita in sette cori, a' due mie' sensi
> faceva dir l'un 'No', l'altro 'Sì, canta.'
> Similemente al fummo delli 'ncensi
> che v'era imaginato, li occhi e 'l naso
> e al sì e al no discordi fensi.
> Lì precedeva al benedetto vaso,
> trescando alzato, l'umile salmista,
> e più e men che re era in quel caso.
> Di contra, effigiata ad una vista
> d'un gran palazzo, Micòl ammirava
> sì come donna dispettosa e trista.[1]

[1] I cite the translation of J. D. Sinclair (Oxford, 1948) and the text of the Società Dantesca Italiana (Florence, 1921).

Dante, after indirectly referring to Uzzah's presumption in touching the ark, focuses his narrative on the paradoxical self-abasement of the mighty king who, by his self-imposed humility before the Lord became less a king to such as Michal but more in the eyes of his Creator. This is a perfect *exemplum* of the favourite Christian paradox of *humilitas-sublimitas*, supremely manifested in the life of Christ, the God-man who voluntarily humiliated himself even though he was simultaneously Lord of the universe. Thus David is a type of Christ, a *figura Christi*, while the ark itself is a figure of the Church, the fortunes of which during its persecutions were prefigured in the removals of the ark from one place to another.[1]

There is a third strain in the typological tradition of David, although it is intrinsically related to the theme of the humble psalmist and perhaps ought to be treated as identical with it. In this tradition the stress is on 'psalmist' rather than on 'humble,' for David was famous as a great musician, the composer of the Psalms. Although this talent may appear to be a possible source of sinful pride, we must recall that he manifested his humility precisely in the great gesture of singing and dancing 'psalms' themselves before the ark.

This tradition, as we shall see, came to be related to the political one and to various classical notions concerning music, although the musical reputation of David was quite important in the early Church, even before its philosophical elaboration, as authority for the use of music in religious rituals.[2] A passage from Augustine's *City of God* reveals both a puritanical ambivalence about the pleasures of music and the application to David of a well-developed conception of music as the art of cosmic harmony. Augustine felt that it was necessary to apologize for a strong interest in music on the part of this

---

[1] Auerbach, 'Figurative Texts,' p. 477, cites Gregory the Great, *Moralia*, in Migne, *PL*, LXXV, col. 444, for the example of David as *humilis psalmista* and *figura Christi*, and Honorius of Autun, in Migne, *PL*, CLXXIII, col. 369, for the significance of the ark as a type of the persecutions of the Church. For this theme as applied to St. Francis, see Auerbach, 'St. Francis of Assisi in Dante's "Commedia" *Italica*,' XXII (1945), 166–79, and 'Rising to Christ on the Cross (*Paradiso*, XI, 70–72),' *MLN*, LXIV (1949), 166–68.

[2] Leo Spitzer, 'Classical and Christian Ideas of World Harmony,' *Traditio*, II (1944), 409–64; II (1945), 307–64, 432.

ancestor and *figura* of Christ, and explains that David loved his music mystically, as an image of that unity in variety which is the essence of a well-ordered city. In this way Augustine makes David's musicianship an intrinsic part of his rôle as a ruler. As we shall see, Marvell makes exactly the same kind of use of Cromwell's fondness of music, a trait of his character which attracted a certain amount of comment.

In the progress of the city of God through the ages, therefore, David first reigned in the earthly Jerusalem as a shadow of that which was to come. Now David was a man skilled in songs, who dearly loved musical harmony, not with a vulgar delight, but with a believing disposition, and by it served his God, who is the true God, by the mystical representation of a great thing. For the rational and well-ordered concord of diverse sounds in harmonious variety suggests the compact unity of a well-ordered city.[1]

Such conceptions of music as Augustine applied to David were by no means new. Greek speculation, beginning in pre-Socratic times, had worked out a complete cosmogony of music based on the notion of cosmic harmony in the world-soul, a harmony reflected in the movements of the heavenly bodies, in the individual soul where it was achieved through musical education, and in the body-politic where it was established through the rule of a good king. The first and most famous synthesis of such ideas of universal harmony is Plato's *Timaeus*, a work which in turn was the source of Cicero's conception of a 'musical' world-soul and of his conception of the music of the spheres as a cosmic analogue of the order of the state. Boethius, of course, was for the Middle Ages the most important source of medieval preoccupation with music as the symbol of world

---

[1] *De civitate Dei*, XVII, 14, in Migne, *PL*, XLI, col. 547: I cite the new text of the *Corpus Christianorum, Series Latina*, XLVIII (Turnholti, 1955) with 'v' for consonantal 'u'. The translation is by Marcus Dodd, in *A Select Library of the Nicene and Post-Nicene Fathers of the Christian Church*, vol. II (Buffalo, 1887): Procurrente igitur per tempora civitate Dei, primo in umbra futuri, in terrena scilicet Hierusalem, regnavit David. Erat autem David vir in canticis eruditis, qui harmoniam musicam non vulgari voluptate, sed fideli voluntate dilexerit eaque Deo suo, qui verus est Deus, mystica rei magnae figuratione servierit. Diversorum enim sonorum rationalibus moderatusque concentus concordi varietate compactam bene ordinate civitatis insinuat unitatem.

harmony, and the references to him in this connection are abundant in this period. Later references to him would indicate that the influence of *De Musica* extended well into the seventeenth century.[1]

For our purposes, we need to stress the political aspect of these traditions of cosmic harmony to which the figure of David was assimilated and to which, in turn, Marvell assimilated Cromwell through David. Indeed, politics is the essential link between the 'humble psalmist-cosmic musician' on the one hand and the 'sublime,' divinely anointed king, on the other. The Davidic archetype we discern in the *First Anniversary of the Government* and the *Poem on the Death of O.C.* is a model political figure who is, as it were, our focus for Cromwell. Around the *figura* and its fulfilment cluster many of these ideas of divine election, humility-sublimity, and charismatic mystical insight into those universal principles of order which were presumed to underlie all great statecraft.

III

The first correspondence which Marvell establishes for Cromwell in *The First Anniversary of the Government under O.C.* is with the sun, the ruler of the cosmos. As the king of celestial bodies moves with greatest rapidity through the signs of the Zodiac exceeding the other planets, so Cromwell exceeds all other princes in his efficiency and ability. The lesser princes, indeed, do not even approximate the speed of the next most swift heavenly bodies but function in analogy with Saturn, the slowest and most malignant planet.

> *Cromwell* alone with greater Vigour runs,
> (Sun-like) the stages of succeeding Suns:
> And still the Day which he doth next restore,
> Is the just Wonder of the Day before.
> Cromwell alone doth with new Lustre spring,
> And shines the Jewel of the yearly Ring.

[1] For a masterly survey of these concepts see Spitzer's work already cited, and cf. G. L. Finney, 'A World of Instruments,' *ELH*, XX (1953), 87–120. On the analogies between human organism, state, and universe see Rudolf Allers, 'Microcosmus,' *Traditio*, II (1944), 319–407. esp. 368 ff., and on the musical terminology for these same analogies see pp. 375 ff.

> 'Tis he the force of scattered Time contracts,
> And in one Year the work of Ages acts:
> While heavy Monarchs make a wide Return,
> Longer, and more Malignant than *Saturn*:
> And though they all *Platonique* years should raign
> In the same Posture would be found again.[1]
>
> (7–18

Not only can Cromwell accomplish more than other rulers, but he does the right things. He is, indeed, of the type of Solomon, a ruler who will actually 'build the Temple in their days.' Thus Marvell begins to interweave the 'astronomical' with the biblical conceptions of the ruler and prepares us for the assimilation of Cromwell to David by the allusion of Solomon. While lesser rulers passively consult astrologers to learn how much time Fate has decreed in which they can remain free of their deserved punishment, Cromwell is himself, as sun or 'star,' a maker of destiny, or like any star, an instrument of Destiny in the sense of divine providence. The stars or planets, from antiquity believed to be the instruments of necessity or fate (with some allowance for free-will on the part of the ortho-dox), do not control Cromwell. Like a true man of *virtù* he is himself the fate of others, and we can assume that his only over-lord is Providence itself. In his freedom from blind astrological necessity and his rapid effective action we discover that Crom-well is also a Machiavellian ruler, the new ruler of sure ability who will also build the Temple of the state in his own time, a true master architect of the nation.

> No other care they [i.e. heavy Monarchs] bear of things above,
> But with Astrologers, divine, and *Jove*
> To know how long their Planet yet Reprives
> From the deserved Fate their guilty lives:
> Thus (Image-like) an useless time they tell,
> And with vain Scepter strike the hourly Bell;
> Nor more contribute to the state of Things,
> Then wooden Heads unto the Viols strings.

[1] I cite the edition of Hugh MacDonald, *The Poems of Andrew Marvell* (Cambridge, Mass., 1952), since it reproduces the unique copy of Marvell's *Miscellaneous Poems* (1681) containing the Cromwell poems. I have, of course, had continual recourse to the standard edition of H. M. Margoliouth, *The Poems and Letters of Andrew Marvell* (Oxford, 1952; 2 vols., 2nd ed.).

> While indefatigable *Cromwell* hyes,
> And cuts his way still nearer to the Skyes,
> Learning, a Musique in that Region clear,
> To tune this lower to that higher sphere.
>
> (37–84)

Cromwell, the 'sun,' rises to the skies, where he learns the music of cosmic order, the music of the spheres, an order which he will transmit to the microcosm below, imposing thereon the political form of universal harmony. It effect, these lines tell us that Cromwell fulfils the function of a truly providential ruler, one who can attune the microcosm of the state to the orderly motion of the heavenly bodies and the harmonic proportions between them which is their music.

This identification of Cromwell as a political and cosmic 'musician' leads immediately to a further identification with him as Amphion, the artist who built the walls of Thebes by playing on his lute, the heavenly gift of Hermes, with such skill that the stones moved of their own accord to form a wall. Cromwell is thus not only a musician but by virtue of being the kind of musician he is, also an architect. Marvell develops this notion by describing the miraculous building of the walls of Thebes in terms of the variations of Amphion's music:

> So when *Amphion* did the Lute command,
> Which the God gave him; with his gentle hand,
> The rougher Stones, unto his Measures hew'd,
> Dans'd up in order from the Quarreys rude;
> This took a Lower, that an Higher place,
> As he the Treble alter'd, or the Base:
> No note he struck, but a new Story lay'd,
> And the great Work ascended while he play'd.
>
> (49–56)

The order of music is here transformed into the hierarchical order of architecture, levels of the building of the state corresponding to the various notes, high and low, of a musical structure, making a kind of 'Harmonious City of the seven Gates' (66):

> Such was that wondrous Order and Consent,
> When *Cromwell* tun'd the ruling Instrument;
> While tedious Statesmen many years did hack,
> Framing a Liberty that still went back;

Whose num'rous Gorge could swallow in an hour
That Island, which the Sea cannot devour:
Then our Amphion issues out and sings,
And once he struck, and twice, the pow'rful Strings.   (67–74)

Cromwell thus is transformed into the ruler as artist, the man who by his *virtù* constructs that supreme work of art which is the state. His 'instrument' is both the apparatus of state and the instrument of government of 1653 which regulated the position of Cromwell as protector. From one point of view, we discover here the traditional Machiavellian conception of the successful new ruler, the man with great ability but with no hereditary authority or traditional supports of his rule, a prince who must create his own 'legitimacy.' For Machiavelli, of course, success and efficiency are the only warrants the new ruler needs. If he can gain and hold power, order the state, and win the support of his subjects, he is as 'legitimate' as he needs to be. There was nevertheless a strong impulse on the part of the new rulers and their supporters—one shared by Marvell as well—to legitimize their rules. In the Italian city-states the new rulers attempted to substitute the fresh symbols of art and culture for the old traditional symbols of authority to which they had no right. The positive revaluation of the arts and artists which is so important a motif in Renaissance culture in part rests on this phenomenon, although of course legitimate hereditary monarchs also employed the arts as extensions of their power and glory.

But Cromwell does not need these trappings. He is not simply a successful ruler in the strictly secular sense, but a divinely chosen ruler who has been given insight into the workings of the macrocosm, whose love of music implies that he possesses that order in the microcosm of his soul, and who knows how to impose it on the microcosm of the state with speed, unlike 'heavy Monarchs' for whom a platonic year would not suffice, or 'tedious Statesmen' who hack away in vain to shape the building blocks of the state.

> The Commonwealth then first together came,
> And each one enter'd in the willing Frame;
> All other Matter yields, and may be rul'd;
> But who the Minds of stubborn Men can build?
> No Quarry bears a stone so hardly wrought,
> Nor with such labor from its Center brought;

None to be sunk in the foundation bends,
Each in the house the highest Place contends
And each the Hand that lays him will direct,
And some fall back upon the Architect;
Yet all compos'd by this attractive Song,
Into the Animated City throng.   (75–86)

Not only does Cromwell place all the units of the state in their proper places, but his architectural skill is so great that the opposition, like the counter-thrusts in a properly constructed building, only serve to strengthen the whole edifice. It is obvious that Cromwell, in Marvell's eyes, created a mixed constitution on the model suggested by Polybius' analysis of Roman institutions and strongly advocated by Renaissance political theorists such as Machiavelli and Guicciardini. In a famous chapter of the *Discorsi* (I, 2) Machiavelli adopts Polybius' version of ancient political theories concerning the cycle of the state and maintains that the three forms of government, monarchy, aristocracy, and commonwealth, run through a cycle of decay passing over into their bad counterparts, tyranny, oligarchy, and 'licentiousness.' The only way to interrupt this cycle is to establish a mixed form of government in which the same constitution combines a prince, a nobility, and the power of the people. The three powers would then be able to keep watch on one another and to keep each other in check. In such a government a tyrant could not rise, and both nobles and people would have liberty. In addition, disputes would become a source of strength, since they would lead to a readjustment of the internal balance of stresses and not to revolution:

The Common-wealth does through their Centers all
Draw the Circumf'rence of the publique Wall;
The crossest Spirits here do take their part,
Fast'ning the Contignation which they thwart;
And they, whose Nature leads them to divide,
Uphold, this one, and that the other Side;
But the most Equal still sustein the Height,
And they as Pillars keep the Work upright;
While the resistance of opposed Minds,
The Fabrick of the Arches stronger binds,
Which on the Basis of a Senate free,
Knit by the Roofs Protecting weight agree.   (87–98)

Marvell then returns to the conception of Cromwell as a 'star' and makes more explicit the theme of his leadership. He, like a heavenly body, influences others and, like the pole star, helps others to steer their course.

> When for his Foot he thus a place had found,
> He hurles e'er since the World about him round;
> And in his sev'ral Aspects, like a Star,
> Here shines in Peace, and thither shoots a War.
> While by his Beams, observing Princes steer,
> And wisely court the Influence they fear.

(99–104)

Note too that he has both benign and malignant aspects as the heavenly bodies do for astrologers, the first hint of a new antithesis, 'creation-destruction' which, as we shall see, is developed later in the poem.

The return to the theme of Cromwell as 'star,' destiny, or fate, is followed by a long attack on the other, so to speak, 'non-observing' princes of Europe who do not 'humbly tread / The path where holy Oracles do lead' (107–08). It is such who delay the unfolding on earth of Providence's 'great Designes kept for the latter Dayes' (110). Such rulers, Marvell tells us, are 'mad with Reason, so mis-call'd of State. / They know not what they know not hate' (11–12). The historical reference here would seem to be to the failure of Cromwell's attempt to include the Dutch and the Swedes in a general Protestant alliance. The latter, although quite as Protestant as Cromwell, found it politically expedient to stay out. There were evidently two kinds of 'reason of state' for Marvell, the kind which appears to be so but is really to be subsumed into the mysterious workings of Providence, and the kind which is not merely apparently unprincipled but actually is. Perhaps a cynic would say that the two kinds are the kind practised by Cromwell and the kinds practised by others who should have agreed with him and didn't.

After the outright political realism of the *Horatian Ode* and similar elements in the *First Anniversary* it is a little odd to follow Marvell through a prophetic interpretation of Cromwell in the apocalyptic mode (105–58) where his rule is seen as a preparation for the fulfilment of biblical prophecy. The passage is complete with a coming reign of saints, the destruction of the Great Whore and the Beast, and an ingathering of peoples, especially of the Jews. Cromwell alone chases the Roman 'monster through every Throne' (128), a certain sign of his election for the providential task of reforming the political structure of the world in preparation for the last days and the end of history. The signs would all appear to be actual and Marvell dares to hope:

> Hence oft I think, if in some happy Hour
> High Grace should meet in one with highest Pow'r,
> And then a seasonable People still
> Should bend to his, as he to Heavens will,
> What might we hope, what wonderful Effect
> From such a wish'd Conjuncture might reflect,
> Sure, the mysterious Work, where none withstand,
> Would forthwith finish under such a Hand:
> Fore-shortned Time its useless Course would stay,
> And soon precipitate the latest Day.
> But a thick Cloud about that Morning lyes,
> And intercepts the Beams of Mortal eyes,
> That 'tis the most which we determine can,
> If these the Times, then this must be the Man.
>
> (131–44)

If this seems incompatible with the political realism of Marvell, it may not prove so on further reflection. The truly Machiavellian view of political activity involves the isolation of that aspect of political behaviour which lies on the other side of customary moral norms and which cannot be understood in terms of an ethic of good intentions regardless of achieved results. What is apparently evil may then from this perspective possibly be good, and *vice versa*. But this perspective is quite close to the human view of the workings of Providence. If all that happens in history has a providential meaning—i.e. will work out for the best—even though many of these events are ethically incongruous, then those ethically ambiguous phenomena and actions which relate to the arrival of a new ruler on the stage of history—and these are the concern of Machiavelli in *The Prince*—are as capable as any other activity of being subsumed into a prophetic interpretation of history. After all, the moral character of Augustine's *terrena civitas* is not very different from that of the state of Machiavelli. For the former, of course, there is a world of true justice and righteousness outside of space and time, a world where intention and result are harmoniously unified and there is no difference between being and seeming. But for political theory this is of little moment, since such a world will continue to remain outside of space and time.

We should not, however, push these resemblances between Machiavelli and Marvell too far. Marvell, like Malvolio, read many 'politick authors' and accepts the Augustinian and Machiavellian view of the problematic character of action, the inevitable mixture of good and evil in it, the way the results of action change their ethical character depending on the 'time' in which they come to pass and the 'time' from which we view them, the gulf which obtains between what the agent of action seems to be doing and what he actually does. However, he does not believe that God or fortune gives dominion to the good and bad alike. Cromwell is good. We have all sorts of divine warrants for that conviction, and any acts which do not seem good, such as regicide, are a result of the fact that he lives on another plane, the plane of destiny, or as Machiavelli would say, the plane of *necessità*. It is also clear that Marvell theologizes *necessità*. Cromwell, the 'star,' the man of destiny and instrument of Providence, simply cannot be completely judged by customary ethical norms. There was ample precedent for this view in biblical exegesis as well as in Machiavellian political theory. Solomon's harem, Samson's suicide, these and many more ethically dubious episodes of Scripture were seen as divinely ordained dispensations for the 'times,' and, 'if these the Times, then this must be the man' (144).

> And well he therefore does, and well has guest,
> Who in his Age has always forward prest:
> And knowing not where Heaven's choice may light,
> Girds yet his Sword, and ready stands to fight.
>
> (145–48)

There is no doubt that, for Marvell, Cromwell is the man for the times, but it is interesting to observe that the prophetic mode the poet has adopted for this passage closely imitates the 'obscure' mode of biblical apocalyptic prophecy. The times are troubled ones, and it is difficult to trace out the designs of Providence in a very real chaos which only the eyes of faith can see as a mere appearance. Marvell then continues by furnishing even more evidence of Cromwell's special destiny. His saintly mother lived to be so old 'That she might seem, could we the Fall dispute / T'have smelt the Blossome, and not eat the Fruit' (163–64). This brief and witty allusion to the fall becomes a very important motif of the rest of the poem in terms of the antithesis 'Fall-Rise,' 'humiliation-exaltation,' 'humility-sublimity.' The point of departure for Marvell's development of this theme is a reference to a very literal fall for Cromwell when, on September 29th, 1654, his coach drawn by six German horses was overturned in Hyde Park while he was at the reins himself.

> How near they fail'd, and in the sudden Fall
> At once assay'd to overturn us all.
> Our brutish fury struggling to be Free,
> Hurry'd thy Horses while they hurry'd thee.
> When thou hadst almost quit thy Mortal cares,
> And soyl'd in Dust thy Crown of silver Hairs.   (175–80)

This fall becomes the Fall. Nature groans, the cosmic order is disrupted, and the edifice of the state cracks.

> Thou *Cromwell* falling, not a stupid Tree,
> Or Rock so savage, but it mourn'd for thee:
> And all about was heard a Panique grown,
> As if that Nature's self were overthrown.
> It seemed the Earth did from the Center tear;
> It seemed the Sun was faln out of the Sphere:
> Justice obstructed lay, and Reason fool'd;
> Courage disheartened, and Religion cool'd
> A dismal Silence through the Palace went,
> And then loud Shreeks the vaulted Marbles rent.   (201–10)

But Cromwell swiftly and gloriously rises, an ascent described with allusion to the ascent of Elijah and to the progress of the sun:

> But thee triumphant hence the firy Carr,
> And firy Steeds had born out of the Warr,
> From the low World, and thankless Men above,
> Unto the Kingdom blest of Peace and Love:
> We only mourn'd our selves, in thine Ascent,
> Whom thou hadst left beneath with Mantle rent.   (215–21)

Cromwell's physical fall and rise not only has a typological significance in biblical history and a contemporary reference to his indispensable position in the state, but it is in turn the physical analogue of his moral character. He literally fell and rose again and the political world fell and rose with him. But in the moral sphere Cromwell, so to speak, rises and falls all the time simultaneously, for he is at once lowly and exalted:

> For all delight of Life thou then didst lose,
> When to Command, thou didst thy self Depose;
> Resigning up thy Privacy so dear,
> To turn the headstrong Peoples Charioteer;
> For to be Cromwell was a greater thing,
> Then ought below, or yet above a King;
> Therefore thou rather didst thy Self depress,
> Yielding to Rule, because it made thee Less.
>
> (221–28)

If Cromwell was first Elijah in his translation to the heavens, he next descends as the cloud of rain which broke the three years' drought Israel suffered under the reign of Ahab. This cloud, which Elijah's servant saw only the seventh time he went to look for it, marked both Jehovah's favour and the destruction of the priests of Baal whose cult had been fostered by Jezebel, Ahab's Phoenecian wife (1 Kings 17 ff., esp. 17.42–46). It is clear that Marvell here alludes to the political and religious evils of Charles's rule, evils which Cromwell swept away. Hence Cromwell, like the biblical cloud, is both beneficial and destructive, good for the 'dry land' but murderous to the king:

> For, neither didst thou from the first apply
> Thy sober Spirit unto things too High,
> But in thine own Fields exercisedst long,
> An healthful Mind within a Body strong;
> Till at the Seventh time thou in the Skyes,
> As a small Cloud, like a Mans hand didst rise;
> Then did thick Mists and Winds the air deform,
> And down at last thou pow'rdst the fertile Storm;
> Which to the thirsty Land did plenty bring,
> But though forewarn'd, o'r-took and wet the King.
>
> (229–38)

Marvell is careful again to accentuate the moral balance in Cromwell, who was not over-ambitious and who possessed the

classical perfection of *mens sana in corpore sano*. He thus prepares us to accept Cromwell's destructive aspect as super-
naturally ordained, not as flowing directly and solely from his
own person. Like nature and many of the providential instruments of Scripture, he rewards and punishes, creates and
destroys in fulfilment of designs which are in part beyond
human comprehension. The force of all the astrological allusions and the references, direct and oblique, to biblical events,
converge finally on a justification of the regicide. Cromwell was
the instrument of Divine Providence, a divinely ordained
architect of the state who must be judged by his magnificent
results (a real as against a seeming king), his unfailing prudence, his ability to destroy only in the interest of greater
creation. We begin to glimpse that there is a further, divinely
sanctioned, antithesis in Cromwell and that is of destruction and
creation.

> What since he did, an higher Force him push'd
> Still from behind, and it before him rush'd,
> Though undiscern'd among the tumult blind,
> Who think those high Decrees by Man design'd
> 'Twas Heav'n would not that his Pow'r should cease,
> But walk still middle betwixt War and Peace;
> Choosing each Stone, and poysing every weight,
> Trying the Measures of the Bredth and Height;
> Here pulling down, and there erecting New,
> Founding a firm State by Proportions true.
>
> (239–48)

Like Gideon, Cromwell knows how to conquer 'Zeba and
Zalmunna' and punish 'Succoths elders,' but he is even more
like this *figura* in refusing the headship of state for himself and
his sons (249–56; cf. Judges 8–9). And if the 'olive' refused to
reign over the other trees, should the bramble be anointed with
the oil that belongs to the olive? (257–60). Without wishing
to stretch Marvell's analogies even further, it would not be
irrelevant to suggest that Cromwell has something better than
royal blood in his veins. He has the very oil of unction which
makes kings into kings. In so far as Cromwell is thus both more
and less than a king, he is assimilated to the figure of David,
and in reference to his refusal to accept kingship he is of the
type of Gideon. Indeed, he is both more and less than an

anointed king; he is a *christus Domini* who, possessing the
internal spiritual unction, refuses the external chrisma. In
the last analysis he is *sui generis*, a ruler as unique as David,
the singular king of Israel.

> Whose climbing Flame, without a timely stop,
> Had quickly Levell'd every Cedar's top.
> Therefore first growing to thyself a Law,
> Th'ambitious Shrubs thou in just time didst aw.
>
> (261–64)

Cromwell, to human eyes, seems like a true Machiavellian
ruler: a law unto himself, a man with a miraculous sense of the
appropriate time and conditions for action, prudent and swift,
thoughtful and impetuous at the same time, qualities he demonstrated in his suppression of the Levellers. But Marvell continually reminds us through image and type that from another
perspective, rationally irreducible to this one, Cromwell is a
divinely endowed and divinely directed instrument.

Political architect, cosmic musician, instrument of destiny,
Cromwell is the saviour of the ship of state, not like the helms-
man who should have saved it but like 'some lusty Mate, who
with more careful Eye / Counted the Hours, and ev'ry Star did
spy, / The Helm does from the artless Steersman strain'
(273–75). From this point of view he is the true man of ability,
of *virtù*, who can count the hours to know the right 'time' and
who in reading every star shows his awareness of that cosmic
order by which we determine our 'place.' He derives his right
to take the helm of state from his artless predecessors because
he has true *virtù*, but we are also reminded that it is a *virtù* in
harmony with the order of things. If Cromwell's achievement
was the imposition of order, the fruit of that order is liberty:

> 'Tis not a Freedome, that where All command:
> Nor Tyranny, where One does them withstand:
> But who of both the Bounders knows to lay
> Him as their Father must the State obey.   (279–82)

> And only didst for others plant the Vine
> Of Liberty, not drunken with its Wine.
> That sober Liberty which men may have,
> That they enjoy, but more they vainly crave.   (287–90)

After a section concerned with the various internal enemies of the state (291–324), Marvell takes up again the analogy of Cromwell to the sun, comparing the fear that he would be only temporarily successful to the fear of the first man that the sun might not return after its first setting (325–42):

> So while our Star that gives us Light and Heat,
> Seem'd now a long and gloomy Night to threat,
> Up from the other World his Flame he darts,
> And Princes shining through their windows starts;
> And credulous Ambassadors accuse. (343–48)

These foreigners express amazement that the Protectorate could create a navy and rebuild itself as rapidly as it did (349–52), and equal amazement at Cromwell's skill in the arts of statecraft. They are puzzled by the sublime ability which in their eyes should mark him as the peer of a legitimate monarch although he is a usurper, and also by his humble refusal to 'legitimize' himself by becoming a king.

> 'Where did he learn those Arts that cost us dear?
> Where below Earth, or where above the Sphere?
> He seems a King by long Succession born,
> And yet the same to be a King does scorn.
> Abroad a King he seems, and something more,
> At home a Subject on the equal Floor.' (385–90)

Cromwell is here presented by his own enemies as the truly successful Machiavellian prince who, through the arts of statesmanship, the arts apparently learned 'below earth,' becomes the equal of a hereditary monarch. It is precisely for such that *Il Principe* is a handbook, and Cromwell learned his lesson well. Simultaneously he carries the stamp of the Davidic king, whose statesmanship comes from 'above the Sphere' and whose moral nature is a paradoxically harmonious fusion of the antithesis *humilitas-sublimitas*.

Let us now turn briefly to *A Poem on the Death of O.C.*, in which some of the themes we have been considering, particularly the Davidic archetype, become more explicit.

It is in great part a conventional eulogy and, for the purposes of this essay, we need not consider it in as much detail as the *First Anniversary*. The very opening of the poem calls our attention to the providential character of Cromwell's rule.

> THAT Providence which had so long the care
> Of *Cromwell's* head, and numbred ev'ry hair,
> Now in its self (the Glass where all appears)
> Had seen the period of his golden years.   (1–4)

This theme is emphasized later in the poem when Marvell alludes to the great efficacy Cromwell's prayers had in inclining the God of battles to his side. Astonished armies fled before Cromwell, and no man had been more obeyed in heaven since the time of Gideon for whom God stayed the sun in its path. This, of course, is the same Gideon who, in the *First Anniversary*, was the prototype of Cromwell in his refusal to be king.

In this last poem on Cromwell, the 'humility-sublimity' antithesis is first suggested in the form of 'valour-clemency' or 'force-mercy.' In the *First Anniversary*, let us recall, Cromwell had been interpreted as a synthesis of various antithetical though generally positive values: a Machiavellian 'prince' and a biblical king, an apparently illegitimate usurper who has a higher form of legitimacy than any so-called legitimate monarch, a man with so much energy and freedom of action that he is as fate to others, but who is nevertheless completely an instrument of the Providence whose service is perfect freedom, a sublime and humble man all at once. Now, on the occasion of his death, Marvell largely emphasizes the moral antitheses in Cromwell, and they were of such a unique blend that, unlike a stage ruler, Cromwell was able to die in bed.

> The People, which what most they fear esteem,
> Death when more horrid so more noble deem;
> And blame the last *Act*, like *Spectators* vain,
> Unless the *Prince* whom they applaud be slain.
> Nor fate indeed can well refuse that right
> To those that liv'd in War, to dye in Fight.
> But long his *Valour* none had left that could
> Indanger him, or Clemancy that would.
> And he whom Nature all for Peace had made,
> But angry Heaven unto War had Sway'd,
> And so less useful here he most desir'd,
> For what he least affected was admir'd,
> Deserved yet an End whose ev'ry part
> Should speak the wondrous softness of his Heart.   (7–20)

It is important to observe that 'valour-clemency' stands in

direct proportion to 'heaven-nature.' Cromwell's force and courage which enabled him to suppress his enemies were functions of his rôle as the instrument of an angry heaven. His mercy, a function of his own nature, disarmed those enemies for whom force was not necessary. Like the best sort of Machiavellian ruler Cromwell was both loved and feared, but his exercise of force is 'moralized' by attributing to Providence the fearful elements in Cromwell's character. It is not insignificant that Marvell makes much of this last poem a description of Cromwell as a tender father watching over his dying daughter Eliza.

As with the death of any truly great man, Cromwell's is preceded by a great storm ('A Secret Cause does sure those Signs ordain / Foreboding Princes falls, and seldom vain,' 101–02). Marvell then continues with an eulogy of his virtues, singling out valour, religion, friendship, and prudence by name, although he possessed all the rest besides (227–28), and with a description of the greatness of his character and of his public achievements as the Great Protector. What is most significant for our theme, however, is an explicit reference to the type of David as the humble monarch, as the archetypal *figura* of which Cromwell was a contemporary fulfilment:

> No more shall heare that powerful language charm,
> Whose force oft spar'd the labour of his arm:
> No more shall follow where he spent the dayes
> In warre, in counsell, or in pray'r, and praise;
> Whose meanest acts he would himself advance,
> As ungirt *David* to the arke did dance.
>
> (237–43)

Earlier in the poem we were prepared for this passage by a *reprise* of the 'sublimity-humility' themes so dominant in the *First Anniversary*, when Marvell says of Cromwell: 'For he no duty by his height excus'd / Not though a *Prince* to be a Man refused' (84–85). What was the implicit type of the *First Anniversary* and of the earlier portions of *A Poem on the Death of O.C.* finally becomes explicit. Any contemporary reader versed in Scripture and the contemporary techniques of exegesis would have recognized the implicit analogies to David in Cromwell's attributes of *sublimitas-humilitas*, his election by heaven for rule by a special covenant like the one God made with

David through Nathan the prophet, and, last but not least, his love of music, the art which in a cosmic and mystical sense is necessary to impose order and harmony on the body politic. They expected that in his death Cromwell's soul would go to join other great law-givers and biblical kings such as Moses (one of Machiavelli's examples of a successful armed prophet, by the way), Joshua and especially '*David*, for the sword and harpe renown'd' (294).

In the *Horatian Ode* Marvell's 'frame,' so to speak, was Machiavellian. Over the years Marvell gradually transformed Cromwell from the 'Machiavellian prince,' in the authentic and not the vulgar sense of that phrase, into a Davidic king, thus moving from a predominantly secular conception of Cromwell to a profoundly religious one. The typological method is apparent in all of the poems, in its secularized form in the *Horatian Ode*, and in an authentically scriptural form in the others. What is also apparent is that Marvell was impelled in the path we have traced by the persistent need to 'legitimize' the man who was, after all, a usurper. After an attempt, filled with tension, to fuse together both conceptions, that of biblical king and Machiavellian 'prince' in the *First Anniversary*, Marvell concludes by settling on the biblical conception, virtually excluding a 'secular' Cromwell, and legitimizes the Great Protector in the only way he could, by canonizing him.

In his treatment of Cromwell, Marvell reveals those same qualities of imagination that we find throughout his poetry, and which derive from the interpretation of experience through a perspective created by the fusion of antitheses. The theme of 'humility-sublimity' so dominant in the Cromwell poems runs through *Upon Appleton House*, where it receives both an aesthetic and a moral application, with all kinds of subtle changes on true and false humility in life and art, and true and false chastity. Similarly, the antithesis 'art-nature' in all of its paradoxical implications, unites *Appleton House* with the Mower poems. From this point of view the Cromwell poems become of a piece with the rest of Marvell's poetry and lose the anomalous character with which much modern criticism seemed to endow them.

Index